The Soviet Occupation of Germany

This is a major new account of the Soviet occupation of post-war Germany and the beginning of the Cold War. Dr Filip Slaveski shows how in the immediate aftermath of war the Red Army command struggled to contain the violence of soldiers against German civilians and, at the same time, feed and rebuild the country. This task was then assumed by the Soviet Military Administration in Germany (SVAG), which was established to impose order on this chaos. Its attempt, however, intensified the battle for resources and power among competing occupation organs, especially SVAG and the army, which spilled over from threats and sabotage into fighting and shootouts in the streets. At times, such conflicts threatened to paralyse occupation governance, leaving armed troops, liberated POWs, and slave labourers free to roam. SVAG's successes in reducing the violence and reconstructing eastern Germany were a remarkable achievement in the chaotic aftermath of war.

FILIP SLAVESKI is an Honorary Fellow in History at the School of Historical and Philosophical Studies, University of Melbourne, Australia.

The Soviet Occupation of Germany

Hunger, Mass Violence, and the Struggle for Peace, 1945–1947

Filip Slaveski

CAMBRIDGE
UNIVERSITY PRESS

CAMBRIDGE
UNIVERSITY PRESS

University Printing House, Cambridge CB2 8BS, United Kingdom

Published in the United States of America by Cambridge University Press, New York

Cambridge University Press is part of the University of Cambridge.

It furthers the University's mission by disseminating knowledge in the pursuit of education, learning, and research at the highest international levels of excellence.

www.cambridge.org
Information on this title: www.cambridge.org/9781107043817

© Filip Slaveski 2013

First published 2013

Printed in the United Kingdom by Clays, St Ives plc

A catalogue record for this publication is available from the British Library

ISBN 978-1-107-04381-7 Hardback

For Sr Lieutenant I. N. Sychkov,
who lost more in victory than in defeat
dod 25.3.1946

Contents

Tables and map

Preface

Soviet soldiers marched into Germany in the winter of 1945 on roads lined with wooden plaques inciting them to wreak vengeance on the country. Their pockets were stuffed with newspaper articles explaining why they should. Red Army propagandists planted more plaques and printed more articles over the winter, worrying that the exhausted soldiers needed a morale boost before launching the final stage of the war. They need not have worried. The horrors of German occupation in the Soviet Union which the articles evoked paled in comparison to the sight and smell of them. The soldiers knew these horrors all too well and were ready to avenge the millions dead.

The prisoners of war (POWs) and slave labourers whom the soldiers had liberated from the camps in Poland and Germany were ready to seek their own justice. Many joined the soldiers in the explosion of violence against anyone and anything German. The Red Army command struggled to contain the violence and, at the same time, feed and rebuild the country that it had once been ordered to destroy. The Soviet leadership soon realised that the Red Army, which had defeated one of the largest and most brutal invading forces in history, could not act as a peacetime government.

The army was relieved of its governing duty in June 1945, one month after the war concluded. The Soviet Military Administration in Germany (SVAG) was then established to try and impose order on this chaos and reconstruct the country. SVAG's war was only beginning. It was surrounded by powerful Moscow-backed groups and organisations which pursued policies contradictory to its own. The army was out of control, with many officers incapable or unwilling to follow orders from the army command to stop their men from robbing and raping. They had even less control over the liberated slaves. Many officers were certainly not going to listen to SVAG 'upstarts' who complained about the violence, leaving the upstarts with little choice but to try to arrest the violent soldiers themselves and denounce their negligent officers. There were about 40,000 SVAG members by summer's end in 1945, facing almost a 1.5 million man army, more liberated slaves, and thousands of unsympathetic Soviet officials.[1]

Many historians can explain convincingly why some soldiers continued to attack German civilians after the end of the war. Such violence was a response to their traumatic experience of war and German occupation.[2] It is more difficult to explain why some of their officers initially sought to protect civilians, more so why they were unsuccessful even when the army command became committed to reining in the violence. The conflict between SVAG and the army is central to answering this question.[3] The indiscipline in the army which erupted during the final stages of the war endured long afterwards. As difficult as it was for officers to bring the troops into line then, when there was still a war to fight, it was almost impossible now in peacetime. Army officers who desired it still could not simply 'go by the book' and discipline their men for every rape, murder, or robbery. They would not have survived long if they did. On the other hand, they could hardly have retained control of their detachments for long if they did nothing. To manage their men in the chaos of 1945, many officers needed to strike a balance between punishing the worst offenders internally and still allowing others (and themselves) to behave like the conquerors they were – a precarious and often unattainable balance that the army command and certainly SVAG refused or failed to appreciate. Most importantly, officers needed to protect their men from SVAG, which, frustrated with the continuation of troop violence, arrested and sought the prosecution of violent soldiers. Army officers understood this as a wanton assault on their authority that cast doubt on the quality of their command. They thus protected their men, in the process reinforcing the very patronage ties essential to maintain control of their units, a task now more difficult with no war to fight and no fear of imminent death. Officers provided alibis for suspects, frustrated SVAG investigations, and

---

[1] Estimates of SVAG membership vary. By September 1945, SVAG officially numbered 46,867 workers, yet the number was actually closer to 40,000. T. V. Tsarevskaia-Diakina, 'Struktura SVAG,' in *Sovetskaia voennaia administratsiia v Germanii, 1945–1949; Spravochnik*, ed. A. V. Doronin, J. Foitzik, and T. V. Tsarevskaia-Diakina (Moscow: Rosspen, 2009), 24.

[2] Norman Naimark, Catherine Merridale, and Elena Seniavskaia all discuss psychological factors accounting for troop violence at length. N. Naimark, *The Russians in Germany: A History of the Soviet Zone of Occupation* (Cambridge, Mass.: Harvard University Press, 1995); C. Merridale, *Ivan's War: Life and Death in the Red Army, 1939–1945* (New York: Metropolitan Books, 2006); E. S. Seniavskaia, *Frontovoe pokolenie, 1941–1945: Istoriko-psikhologicheskoe issledovanie* (Moscow: In-t Rossiiskoi Istorii RAN, 1995).

[3] Naimark does note that the inability of SVAG officers to exert control over the troops did not help to reduce the level of troop violence, yet does not investigate the conflict between SVAG and the army. Naimark, *The Russians in Germany*, 90. This question is dealt with at length in Chapter 4.

demanded the release of their men from SVAG lock-ups. When the release was not forthcoming, some officers stormed the lock-ups with their units, guns blazing, to free their boys.

Despairing, SVAG reacted to this challenge to their authority by arresting more soldiers and denouncing more of their 'negligent' officers. But this approach only exacerbated the troop violence problem. Sensing themselves under attack, many army officers now spent less time punishing and more protecting their men, often effectively, leaving them to trawl the streets for longer. It also sparked the beginning of violence between SVAG and the army. At its height, this conflict could no longer be contained to denunciations, threat-making and sabotage, but spilled over into the street as fistfights and shoot-outs between SVAG and army units raged outside the bars and theatres of the Soviet occupation zone in eastern Germany.[4] This violent conflict, so detrimental to the combatants and the reconstruction of Germany then, has been largely ignored since.

Some historians prefer to understand the continuation of troop violence as a problem of indiscipline in the army and focus on its cooperation with SVAG.[5] Indiscipline certainly was the problem, and not only in Germany. In other Soviet-occupied territories and the Union itself, active and demobilised troops carried wartime violence into the post-war era but were eventually reined in by governments as they established greater control over their chaotic post-war societies. There was no such government to speak of in Germany. SVAG established control over the occupied population, but not over the army and thus not entirely over the country. The harder it tried to bring army officers into line, the more undisciplined they became.

Some historians also assume that the conflicts which developed between organs in Germany were little different to those which raged

---

[4] Hereafter, 'the zone'. Germany was divided into four separate occupation zones after the war. Each zone was administered by one of the four occupying powers (Britain, America, France, and the Soviet Union). The Soviet zone was also formally divided into five states (lands/provinces) on 9 July 1945, which broadly corresponded to traditional boundaries in eastern Germany: Mecklenburg and Western Pomerania, Saxony, Brandenburg, Thuringia, and Saxony-Anhalt (Appendix 1). Although SVAG headquarters were situated in Karlshorst (Berlin), each state was governed by a central Soviet Military Administration (SVA) that controlled the numerous *komendaturas* within its borders, which formed the skeleton of SVAG power in the zone. Each *komendatura* was responsible for governing a set geographical area and was run by a *komendant*, small staff, and guard.

[5] For the focus on cooperation in the Russian literature see Vladimir Zakharov's article, 'Voennye komendatury SVAG v sovetskoi zone okkupatsii Germanii 1945–1949 gg.', in *Deiatel'nost' sovetskikh voennykh komendatur po likvidatsii posledstvii voiny i organizatsii mirnoi zhizni v sovetskoi zone okkupatsii Germanii 1945–1949: Sbornik dokumentov*, ed. V. V. Zakharov (Moscow: Rosspen, 2005).

back home.[6] After all, they were expected to strive for power and resources within Stalinism, sometimes even violently. But this drive for power in Germany was fostered by the structure of the Soviet occupation machinery, where lines of jurisdictional control were blurred to a much greater extent than in the Soviet Union. And without a dominant organ in Germany which could settle the disputes among its subordinates, long drawn-out battles were bound to develop among them. At times, such conflicts threatened to paralyse areas of occupation governance. This is what makes SVAG's successes in reconstructing the zone so remarkable. The greatest of these was surely establishing a functioning food rationing system in the post-war chaos, while armed troops and repatriates (liberated Soviet POWs and slave labourers) roamed the countryside conducting their own requisitions, which threatened to starve the country.

Theoretically at least, this conflict should never have emerged. How could there be a conflict between SVAG and the army when the military commanders appointed to the SVAG brass effectively retained command of their divisions? The famous Marshal Zhukov was head of both SVAG and GSOVG, the new name for Red Army forces in Germany.[7] He and some of the military commanders sat on the SVAG Military Council, which tackled the most pressing problems facing the Soviets and issued orders binding on both SVAG and the army. But the synapse between the brass and the army officer corps was wider now than during the war. Even Zhukov struggled to bridge it and resolve the conflict, which was stifling his attempts to bring order to the zone. And when he could break apart the combatants, he was left to settle their internal disputes and clear the webs of organisational confusion that plagued them – the DNA of the infant Stalinist leviathan that was to rule half of Germany for forty years.

The initial years of the Soviet occupation were marked by this tension between the destructive forces of violence and constructive forces of national regeneration. Despite the official 'pro-German' policies pursued by the Soviet leadership, people were simply uncertain as to which of these

---

[6] For the parallels between Soviet and German state-building see Nikita Petrov's essay on the matter, 'Formirovanie organov nemetskogo samoupravleniia i sovetizatsiia Vostochnoi Germanii', in *SVAG i nemetskie organy samoupravleniia 1945–1949: Sbornik dokumentov*, ed. N. V. Petrov (Moscow: Rosspen, 2006).

[7] The Soviet forces which invaded Germany were reorganised in June 1945 into the Group of Soviet Occupation Forces in Germany (GSOVG), referred to as the 'army'. Many Council members enjoyed dual positions in SVAG and the army, such as Generals F. E. Bokov and V. E. Makarov, etc. The lack of clarity surrounding the nature of the Military Council and the general lack of clarity regarding SVAG–army relations during 1945 and 1946 is discussed in a recent essay, J. Foitzik, 'Zamestitel' glavnonachal'stvuiushchego SVAG po politicheskim voprosam', in *Sovetskaia voennaia administratsiia v Germanii*, ed. Doronin, Foitzik, and Tsarevskaia-Diakina.

forces would emerge dominant in the first years of the occupation. It was only in 1947 that the SVAG–army conflict receded and troop violence ceased to be a staple of occupation life. Now the more positive Soviet policies aimed at engaging the civilian population began to bear fruit. This book is about the fundamental tension between violence and national regeneration, which traces the final victory of those Soviet officers and men who swallowed the pain of their experience under German occupation to rebuild a country with their new German 'allies' on the ruins of the past.

Acknowledgements

I have incurred many great debts in completing this book, none more so than to the eminent Soviet historian Stephen Wheatcroft, under whom I worked for almost a decade. His intellectual guidance and enduring friendship have enriched both this book and my life. In early 2010 I also first met the Australian historian John Hirst, who agreed to assist in preparing the original manuscript and who, years later, continued to do so well beyond his initial obligation. I am most grateful for his advice, friendship, and generosity, without which this book and especially its prose would have suffered enormously.

My fruitful collaborations with Mark Edele on the demobilisation of the Red Army after the Great Patriotic War and with L. H. Lumey on European famines have provided many insights to improve this book and to focus the original research upon which it is based. This research was assisted greatly by the excellent archivist Dina Nokhotovich at the State Archive of the Russian Federation (GARF) and Oleg Khlevniuk, who offered me his valuable time and wealth of archival knowledge in Moscow. Robert Horvath, Steven Welch, and Stanislav Kulchytsky were kind enough to read earlier versions of my work and offer their valuable suggestions, as did my editors at Cambridge, Michael Watson, Gaia Poggiogalli, and particularly Dr Iveta Adams who, as copy-editor, has done much to improve the final version.

I have presented elements of my research at numerous conferences/ workshops since 2007, most notably the biannual conferences of the Australasian Association for European History (AAEH) and at the 'International Workshop on Grain and Politics in the Twentieth Century' at Jiao Tong University in Shanghai. I am very thankful for much of the feedback from attendant colleagues. Other colleagues and friends too have always been ready to offer their opinions on the book and help with research, particularly Jared McBride in Russia and, in Melbourne, Shawn Borelli-Mear and Anthony Garnaut.

The most enduring debts are inevitably personal. My wonderful *khoziaika*, Nina Nikeshina, made a home for me in Moscow not unlike the one that I left in Melbourne. Here I have been blessed with a most supportive family, whose encouragement for my work and tolerance for the discomforts that it sometimes brings always buoy my spirits. Without their support, particularly that rendered by my parents, this book would never have been written.

The original manuscript was produced with the assistance of the Writing Centre for Scholars and Researchers at the University of Melbourne, for which I am grateful – as I am to Nova Science Publishers Inc. for granting me permission to reprint in Chapter 7 sections of another of my works, F. Slaveski, 'The Occupiers' Burden: Tackling Food Shortage and Related Health Problems in Post-War Germany, 1945–47', in *Early Life Nutrition, Adult Health, and Development: Lessons from Changing Diets, Famines, and Experimental Studies*, ed. L. H. Lumey and A. Vaiserman (New York: Nova Science Publishers Inc., 2013).

Of course, any errors in this book are mine alone.

Abbreviations

ACC	Allied Control Council
Agitprop	Department for Agitation and Propaganda in the Central Committee of the VKP (b)
ARC	Allied Reparations Commission
CDU	Christian Democratic Union
DWK	German Economic Commission
GARF	State Archive of the Russian Federation
GDR	German Democratic Republic
GKO	State Defence Committee
GlavPURKKA	Main Political Administration of the Workers' and Peasants' Red Army
Gosplan	State Planning Committee
GSOVG	Group of Soviet Occupation Forces in Germany
Komendant	Soviet commander in charge of *komendatura*
Komendatura	Area of Soviet administration in Germany
KPD	German Communist Party
KPÖ	Austrian Communist Party
KS	*Komendant*'s Service
LDP	German Liberal-Democratic Party
LIP	Level of Industry Plan
MGB	Ministry of State Security
MVD	Ministry of Internal Affairs
NCO	Non-commissioned officer
NKGB	People's Commissariat of State Security
NKVD	People's Commissariat of Internal Affairs
NKID	People's Commissariat of Foreign Affairs
NSDAP	National Socialist German Worker's (Nazi) Party
OGPU	Joint State Political Administration
OMGUS	Office of Military Government Unites States (Germany)
POW	Prisoner of war
RGAE	Russian State Economic Archive

RGASPI	Russian State Archive of Socio-Political History
SED	German Socialist Unity Party
SGAO	Soviet–German Joint Stock Company
SMERSH	Death to Spies (Soviet Military Counterintelligence)
Sovmin	Council of Ministers
Sovnarkom	Council of People's Commissars
SPD	German Social-Democratic Party
SPÖ	Austrian Social-Democratic Party
SVAG	Soviet Military Administration in Germany
TsK VKP (b)	Central Committee of the All Union Communist Party (bolsheviks)

Part I

The explosion of violence

1   The Soviet advance into Germany

> The commander of the Yanovskii camp, *Oberführer* Vilgas, habitually fired his rifle from the balcony of the camp office at the prisoners working on the camp grounds ... His wife did the same. Now and then, Vilgas ordered his guards to throw camp infants into the air and shot them to the ground to the applause of his nine year old daughter who cried, 'Daddy, again, again!'[1]

Red Army soldiers arrived at the Yanovskii camp in Ukraine in the middle of the hot summer of 1944. The fleeing Germans had left them fresh corpses in shallow, sandy graves behind the camp. It wasn't difficult for the soldiers to find them. The stench was sickening, attracting the fat summer flies that feast on rotting skin. They tore at the nerves of the soldiers no end. But at least they didn't have to dig for long. The corpses were hardly buried, only flung upon one another in narrow ditches and covered with loose sand. The dead had their hands tied behind their back and a bullet hole in the front and back of their skulls. The women's hair had been ripped out by the German guards as they dragged them to the edge of the ditch. Hair was scattered everywhere in sandy clumps both within and above the graves. Army photographers shifted the women's corpses into poses that would allow them to snap the raw patches on their scalps in the best light.

The prisoners at Yanovskii and other camps sought out anything on which to scribble their semi-literate testimonies to these crimes. They abound in the Russian archives, presenting us with a mosaic of discoloured papers, newspaper sheets, and cheap cardboards bearing witness to what Germany's war of annihilation in the Soviet Union meant to its victims. These records help us to understand the conduct of Soviet soldiers towards German civilians once the tables were turned, that is, when the Red Army swept through Eastern Europe and invaded Germany in January 1945.

---

[1] State Archive of the Russian Federation (GARF) – f. (*fond*) r-7021, op. (*opis'*) 128, d. (*delo*) 157, l. (*list*) 6.

The soldiers who liberated the camps had seen mass graves and extermination camps across Europe, their indignation and feeling of injustice rising with every step westward. Now it had reached a climax, face to face with their emaciated countrymen. Girls as young as sixteen who had been kidnapped from their homeland by German forces cried in their arms confessing the sordid details of their defiled youth.[2] If the emaciated and disease-ridden camp survivors couldn't muster the breath to ask their liberators to avenge them, the sight of corpses rotting in shallow graves screamed for it.

Most soldiers, however, never set foot in the camps. The clarity of this sight and pitch of this scream was thus set by journalists who published endless news stories about the camps in army newspapers. These stories were replete with photographs of emaciated prisoners and piles of corpses which managed to shock even the most battle-hardened, literate and not.[3] Nonetheless, for many of them, the camps were not the essence of German criminality that they would later become in contemporary understandings of the war and certainly not the source of their wrath in 1945. This source was inexorably personal, impassioned, but underlain by the logic of this war that called for it to be waged without restraint.

As the Red Army advanced through the western parts of the Soviet Union it found them totally devastated by German forces. In large swathes of 'partisan-infected areas' in Belorussia and Ukraine as Hitler called them,[4] German forces waged a war behind the front line, killing partisan suspects, mostly civilians, en masse. Particularly telling was the practice of torturing wives of suspect partisans for information in open squares to 'root out' their husbands hiding in the woods, supposedly watching on.[5] Other suspects were shot, hung, or if they were luckier, deported to Germany as slave labour along with the other 'able-bodied' people. The areas were stripped not only of manpower, but of foodstuffs, animals, clothing, and their housing and infrastructure destroyed.[6] By 1943 German forces were thus no longer pacifying these areas to administer them better, but

[2] Russian State Archive of Socio-Political History (RGASPI) – f. 17, op. 125, d. 318, ll. 23–5.

[3] A. Kondoyanidi, 'The Liberating Experience: War Correspondents, Red Army Soldiers, and the Nazi Extermination Camps', *The Russian Review* 69 (2010).

[4] M. Edele and M. Geyer, 'States of Exception: The Nazi–Soviet War as a System of Violence, 1939–1945', in *Beyond Totalitarianism: Stalinism and Nazism Compared*, ed. M. Geyer and S. Fitzpatrick (New York: Cambridge University Press, 1999), 381.

[5] GARF – f. r-7021, op. 128, d. 104, l. 43.

[6] B. Shepherd, 'Hawks, Doves and Tote Zonen: A Wehrmacht Security Division in Central Russia, 1943', *Journal of Contemporary History* 37, no. 3 (2002): 353. For the number of people evacuated to Germany see Hamburger Institut für Sozialforschung, *Verbrechen der Wehrmacht: Dimensionen des Vernichtungskrieges 1941–1944. Ausstellungskatalog*

destroying them to make them uninhabitable for the advancing Red Army. As some historians have recently noted, the German 'term for this *Verwüstung* (desertification) is telling and entirely appropriate'.[7]

The logic of the war that eventually led to these human deserts, or *Tote Zonen* (dead zones) as the Germans called them, was that it was to be fought without restraint against men, women, and children 'with every means ... in which the winner took all'.[8] Even before the Red Steamroller rolled into Germany in January 1945, it was clear who the winner would be. Millions of terrified German civilians cognizant of this logic or at least of the sense that one reaps what one sows fled westward to escape the Red Army in January 1945. Years of Nazi propaganda featuring the terrifying 'Russian beast' accelerated their progress. It was left largely to those who could not flee in time to answer for the crimes of a nation – German women and children, the elderly, and the infirm. Some had no idea that the Red Army was near. Their local Nazi chiefs had prohibited them from evacuating their towns while fleeing secretly themselves, leaving them to find out the hard way that they had been abandoned.

The question now was whether the Red Army would allow the Germans who remained to live – 'life which the Germans had denied their enemy'.[9] They did, but the logic of the war without restraint seemed clear in the explosion of troop violence during the advance that left eastern Germany in flames and its women ravished. Violence against women had always been part of this logic. German forces took millions of Soviet women as slave labour to Germany, fewer as sexual slaves into the bordellos that dotted the Soviet occupation landscape. Where the bordellos did not suffice in number or taste, the Germans raped widely in the chasms between.[10] Women's labour was booty and their bodies a spoil of war. This sparked a fierce propaganda campaign in the Soviet press, calling soldiers to protect their womenfolk from the 'fascist beasts' and avenge those whom they could not.[11] At times, propaganda leaflets appeared that described the rapes in detail, complete with photographs of the mutilated bodies.[12] It is not surprising, then, that some soldiers raped the women

(Hamburg: Hamburger Edition, 2002), 387–9. Soviet forces also tried to conduct a scorched earth policy in 1941, removing their citizens and valuable machinery, livestock, etc. to the rear while retreating from German forces.

[7] Edele and Geyer, 'States of Exception', 380.   [8] Ibid.   [9] Ibid., 381.

[10] Official race laws prohibiting race-mixing (*Rassenschande*) between German forces and Soviet civilians were largely ignored by the Wehrmacht. J. Burds, 'Sexual Violence in Europe in World War II 1939–1945', *Politics and Society* 37, no. 1 (2009): 42.

[11] M. Edele, 'Paper Soldiers: The World of the Soldier Hero according to Soviet Wartime Posters', *Jahrbücher für Geschichte Osteuropas* 47, no. 1 (1999): 102.

[12] Pisiotis argues in his study of wartime propaganda that it was rare for images of raped women or detailed accounts of such crime to appear in the Soviet press, A. K. Pisiotis, 'Images of Hate in War', in *Culture and Entertainment in Wartime Russia*, ed. R. Stites

who remained in eastern Germany indiscriminately, old and young, fascist and communist, attractive and not. Historians have offered further explanations for the rapes, exploring the symbolism of rape in war and the sexual peculiarities of the Red Army and, indeed, Stalinist society. They help to explain why soldiers raped so extensively and publicly, often in front of German men.[13] They also help explain how a soldier's pain at any aspect of the German occupation – the murder of his relatives or the destruction of his village – could be channelled towards sexual violence. But in the chaos of the advance and disintegration of military discipline where much became permissible, more direct, less symbolic reasons remained in play. Soldiers were often blind drunk, sex-starved for years and couldn't be bothered looking for four standing walls in the rubble to rape women in private, German or not. In the place of slavery, forced starvation and mass exterminations – the hallmarks of the German occupation – rape became widespread in 1945.

Looting and wanton destruction more so. Soldiers marvelled at the solid-cut stone manors in the countryside of East Prussia, filled with preserved foods, polished furniture, and full-sized mirrors, filled with everything unavailable in their impoverished villages back home. Faced with the question of why such a rich nation as Germany would invade and try to enslave their own poor utopia, the soldiers simply smashed to pieces all the wonderful things they couldn't loot. They razed the mansions to the ground and killed the remaining rich landowners as their fathers had done to their own back in 1917 at the time of the revolution.

Stalin excused them then and now. He said he would not indict his soldiers for having 'fun with a woman or some trifle' when they had crossed Europe over the dead bodies of their comrades and dearest ones to liberate the continent.[14] Many of his military commanders agreed with him out of conviction or necessity. They did little to stop the violence meted out to German civilians during the advance, feeling that it was

(Bloomington, Ind.: Indiana University Press 1995), 143. Any reading of the soldier newspapers, such as *Krasnaia Zvezda* (Red Star) supports this viewpoint. There were, however, many exceptions to this trend, most notably during the latter stages of the war in other forms of media subject to less central control such as leaflets, etc. A full reprint of one such leaflet can be found in Burds, 'Sexual Violence in Europe', 48.

[13] Naimark and Merridale offer the most useful explanations. Naimark, *The Russians in Germany*, 109–16, Merridale, *Ivan's War*, 309–20. For a discussion of wartime rape in Germany and its relationship to historical memory see A. Grossman, 'A Question of Silence: The Rape of German Women by Occupation Soldiers', *October* 72 (1995) as well as articles in the special edition of the following journal dedicated to this topic: *Violence against Women* 12, no. 7 (2006), especially J. W. Messerschmidt, 'The Forgotten Victims of World War II Masculinities and Rape in Berlin, 1945', and K. V. Bletzer, 'A Voice for Every Woman and the Travesties of War'.

[14] M. Djilas, *Conversations with Stalin*, trans. M. B. Petrovich (New York: Harcourt, Brace & World, 1962), 110.

simply a natural process of justice playing itself out, one in which they need not interfere.

Unlike their German counterparts, however, Soviet commanders had not ordered that mass violence be meted out to civilians as a policy of pacification and certainly not desertification. But it didn't matter. Now the logic of the war did not need to be articulated in orders and, in any case, commanders could do little to change it. Crossing the dead zones, soldiers had learnt how civilians should be pacified. The reams of army newspapers calling for vengeance against anyone and anything German reflected the mood of the troops as much as it exacerbated it. Yet it soon became clear to many commanders in a matter of days and weeks that the violence and the propaganda could not continue, if they were to finish the war anytime soon and have any chance of administering the lands they had conquered. The logic of the war which demanded it be waged without restraint no longer made sense in Germany.

Even at the beginning of February, military operations were suffering with so many soldiers binge-drinking, seeking out women and loot rather than preparing for battle. Insubordination was rife. Those officers who cared to look struggled to keep track of their men's whereabouts, especially when they exchanged their military uniform for smart German suits. Expectedly, German military resistance stiffened as news of Soviet violence fused with old images of the 'Russian beast' sped westward ahead of the advance. Commanders also feared that, far from the violence pacifying civilians, it would spark a partisan movement as it did back home. Something had to be done to save the army from disintegrating before it could reach Berlin and end the war.[15]

Then there was the question of what to do once the war was over. The plan was to defeat German forces and pacify conquered areas to administer them better, even to feed the population, not evacuate them and make eastern Germany uninhabitable. But soldiers were burning towns to the ground for no apparent military reason, exacerbating housing shortages in eastern Germany, not only for the Germans but for their own liberated citizens as well. They were destroying factories that dismantling teams were lining up to remove and send back to the Soviet Union as war reparations. The threat of violence was discouraging Germans from working with the Red Army to help reconstruct essential services. Farmers were too afraid to work in the fields.[16] This is to say nothing of how the

---

[15] See the reprint of a speech delivered to 'political workers' in the Red Army on 6 February 1945, which discusses the multitude of these self-inflicted problems facing the army and their proposed solutions. Seniavskaia, *Frontovoe pokolenie*, 199–202.

[16] See Chapter 8.

long-term impact of mass rape would complicate any political structures that the Soviets planned to build in post-war Germany.

Even though many military commanders became aware of this looming catastrophe quickly and began to issue orders to stamp out the violence and restore order, they did so in a language unrecognisable to the troops – officers and men.[17] They lamented that no one understood Stalin's clear distinction between Hitlerite criminals and ordinary Germans, especially those whose families had suffered under German occupation. No one understood the new propaganda line that now specified that they were supposed to wreak their vengeance on the battlefield, not in the rear.[18] Commanders sometimes executed rapists in front of their units to make the men understand that rape was not permissible,[19] but with insubordination rife, such executions could only be staged sparingly.

If commanders experienced trouble communicating with soldiers whose families suffered, had been killed, kidnapped, or wounded by German occupation forces, then what of those soldiers who had suffered themselves? Commanders looked with hope upon the POWs whom they had liberated from captivity in Germany as a new source of manpower, perhaps physically drained, but seething to avenge their bondage on the battlefield and prove their loyalty to the motherland. That loyalty was in doubt as, according to Soviet law, a soldier was either dead or in service. A POW was a traitor who had failed to fight to the death and, if an officer, should be shot upon discovery and his family arrested.[20] Understandably, the POWs went to great lengths to convince their liberators that they had not surrendered to the Germans, but had been knocked unconscious in battle or wounded severely.[21] They tore off their shirts to reveal old, unhealed wounds to prove to their interrogators that they weren't able to shoot themselves before falling into captivity, like all good and dead soldiers.

But the commanders were interested less in their excuses and more in their redemption. In March 1945, 40,000 liberated POWs were re-enlisted into the armies on the 1st Ukrainian Front in south-eastern

---

[17] Seniavskaia, *Frontovoe pokolenie*, 197.

[18] Ibid. For an extract of Stalin's order to the troops in early 1942, see Edele and Geyer, 'States of Exception,' 369.

[19] See Merridale's study of memoir literature on this point, Merridale, *Ivan's War*, 320.

[20] Stalin's orders no. 270 (August 1941) and no. 227 (July 1942) were unpublished, but were conveyed verbally in each company of the Red Army, in *Russkii arkhiv: Velikaia Otechestvennaia voina: Prikazy narodnogo komissara oborony SSSR, 22 iiunia 1941g.–1942 g.*, vol. XIII (Moscow: Terra 1997), 57–8, 275–9.

[21] *Russkii arkhiv: Velikaia Otechestvennaia voina: Bitva za Berlin*, vol. xv (Moscow: Terra, 1995), 148–52.

Germany for the final offensive on Berlin.[22] Thousands of others too ill or suspect to fight were sent to field hospitals or detainment camps run by the feared secret police. At the political classes where German brutalities were discussed to rouse the troops before battle, those enlisted offered first-hand accounts of how their comrades had been exterminated, worked to death and tortured in captivity. They spoke of the Germans as wretched vermin. Now that they were armed, they relished the opportunity to take their vengeance. Their enthusiasm was infectious. They promised to fight bravely to avenge the wrongs committed against them and prove their loyalty to the motherland. One private told his liberator/interrogator that he and his fellow POWs 'needed to fight especially hard to cleanse them-selves of the shameful stain of fascist captivity' and, implicitly, avoid the Gulag upon their return home.[23] Most fulfilled their promise. One officer was re-enlisted to a rifle battalion on the Front after spending two years in German captivity, killed ten German soldiers and took nine prisoner in his first battle – his unit killed fifty.[24] Others died charging into German fire and undertaking suicide missions, earning posthumous medals for brav-ery. The examples are endless.[25]

Commanders were elated with the progress of many of their POW recruits in the final battles of the war, especially with those who died on the field. But many of the new recruits survived, and the end of the war did nothing to dampen their enthusiasm for revenge and 'cleanliness'. Some had deserted in battle and had wreaked havoc in Germany along with repatriates, but most were still serving in Red Army ranks after the war. Commanders who had lauded the recruits' courage and ferocity in battle now complained about their violent behaviour towards the occupied population. Some commanders derided the recruits as worse than the liberated slaves for the continuing raping and pillaging.[26]

If they were right, it would have been much easier to stop the violence after the war. But they were wrong. It was convenient to blame the 'mentally unstable' POWs, but they did not attack the Germans any

---

[22] Ibid., 148.   [23] Ibid., 152.   [24] Ibid.

[25] Depending partly on their 'reliability', POWs were enlisted into their old, ordinary, or penal units advancing into Germany. In an attempt to shore up failing discipline in the Red Army and stop disorganised retreats, penal units were established by Stalin in July 1942 (order no. 227). Servicemen now found guilty of serious and, eventually, not so serious offences were to be transferred to penal units to 'atone for their crimes against the Motherland with their blood'. These units, as in the Russian Civil War, were often sent to the most dangerous areas of the front and charged with suicide missions. See A. Statiev, 'Penal Units in the Red Army', *Europe–Asia Studies* 62, no. 5 (2010).

[26] Some of the 'liberated slaves' were, in fact, POWs who were not drafted into military service or placed under arrest upon their release. For POW violence in Brandenburg, see GARF – f. r-7077, op. 1, d. 178, l. 7, for Saxony GARF – f. r-7212, op. 1, d. 51, l. 94.

more or less than other soldiers. This was really the problem – each soldier had his own tragedy, his own memories of burnt-out villages and murdered relatives to draw upon. Many felt little difference between their own suffering, that of their families, or, indeed, that of their nation. In any case, the troops had been constantly reminded of all these sufferings by the visceral anti-German propaganda with which the army was saturated. The impact of such trauma and propaganda on millions of individual soldiers defies accurate analysis, allowing us to speak only generally about the links between it and their behaviour. Many attacked German civilians, many did not. Alcohol was usually an important factor. When it was involved, the violence could be so chaotic that not only German women, but any women, were targeted.

The ability of commanders to make their conquered areas habitable by reconstructing essential services and a rationing system within this chaos was nothing short of remarkable. Many of them who laboured so constructively were studious communists, but poor students of their erstwhile German occupiers. Although subjected to severe anti-German propaganda during the war, they had difficulty in assuming the same dehumanised attitude towards 'enemy civilians' that the Germans had mastered. They could not look on other human beings as subhumans who could only muster some unintelligible speech and were fit for slavery and nothing else. This distinction is most evident in the other scribbled testimonies that fill the archives – those of captured German soldiers under interrogation. Soviet interrogators poked and prodded the men to confess the sordid details of their conduct in the Soviet Union. They wanted names, dates, and locations of mass killings, rapes, robberies, and every single humiliation wrought on the Soviet people. But they often received little insight from the frightened soldiers. The interrogators were not surprised by the reluctance of the soldiers to speak about their crimes, but by the reason they gave for it. A young German soldier from the 267th Infantry Division interned in a makeshift POW camp during 1945 explained:

It is difficult to remember all the crimes committed by our division, as they occurred quite frequently. Brought up on contempt towards the Russian people, we officers and soldiers of the German army did not pay any attention to them, as the life of a Russian person has no value whatsoever in our understanding.[27]

Many civilians in Germany felt the same. Pounded by years of Nazi propaganda that radicalised old anti-Slavic stereotypes, many understood the mass rapes in eastern Germany only as an affirmation of the Russian 'subhuman' character. If Russians were sub-human, then according to the

---

[27] GARF – f. r-7021, op. 148, d. 30, l. 2.

German racial hierarchy the 'Mongolians' in the Red Army were simply animals. Wide-eyed with supposedly yellowing sharp teeth and flat, ape-like faces, the Germans scoffed at their raping as a form of bestiality rather than sex. Many of them felt that it was just another example of how fate had dealt them an unfair hand.[28] After all, they were just the innocent civilians led astray by a criminal leadership. Many Red Army officers committed to stopping the violence found this attitude exceedingly obnoxious. Even when Stalin began speaking more and more of good Germans and bad Nazis near the end of the war, these attitudes tested the resolve of the officers to risk their lives to restrain their men. They were buoyed, however, by their interactions with many Germans who adopted a different approach to dealing with the Red Army. Upon seeing his house burned to the ground by marauding Red Army soldiers in East Prussia in February 1945, one farmer confided to an onlooking Soviet officer, each as helpless as the other to put a stop to the carnage:

I know what German soldiers did in Russia. I know the Russian attitude towards the Germans. Thus I understand that malice, with which you Russians look at us.[29]

Such attitudes were widespread among 'anti-fascists' in Germany. The Soviets recruited allies from their ranks to rebuild war-torn Germany. Together, they laboured towards this end, and were equally disappointed at how the violence compromised their ability to achieve it. The violence got worse in the final stages of the war and its immediate aftermath, when the Red Army liberated millions of slave labourers in Germany. As discussed above, some had been POWs and were drafted back into the army for the final battles, but most were deemed unfit for service. Others were just civilians who had been kidnapped from their homelands by German forces or been duped into volunteering for work in Germany by the placards strewn across Ukraine and Belorussia promising them an escape from the ravages of occupation. Whoever they were, they now either had scores to settle with the Germans or good reason to avoid the Soviet authorities, who considered the volunteers traitors. Either way, the liberated could not have cared less about how their rampaging for food, booty, and justice in eastern Germany made SVAG's task of administering the country difficult, if not impossible to carry out. This was one of many 'bad inheritances' received by SVAG after the war, which they would fight tooth and nail to disavow.

---

[28] German complaints about low food rations were especially a source of frustration for Soviet officers. See Chapter 8.
[29] RGASPI – f. 17, op. 125, d. 318, ll. 20–1.

2   Inheriting wartime chaos

Before SVAG could turn its full attention to bringing violent soldiers to heel, or even combat the Moscow-backed dismantling groups that threatened to strip Germany's economy bare, it had to deal with its own liberated citizens. Millions of them had been forced to work in German mines, factories, farms, and some even in German concentration camps. Just what they had experienced can be gleaned from their testimonies, and in the camps from those of other prisoners who had worked directly for the German camp staff. Testimonies not only help to explain the extent to which German civilians exploited slave labourers and the intimate workings of the camp system, but also why so many labourers wreaked havoc on Germany after their liberation.

An old German communist called Willi Feiler was imprisoned at the Sachsenhausen concentration camp located 40 km north of Berlin when Soviet POWs first arrived. With the help of a friend who provided him with a dress and a wig, Willi escaped from the camp on a bicycle disguised as a townswoman in July 1943. Notwithstanding his ingenuity, Willi's time in the camp and subsequent years hiding underground had damaged him greatly. Near the end of the war in April 1945, he still lacked the strength to write his testimony, dictating it to his wife instead. Although his body may have been weary, his mind was still sharp. The American military officers who received Willi's testimony quickly realised this and hurried to translate and send it to their superiors. In their haste they offered only a trite apology for their failure to correct all the spelling and typographical errors that abound in such documents written by soldiers with bad typewriters and only an elementary grasp of the enemy's language.[1]

Since the majority of victims at Sachsenhausen were Russians and Ukrainians, the Americans sent Willi's testimony to their Soviet Allies. It makes for chilling reading. It offered the Soviets much more precise

---

[1] GARF – f. r-7021, op. 148, d. 104, l. 174.

information on the mechanics of death in the camp than could most of the survivors. Many told stories of torture which rallied their liberators, but few could offer precise information on how the camp operated before they arrived and how many people were killed there. Willi remembered the first Soviet POWs who arrived at the camp on 1 September 1941 from the battle of Bialystok. On this first morning of autumn, 18,000 of them began to stagger into the camp after travelling for days, stuffed in cattle cars without food or water. As they descended from the cars in ranks of three, two stronger soldiers supporting a weaker between them, they were beaten with clubs by guards standing at 5 metre intervals. Instead of hurrying along the procession, the beatings only felled the exhausted men, causing human bottlenecks at the narrow entrances to the camp parade grounds. The guards became impatient and beat them more severely. They were soon joined by other guards who rushed to meet the procession. They fell upon the prostrate POWs in the parade grounds with sharper, deadlier weapons. Some cut into their flesh using bayonets, others shot at them with pistols, and all with a special enthusiasm. After all, this was the first time that many of the guards had seen Soviet soldiers.[2]

Some camp inmates worried that their cramped barracks could not house such a large number of new arrivals. But housing them was never the intention. The next morning, surviving POWs who could be made to walk or crawl into the camp trucks were herded to the other, secret, side of the camp – the '*Industriehof*'. The execution trench lay at the centre of this industrial yard used for the destruction of human bodies. Dug out of a sandpit, the trench was hardly stable, its sides having to be lined with thick planks of wood to keep them from collapsing. Next to the trench stood a large, old shed used for parking camp trucks, 50 metres long. To prepare for the POWs' arrival, two hundred camp inmates had worked feverishly to turn the shed into an execution barracks. There, more than 10,000 of the POWs were shot in little over two months.[3] Each man was hustled through a series of rooms and told to undress in front of a guard masquerading as a doctor. A guard hiding in an adjacent room then opened a flap in the wall and shot the naked man in the back of the neck. Some guessed what was coming and put up fierce resistance, often succeeding in strangling and biting some of the guards to death. But live guards replaced dead ones and, like their predecessors, continued to murder, extract the POWs' valuable metal teeth, and then drag the corpses into the next room. There, they piled the corpses into the four small, mobile crematoria, which burnt

[2] GARF – f. r-7021, op. 148, d. 104, l. 180.
[3] G. Morsch, ed., *Mord und Massermord im Konzentrationlager Sachsenhausen 1936–1945* (Berlin: Metropol-Verlag, 2005), 34.

them slowly and inefficiently. Camp inmates would need to clear the crematoria regularly of ashes and remaining bones which clogged their incinerators. Political commissars were spared the bullets and crammed into the crematoria alive, kicking, and screaming.[4]

While these POWs burned, the camp guards wondered what to do with the rest of them. SS-Sturmbannführer (Major) Lauer, in charge of supplying the camp with food, provided a solution. Lauer ordered that some of the remaining POWs be transported to nearby woods and locked in a clearing enclosed by barbed wire, usually reserved for the guards' pagan worship. The guards denied the POWs food or water and left the most desperate to feed on the flesh of their dead comrades until everyone had perished.[5]

The Germans rapidly developed more efficient methods to exterminate inmates as the war continued. But torture was always central to the killing. Willi counted forty-seven torture stations to the left of the execution trench where thousands were killed quickly and as a matter of course. There camp guards could take their time to punish the inmates before killing them. On some stations the guards tied the inmates' hands and feet around hollow drums so that their rump could be as taut and exposed as possible to the lashes from their oxtail whips. Anywhere from twenty-five to a hundred lashes would usually be given. On other stations they simply tied inmates' hands behind their backs, attached a chain to them, and, with the aid of a pulley system, hoisted their bodies 10 centimetres above the floor so that all their bodyweight was supported by their bound wrists for hours on end. And if it were necessary to eliminate from the inmates any lingering hopes for escaping certain death, there were fifteen gallows which stood next to the torture stations and on which corpses were always hanging.[6]

Some guards were more creative torturers than others. One of the camp's senior non-commissioned officers (NCOs), Juhren, was quite fond of drowning inmates by attaching one end of a rubber tube to a tap and shoving the other down an inmate's throat. On other occasions, he would lock twenty-five inmates in a small non-ventilated room. The inmates would fight to get closer to the small chink in the door where air could be sucked in, clawing at each other's skin and hair, leaving clumps of them across the floor which camp workers swept up after they had removed the suffocated corpses from the room.[7] A gas chamber was later

[4] GARF – f. r-7021, op. 148, d. 104, l. 180.
[5] GARF – f. r-7021, op. 148, d. 104, l. 181.
[6] GARF – f. r-7021, op. 148, d. 104, ll. 177–8.
[7] GARF – f. r-7021, op. 148, d. 104, l. 182.

constructed with a mechanical door which slid corpses into the fixed crematoria capable of incinerating hundreds a day.[8] The crematoria were rarely used to their capacity, however, as after 1941 POWs were used more as slave labourers for the war effort. They were burnt after they had been worked to death. In any case, the guards persisted with their tortures.

They did their best to obscure the bleak reality of the mass killings from the inmates. The barracks, parade ground, and work areas were situated on the other side of the camp and separated from the '*Hof*' and killing area by high walls. It was only the billowing black smoke from crematory chimneys and the echoes of gunfire sometimes heard on the western wind that raised the suspicions of those who were left behind. But even inmates who were taken to the '*Hof*' for execution were driven in window-less trucks and along complex, winding routes. And there the guards persisted with their ruse, with sham doctors and hidden gun flaps.

The relatively few Soviet POWs and civilians who survived these tortures across the web of concentration camps in Germany were unleashed on the country in the final months of the war. They were joined by millions of Soviet slave labourers who had been kidnapped from their homelands by German forces. Many were rounded up in the city squares of Minsk, Kiev, and across the western USSR by soldiers on horseback and herded into cattle cars with whips and rifles for shipment to German mines, factories, and fields. After the war they were ill, both physically and mentally, but many of those with enough strength and anger went on a rampage.[9] The rank and file soldier-liberators who joined them were just as sceptical of the distinction between Nazi criminals and ordinary Germans which the Soviet propaganda machine began to peddle force-fully in April 1945. Stalin hoped that the new policy and his order to the troops to treat German civilians humanely would stem the mass outburst of troop violence against German civilians and convince German forces defending Berlin to surrender quickly. His hopes were in vain.[10] The years

[8] GARF – f. r-7021, op. 148, d. 104, l. 178.
[9] Earlier in the war, some Soviet citizens 'volunteered' for work in Germany under the false impression peddled by German propagandists that pay and living conditions in Germany were much better than in the Soviet Union. It is not difficult to see how such propaganda may have been appealing in those areas whose economies had been devastated by war and the pressures of occupation. However, mail from 'eastern workers' received back home revealing the truth of their bondage reduced volunteer numbers significantly, encouraging German forces to forcibly recruit workers to meet growing labour demands. Polian's study of 'eastern workers' remains the benchmark, P. Polian, *Zhertvy dvukh diktatur: Ostarbaitery i voennoplennye v Tret'em reikhe i ikh repatriatsiia* (Moscow: Vash Vybor TSIRZ, 1996).
[10] For an extract of Stalin's order and the shift in Soviet propaganda see N. V. Petrov, *Pervyi predsedatel' KGB Ivan Serov* (Moscow: Materik, 2005), 47–8.

of Soviet wartime propaganda which had hammered into the Soviet people the message that all of German society was responsible for the war could not wash off so easily, the Soviet experience of German occupation and bondage even less so. There was simply a common feeling among liberators and liberated that the tortures at Sachsenhausen and the many other camps across German-occupied Europe were extraordinary crimes not committed by individuals but by an entire country. These crimes could not be prosecuted within an ordinary legal framework. The liberated would bring the Germans to justice by the best way they knew how – *samosud* – the old Russian tradition of mob law.

The battles in eastern Germany and the troops' rampages had destroyed so much housing in urban centres that the Red Army had little choice but to keep the former slaves in barracks from which they had just been liberated. By May 1945 some of those liberated were thus billeted at Sachsenhausen. The camps were poorly guarded, if at all, by the Red Army, which in April and early May was still mopping up German forces. These people were essentially let loose. The result at Sachsenhausen and, indeed, throughout the city of Oranienburg where the camp was located was not surprising. Along with Berlin located all but 40 km to its south, Oranienburg was, by mid 1945, one of the most dangerous and chaotic places in Germany and, indeed, post-war Europe.

The *Ostarbeiter* or 'eastern workers', as the Germans called the slaves, attacked young and old in Oranienburg, robbing, raping, and murdering indiscriminately. The worst of the offenders were, expectedly, those billeted at Sachsenhausen. They organised themselves into bands and rampaged through the city every night since their liberation in April, beating anyone who offered the slightest bit of resistance. The indiscriminate nature of the violence shocked Oranienburg communists who appealed to Soviet officers to arrest the offenders.[11] Like the soldiers the eastern workers, contrary to Stalin's order, simply failed to distinguish between the majority of innocent Germans and those Nazis who deserved to be punished.

Most were unaware of the propaganda shifts made by the Soviet leadership which promoted the above distinction. If they had been made aware of this distinction, they invariably dismissed it. They had their own experience to draw upon. The slaves who had laboured under German civilian bosses in industry and agriculture were more dismissive than their comrades who suffered the tortures of camp life at the hands of the German military and SS. Those unfortunate enough to have been sent to the mines

---

[11] GARF – f. r-7077, op.1, d. 178, ll. 30–3.

in Würselen, close to the Belgian border, were subject to the daily beatings and humiliations meted out by their German foremen who took so much pleasure in building their reputations as 'Russian killers'. One of the foremen, Koch, habitually beat the thirty or forty Russian and Ukrainian labourers under his control, some as young as sixteen. Any time one of his workers left the work column to relieve himself, Koch, waiting for him to finish, would beat him to the ground, seize him by the collar and shove his face into the shit. In the absence of toilet blocks for the workers, this was the only way the workers could relieve themselves during their long shifts.[12] More and more of these liberated slaves from western Germany were arriving in Oranienburg and across the zone after the war. They too joined in the rampage and increased the scale of violence.

The Soviets were accepting their citizens from western Germany at a much faster rate than they could register, feed, house, and repatriate them back to the Soviet Union. According to the citizen exchange programme worked out by the Allies and the Soviets in late May, the number of Soviet citizens to be transferred to the east of Germany under Soviet occupation, and German and Western European citizens to be transferred west under Allied, should not have exceeded 50,000 per day. But from the second week of June, an average of 60,000 Soviet repatriates was being transferred daily.[13] Probably just over 600,000 were thus returned to the Soviet zone over this period, and more over the summer, each of whom had to be fed, housed, and guarded.[14] This was simply impossible. SVAG was having enough trouble dealing with millions of their own repatriates. The new arrivals placed significant pressure on SVAG to try and relieve the chaos of the immediate post-war period and govern the zone. Perhaps as significant was the pressure exerted by the millions of penniless, disease-ridden, and hungry ethnic German refugees who flooded Germany's eastern borders at this time. Zhukov was besieged by waves of human misery from east and west as soon as he took command of SVAG.

If the liberated were hungry for justice, they were hungrier for food. They raided farmsteads and fields in the summer of 1945, so that German farmers were reluctant to collect the harvest – women agricultural labourers more so for fear of rape. When they did collect, it was often only enough to feed their families. The scattered collection of the harvest thus threatened SVAG's ability to feed the zone. This problem had been brewing for months. With the mass exodus of German forces and millions of

---

[12] GARF – f. r-7021, op. 148, d. 104, l. 27.
[13] M. Elliott, 'The United States and Forced Repatriation of Soviet Citizens, 1944–47', *Political Science Quarterly* 88, no. 2 (1973): 269.
[14] Polian offers more specific figures, Polian, *Zhertvy dvukh diktatur*, 229–30.

civilians westward ahead of the advance, there was little chance of the spring sowing proceeding as normal in the eastern, most fertile, part of the country. That most large landowners were the first to flee in fear of the Red Army did not help, as they were the greatest commercial producers of grain and other foodstuffs in the country. In any case, some of their land had now fallen under Polish occupation. With the harvest itself only promising limited relief from food shortages, full collection became even more important. However, SVAG could find no apparent solution to this problem. The millions of repatriates who remained in camps were awaiting immediate transport back to the USSR and were required to collect the Soviet, not German, harvest. However much the millions of ethnic German refugees who poured over the border helped alleviate the labour problem, they compounded food shortages even more. In some cases, overstrained Soviet authorities refused to accept refugee trains and sent them back into Polish territory.[15]

Those repatriates who resisted repatriation back to the Soviet Union were often the worst raiders. Some had collaborated with German forces, volunteered for work in Germany, or could not prove that they were victims of German repression. Either way, many faced years of imprisonment in the Gulags upon their return home. They fled at exchange points or shortly thereafter and, with no source of food or material supply, took them from the occupied population by the only means available to them, force.[16] The problem of food scarcity both gave rise to violence and was exacerbated by it.

Liberated Soviet POWs were as angry and hungry as their civilian comrades. Those liberated by the Americans in the state of Thuringia found themselves under Soviet occupation in July 1945 when the Americans evacuated.[17] The Americans left the POWs without provisions, forcing them to fend for themselves. It is little wonder that they roamed in search of food, materials, and weapons, inevitably from German locals. They were bound to run into trouble with the Red Army, which was now establishing control over the area. Gunfights

---

[15] For the greater strains that refugee trains caused to food and medical services in Mecklenburg see Chapter 7. For the refusal to accept German refugees from Polish areas see M. Holz, *Evakuierte, Flüchtlinge und Vertriebene auf der Insel Rügen 1943–1961* (Cologne: Böhlau Verlag, 2004), 95–7.

[16] Ibid., 237–50.

[17] According to the 'Protocol on the Zones of Occupation in Germany and the Administration of Greater Berlin' signed by the Soviets and the Allies in September 1944, Berlin was to be divided into four separate sectors, each administered by one of the occupying powers. As the Soviets took the city first, the Allies handed over territories they had occupied in the eastern parts of the country to the Soviets in return for their slice of Berlin in July 1945.

between regular soldiers and the POWs occurred during this period, resulting in serious casualties. Most took place at supply warehouses containing food or goods which could be traded on the bourgeoning black market.[18]

In this precarious situation with SVAG providing food rations to millions of German urban dwellers, the last thing that it needed was more mouths to feed. From the beginning of the harvest season, even soldiers had been carrying out food requisitions, often under orders, to feed their units. Others had been conducting their own requisitions to sell on the black market.[19] These sporadic requisitions became systematic from August 1945, when the poor Soviet harvest dashed the hopes of the leadership, who were expecting a massive bump in grain levels. Now it was clear that they could no longer supply occupying forces in Germany with food, leaving the entire Red Army to live off the land. This put SVAG into an impossible situation, as it had already worked out grain and foodstuff quotas with German farmers to fund the rationing system. This system, which was tentative at best, was thrust into chaos with the army conducting its own requisitioning or even demanding food supplies from SVAG. There simply was not enough grain for German farmers to satisfy both masters. To make matters worse for farmers, many repatriates, especially Poles, sought to claim their own form of reparations by stealing German agricultural machinery and equipment and carting them back home. And Polish removals were minor compared with those conducted by Soviet reparations teams. They sent thousands of tonnes of working agricultural machinery and livestock back to the Soviet Union at a fantastic pace during this period. Naturally, civilian rations suffered and the bourgeoning conflict between SVAG and the army centred on the troop violence

---

[18] GARF – f. r-9401, op. 2, d. 97, ll. 307–8. Black market problems were exacerbated by the still porous border between the zones, see P. Steege, *Black Market, Cold War: Everyday Life in Berlin, 1946–1949* (New York: Cambridge University Press, 2007), 255. To make matters worse, Soviet soldiers too were keen patrons of the black market. Many of them traded with German black marketeers for moonshine or cigarettes, and in some cases developed long-term trade relations with them. For instance, a senior officer of the Plauen *komendatura*, Lieutenant 'A', regularly stole foodstuffs from the *komendatura* storage house and provided them to a local German tailor in return for civilian clothing during mid 1946. Upon questioning, the tailor's wife admitted that the officer visited them two or three times a week with parcels of butter, meat, and sugar. For the report, see GARF – f. r-7103, op. 1, d. 22, ll. 3–10.
[19] Some soldiers adopted less violent and more sophisticated methods for this purpose. Soldiers in Saxony were known to steal officers' documentation such as sequestration orders, fill them out, and then attempt to enforce the orders at stores and supply depots. SVAG became aware of the practice when they found a fabricated order on the body of a drunken soldier picked up by a patrol on 26 October 1945. GARF – f. r-7212, op. 1, d. 55, l. 50.

problem now broadened into a resource battle that threatened a food crisis in the winter.[20]

The only way SVAG could avert this crisis was to wait for the mass demobilisation of forces begun in June to take effect and reduce the number of people it had to feed. In August, Zhukov launched a massive 'clean up' operation against the 'many thousands of those who hide from our military government to avoid repatriation to the Soviet Union and have taken up banditry and armed robbery as their profession'.[21] From June to September 1945, millions of liberated Soviet POWs and slave labourers, some of whom had been picked up in the August operation, had been repatriated back to the Soviet Union or were at least on their way.[22] The operation targeted other 'enemy elements' as well, mostly members of Nazi organisations. Over 3,000 members were arrested by the People's Commissariat of Internal Affairs (NKVD), the chief security service which Zhukov enlisted for support, while a much larger number of repatriates were interned by the Red Army, which set up filtration points across the zone to check people's documentation.[23] Along with the massive demobilisation of troops, this was a significant achievement by a severely underdeveloped occupation government.

But angry and hungry repatriates were only a symptom of a deeper problem which these mass operations could not resolve. Many army officers were still allowing the violence to continue and failing to punish those responsible months afterward. Permissiveness was an enduring problem which required a permanent solution, and while these operations may have been effective, they were only temporary. SVAG could do little to address this problem in 1945 and 1946. How could they arrest rampaging repatriates when they had been recruited into units by Soviet officers from different occupation organs and were thus under their protection? In addition to performing the tasks assigned to them, such as dismantling factories for dispatch back to the Soviet Union, some of these units, heavily armed, rampaged through the countryside and did as they pleased with their officer leading the charge. One such officer, Colonel 'Sorokin', an economist who, like all specialists who had come to Germany to work, was afforded a military rank, had seventy-one repatriates under his

[20] See Chapter 7.   [21] Zakharov, ed., *Deiatel'nost' sovetskikh voennykh komendatur*, 96.
[22] By 1 September 1945, the total number of repatriates removed from Germany and its other formerly occupied countries reached 5,115,700. Approximately 560,000 remained. T. V. Tsarevskaia-Diakina, 'Otdel repatriatsii i rozyskov sovetskikh grazhdan SVAG', in *Sovetskaia voennaia administratsiia v Germanii*, ed. Doronin, Foitzik, and Tsarevskaia-Diakina, 517.
[23] S. V. Mironenko, ed., *Spetsial'nye lageria NKVD/MVD SSSR v Germanii 1945–1950: Sbornik dokumentov i statei*, vol. II (Moscow: Rosspen, 2001), 30.

command in a regional area of Grimmen near the north-eastern tip of Germany.[24] Armed with rifles, pistols, and machine guns, the colonel and his men habitually descended upon the town square, blind drunk, terror-ised locals, and took from them what they pleased.[25] The men often became so drunk that they forgot their weapons on their rampages, leaving machine guns lying about the town for anyone to pick up. Not that many locals bothered to do so, understanding resistance as futile.[26] Yet, con-sidering that SVAG was trying to remove all weaponry from the occupied population at this time, the unit's negligence was just another reason for SVAG to try to compel 'Sorokin' to restore order in his ranks. He, however, was having none of it. This pattern of officers not under SVAG jurisdiction resisting SVAG intervention at every turn became a dominant feature of the occupation and significantly hampered SVAG's attempts to restore order.

That the Red Army and even the NKVD provided much of the man-power for SVAG's mass 'clean up' operations from July to August was central to their success and, eventually, to bringing men like 'Sorokin' to heel. Yet this posed a problem as well. For all of the soldiers willing to battle armed repatriates and POWs to fulfil their orders, many regular soldiers as well as their commanders were sympathetic to repatriates and/or apathetic about occupation duties. Either way, they were reluctant to round up repatriates, especially if they had to use force. Similarly, camp guards were often unwilling or unable to force repatriates, especially former POWs, to remain in their confinement. POWs housed in intern-ment camps across the zone habitually left the camps to wander around surrounding areas. When alcohol was involved, these wanderings became violent and turned into rampages which could last for days before many of the POWs would return to their camps. Others who were more fearful of punishment would remain at large. At the POW camp near Riesa, just north of Dresden, in October 1945, POWs wandered into nearby villages to rob houses and upon being confronted by homeowners or townspeople ended up shooting them. Liberated slave labourers in the area did the same, but raped rather than killed the women.[27]

The poor guarding of camps remained a pressing problem for SVAG and especially for those unlucky enough to live near them, despite a significant reduction in violence and stabilisation of occupation condi-tions over the winter of 1945–6. As late as April 1946, the citizens of

---

[24] All surnames given in quotation marks are pseudonyms.
[25] GARF – f. r-7103, op. 1, d. 26, l. 65.
[26] For the 'muted' German response to Soviet violence see Chapter 6.
[27] GARF – f. r-7212, op. 1, d. 51, l. 94.

Luckenwalde, a small city 50 km south of Berlin, became the next victims. A camp housing soldiers suffering from venereal disease in the city was poorly guarded, allowing the inmates to descend upon the city and terrorise its inhabitants for weeks. Reports began to filter up the SVAG chain of command in April about the 'amoral developments' in Luckenwalde and the lax attitude of the camp guards towards the problem. SVAG officers in the region were not surprised, given that many of the soldiers had contracted the disease by having sex with German women, forced or consensual, and the camp was notoriously poorly guarded. One such officer, Lieutenant Gusenko, immediately appealed to his superiors for assistance in dealing with the bands of 'venereals' as they were called. He and his unit could only do so much. By the end of the month they had arrested only three soldiers for kidnapping women from the town, dragging them to the woods, and raping them. This made a mockery of SVAG policies aimed at reducing the spread of venereal disease.

Other soldiers were not so discreet. Five were at large after attacking a German restaurant and raping three of the female diners in front of the crowd, stabbing another German who tried to intervene. Even high-ranking communists were not safe. Soldiers stabbed to death Comrade Andress after he refused to provide them with alcohol and cigarettes. This well-regarded local party chief in Luckenwalde was left to bleed to death in the street. Andress hoped that on producing his communist party card, his 'comrades' would leave him alone, perhaps even listen to his call for calm. Sometimes this worked, but not that night. The soldiers tore his card to pieces. They may well have been too drunk to care.[28] But some of the 'venereals' had come to despise the army/party authorities which were punishing them for contracting such diseases. By early 1946 SVAG also

---

[28]   GARF – f. r-7077, op. 1, d. 196, l. 80. There are numerous other cases of left-wingers attacked during the drunken rampages of some troops or 'unofficial elements' during late 1945. In Brandenburg, for instance, a KPD worker reported to SVAG on the alarming incidence of indiscriminate Soviet violence in the area: 'In the village Hertzberg a group of your soldiers headed by an officer stole things from the burgomaster and KPD leadership during the night, raped their women, and tore their party documents to pieces as well as their documents about the [land] reform. These things are quickly made known to the populace and evoke terror among them', GARF – f. r-7077, op.1, d. 179, l. 69. Another report taken from a villager of the Cottbus region in the same month testifies to the seriousness of the problem: 'An incident took place in the night of the 14th to the 15th of November, where a former communist called Klese was killed with his wife and daughter, shocking the entire populace. After this how can we be well disposed to the occupation authority?' This quotation is taken from the seminal report prepared by the newly appointed head of the Political Department in Brandenburg, Colonel Ia. I. Mil'khiker, on 28 November 1945. In the report Mil'khiker outlined what he felt were the most damaging forms of behaviour in Mecklenburg, as evident from the reams of regional reports provided by subordinate political officers. Rape and robbery were high on his list. GARF f. r-7077, op. 1, d. 199, ll. 70–8.

tried to exert much greater control over drug supplies, reserving penicillin and other medicines required to treat venereal diseases for high-ranking officers.[29] The soldiers may well have judged Andress guilty by association. Gusenko's report was quickly passed up the SVAG chain of command. The uncommon speed of this process was due to the extreme nature of the offences and frequency. As many as ten to fifteen cases of rape and murder were reported daily in April. Many more went unreported because the victims were killed in private or were too afraid to speak out.

The SVAG brass was also concerned that this calamity coincided with May Day preparations. Just as SVAG forces in Luckenwalde were hanging grand red flags in the town square and encouraging locals to go out and watch the classics of Soviet cinema and come to party meetings – winning the hearts and minds to use a modern term – a battalion of 'venereals' was rampaging across the city. They caused such panic among locals that few dared to venture out at night. During the day the locals established citizen patrols in villages which raised the alarm upon sighting any soldiers.

SVAG forces in Luckenwalde were outnumbered by the 'venereals', who, in many cases, had managed to arm themselves. The only way that SVAG could deal with the problem was to force the camp guards to do their job or push for their replacement. Eventually the deputy head of SVAG in Brandenburg, the state in which Luckenwalde is located, had to intervene personally. He demanded that the guards do their job and establish control over the camp, which, in time, they did.[30] But this was the main problem. No matter how hard SVAG pushed, it was always relying on the occupation organs to enforce the level of discipline that was required to establish law and order in Germany and rebuild the country – aims to which the other organs and many among the Moscow leadership were largely unsympathetic in 1945 and for much of 1946.

From 1945 onward the chief purpose of the occupation was to destroy Germany's war-making ability and to reconstruct the shattered Soviet economy with the assistance of German reparations. SVAG would need to reconstruct war-ravaged Germany so as to make it habitable and sustain its population, but also assist in achieving Moscow's chief purpose. The best way to do so was to establish a monopoly on political power through

---

[29] GARF – f. r-7184, op. 1, d. 10, l. 176.

[30] The deputy head of the Soviet Military Administration Province Brandenburg (SVAB), Major General V. M. Sharov, forwarded the complaint with some amendments to the SVAG Military Council. He did so in little over a week after the original complaint was made, indicating that some serious complaints could be fast-tracked if detailed evidence against specific detachments or camp administrations were provided (Sharov provided the camp number). GARF – f. r-7077, op. 1, d. 196, l. 89.

its sponsored political party. The problem was that the closeness of the party to the Soviets undermined its popularity as people also blamed it for Soviet excesses and thus made achieving the much sought-after monopoly most difficult. It was not merely this conflict at the heart of SVAG's existence that frustrated its officers so much, nor the attitude of the leadership. It was, essentially, that the very structure of occupation governance which emerged in Germany thrust them into a subordinate jurisdictional position that made its job most difficult, particularly for SVAG's political officers who were charged specifically with establishing this monopoly.[31]

The structure was characterised by the absence of a central executive body that could control policy implementation and mediate between the different occupation organs. In the absence of such a body, commissariats and relevant state commissions in Moscow were able to assign their subordinate organs operating in Germany specific tasks that conflicted with those assigned to SVAG (not to mention assigning different SVAG departments conflicting tasks). As such, conflicting occupation policies were carried out by an array of organs that often competed with one another. The competition was most intense during 1945 and 1946, when the lines of jurisdictional responsibility and power between occupation organs remained most undefined. Within this bureaucratic mess, however, those occupation organs that were entrusted with carrying out 'more important' policies maintained superior levels of power in comparison to SVAG, creating a power hierarchy within the structure of Soviet occupation governance that broadly corresponded to the hierarchy of occupation aims in Germany. At the top of this hierarchy stood the policies of security and reparations, with the thousands of security agents and dismantlers who carried them out. They expressed little concern as to how their operations and reckless behaviour diminished SVAG's ability to govern and inhibited its attempt to construct more positive relations with the occupied population.

Charged with nullifying the threat posed by 'anti-Soviet' elements, the security services operated as a law unto themselves. Arbitrary arrests of local German officials, violence, and foodstuff requestioning committed

---

[31] Most political officers were members of the SVAG Political Administration established by Zhukov on 22 July 1945. The new administration assumed control of both central and land/provincial SVAG political departments. The new political administration also consumed the army political departments in Germany dedicated to conducting political work among the occupied population. For a short history tracing the multifarious functions and historical development of the administration see J. Foitzik, 'Politicheskoe upravlenie SVAG', in *Sovetskaia voennaia administratsiia v Germanii*, ed. Doronin, Foitzik, and Tsarevskaia-Diakina.

by security troops upset the tenuous balance of administrative control that had emerged in any given area and made it most difficult for SVAG to administer it effectively. NKVD agents may have worked with SVAG on some issues and even enjoyed some integrated command structures, but they couldn't have cared less about SVAG's attempt to construct more positive relations with the occupied population for the sake of its political aims.[32] NKVD units in charge of 'special projects' such as the infamous Wismut uranium mine were the worst offenders, forcibly recruiting German labour and working it to the bone in dangerous radioactive conditions.[33]

Dismantlers were similarly unmoved by the political and economic consequences of their work. They hardly differentiated between military and non-military industries when dismantling factories and machinery to send back to the USSR as reparations. They thus removed factories geared towards peacetime production that SVAG hoped to use to help rebuild local economies, at least to a subsistence level. Then there was the problem of meeting equipment or even production quotas demanded from Moscow for finished industrial products manufactured by the very German factories that the dismantlers were removing.[34] The dismantlers' success was SVAG's failure. Despite SVAG complaints, the leadership supported dismantling organs and similarly disregarded the consequences that their operations entailed, particularly high German unemployment and negative public opinion. Try as they might to establish a connection between the efficiency of the Soviet administration and the necessity of garnering support from the locals, SVAG officers failed to convince their superiors in Moscow that drastic measures should be taken to meet these concerns until mid-to-late 1946, when broader occupation policy changed.[35]

Until then, they could do little else but complain. At an August 1945 meeting of leading SVAG officers, Lieutenant General E. V. Dobrovol'skii

---

[32] See Chapter 4.

[33] Naimark offers an in-depth discussion of the Wismut mine, Naimark, *The Russians in Germany*, 238–50.

[34] RGASPI – f. 644, op. 1, dd. 402, 405, 406, 429, 430. These *dela* contain numerous orders issued by the State Defence Committee (GKO) for German industrial, agricultural, and military equipment. For the complex relations among GKO, SVAG, and the Special Committee see the work of K. I. Koval', the first deputy to the SVAG commander-in-chief on economic matters. K. I. Koval', 'Na postu zamestitelia glavnonachal'stvuiushchego SVAG 1945–1949 gg.', *Novaia i Noveishaia Istoriia 3* (1987), 'Zapiski upolnomochennogo GKO na territorii Germanii', *Novaia i Noveishaia Istoriia* (1994), no. 3, 'Rabota v Germanii po zadaniiu GKO', *Novaia i Noveishaia Istoriia* (1995), no. 2.

[35] Internal problems within SVAG also inhibited political officers from offering more support to their sponsored political parties. See Chapter 9.

added to the chorus of complaint against the dismantling organs, particularly the Special Committee (*Osobyi Komitet*),[36] by recounting his altercation with a dismantler outside a camera factory in the city. When Dobrovol'skii reproached the dismantler for failing to dismantle the factory's equipment properly, rendering it useless, the following conversation ensued:

DOBROVOL'SKII: What are you doing, that is not how you are supposed to conduct business?
DISMANTLER: My business is to scatter and terminate. I have been ordered to dismantle, and I am doing it so that not even grass grows there.[37]

Dobrovol'skii and the other SVAG commanders tried to limit the dismantlers from operating on such a large scale, or at least with such recklessness, in a number of different ways. In the end, however, they had all proved unsuccessful during the 'crazy summer' of 1945. They pinned their hopes on convincing Zhukov to put a brake on the practice and to allow them to regulate their area's economies and fulfil their own production orders to Moscow without interference. In this venture, they too were unsuccessful. As much as he sympathised with his commanders' plight,

---

[36] The Special Committee was formed by GKO on 25 February 1945. The committee was administered through the Administrative Department of the Central Committee of the VKP (b) under the presidency of G. M. Malenkov. It incorporated representatives from the State Planning Office (Gosplan), the Defence Commissariat, the Commissariat of Foreign Affairs, and Heavy Industry. Most issues concerning dismantling and related economic matters in the zone were dealt with by the committee. Its decisions were carried out by its considerable army of representatives in the zone. For the order establishing the committee see RGASPI – f. 644, op. 1, d. 373, ll. 48–9.

[37] GARF – f. r-7317, op. 7, d. 14, ll. 44–5. The dismantler's response to a high-ranking SVAG officer, a general no less, is indicative of the capricious attitude of these civilian bureaucrats who had been conferred military rank and significant jurisdictional power to conduct their business. In their haste to remove as many industrial plants and as much equipment as possible, dismantlers payed little attention to the technical aspects of dismantling, often damaging the plant equipment beyond repair and failing to remove factory blueprints and operating manuals. Moscow and even Zhukov believed that the problems that improper dismantling posed for the eventual reconstruction of these factories could be dealt with by minor adjustments to dismantling practice that would pose few obstacles to its speed. GARF – f. r-7317, op. 8, d. 1, ll. 101–2. This proved not to be the case. It is well known that, due to the haste with which industrial plants and equipment were removed, the Soviets were often unable to reconstruct many of the plants successfully and make use of much of the equipment in the Soviet Union. Nonetheless, there were other reasons behind dismantling. A leading dismantling official, Saburov, allegedly articulated them quite well at a meeting of Soviet officials in Germany on 2 July 1945, when he declared, 'If we can't ship it out, it's better to destroy it, so that the Germans won't have it.' V. Rudolf, 'The Execution of Policy, 1945–47', in *Soviet Economic Policy in Postwar Germany*, ed. R. Slusser (New York: Research Program on the USSR, 1953), 41.

Zhukov was painfully aware of Moscow's priorities and his own limitations. He could only voice these priorities to his subordinates:

We must remove everything that requires removal in order to cover the costs of the war more quickly, to heal our war wounds that have been inflicted on our country [and] our industry ... Ideas that have been expounded here today, that dismantling need not be hastened, are incorrect. Dismantling will not cease.[38]

What Zhukov did not say was that SVAG's inability to regulate dismantling and tackle troop violence were two sides of the same coin. Integrated command structures or not, SVAG's relationship with the army exhibited many of the same flawed characteristics as its relationship with the others as well as its own internal dysfunction.[39] In each of its relationships, SVAG was forced to pursue its aims by crawling across the chaotic webs of Soviet bureaucracy, raising the ire of the other organs for which SVAG's gain was their loss. SVAG would defeat the dismantlers by the beginning of 1947,[40] but until then it was army officers on the ground who had most to lose. Soon after their establishment in June 1945, SVAG and the army became embroiled in a serious conflict which stifled post-war reconstruction and was primarily responsible for allowing troop violence to continue years after the war. Such violence was less widespread than that carried out during the advance, or even by the repatriates in the summer of 1945, but far more enduring and damaging to the country.

---

[38] Zakharov, ed., *Deiatel' nost' sovetskikh voennykh komendatur*, 91, 97. This is not to say that Zhukov was happy about this situation. In fact, he told the leading SVAG officers at the meeting that they could no longer allow other occupation organs to continually interfere in their business when it came to raw materials and finished industrial product.

[39] A range of commissariats was involved in the establishment of SVAG, particularly in providing civilian or military personnel to staff the organ. For instance, the Commissariat of Defence (NKO) was responsible for providing personnel to the military departments within SVAG, while the NKID was responsible for providing staff to the SVAG Political Administration. The tendency of commissariats to issue direct orders to different departments compounded organisational difficulties within SVAG, particularly when they conflicted with orders issued by other commissariats or by the SVAG leadership itself. For a list detailing which commissariats provided staff to specific SVAG departments see Sovnarkom resolution no. 1326/301 ss issued on 6 June 1946, published in *Sovetskaia voennaia administratsiia v Germanii*, ed. Doronin, Foitzik, and Tsarevskaia-Diakina, 969–71.

[40] See Chapter 10.

3   Bringing soldiers to heel after the war

The violence carried out by the troops endured long after the war because the whole army, officers and men, was simply incapable of shifting from war to peace. Loyalties which were so important to maintaining cohesion in army units during the war endured long afterwards, with many army officers striving to protect their boys from official prosecution no matter what they had done. The better officers disciplined the worst offenders internally with bouts of incarceration and extra fatigues, but did so cautiously. Heavy-handedness could not maintain their authority over the ranks for long with no more war to fight. As it had been in the wake of the Russian Civil War, it was the officers' ability to balance discipline with permissiveness that helped keep the unit from dispersing or, worse, mutinying.[1] Of course, no punishment was meted out when officers considered violence against the locals necessary.

Throughout the war, officers ordered their troops to requisition what they needed from their own or foreign civilians, with any resistance being met harshly. Since material shortages endured long after the war, the army continued this practice. SVAG officers fought tooth and nail to limit arbitrary requisitioning and prosecute violent soldiers, but struggled to do so throughout 1945 and 1946. They could hardly have done better. Requisitioning and 'protection' spurred on the violence and made it most difficult for them to stabilise the country. Such was the nature of the army and its need to live off the land.

Fuel was always in short supply. Army and SVAG automobiles were often stranded for lack of it, leading officers to fight over those with a full tank. Some doctored automobile permission slips from their superiors when doing so, while the less refined simply carjacked other officers or

---

[1] O. Figes, 'The Red Army and Mass Mobilization during the Russian Civil War 1918–1920', *Past & Present* 129 (1990): 194–8, M. von Hagen, *Soldiers in the Proletarian Dictatorship: The Red Army and the Soviet Socialist State, 1917–1930* (Ithaca, NY: Cornell University Press, 1990), 175–80, and V. I. Shishkin, 'Krasnyi banditizm v sovetskoi Sibiri', in *Sovetskaia istoriia: problemy i uroki*, ed. V. I. Shishkin (Novosibirsk: Nauka, 1992).

Germans on the street. Soldiers exacerbated the problem. They made a habit of siphoning fuel from German automobiles and even their own army trucks to sell on the black market. Some used it to make moonshine, or *samogon* as the Russians call it, sometimes with fatal consequences. By July many units were out of fuel, forcing them to take it from the people. Soldiers from the 391st Rifle Division on the First Ukrainian Front were sent to a Saxon village to fetch some fuel on 9 June 1945, as many others had been across the zone at this time. They conducted house-to-house searches and, failing to locate any, stole some gramophones instead. Just before they left, twenty-five locals confronted the soldiers about the theft – a sure sign that they had had little experience with the Red Army. They rushed at the soldiers and tried to reclaim the goods, wounding one in the process. Upon returning to their headquarters the soldiers informed their commanding officer, Major 'Katz', that they had been attacked while fetching fuel. Of course, they left out any references to the robbery and the two villagers whom they had wounded. Incensed with rage, 'Katz' rounded up his men and set off for the village. He lined up fifteen of the suspects in the village square, whipped them, and shot two dead; seeing no reason to continue the German practice in the Soviet Union of shooting or hanging ten to a hundred civilians for every one soldier killed or wounded, he maintained the 1:1 ratio like most of his comrades.[2] The lying soldiers were investigated, but there was no change in requisitioning practice. The next month SVAG arrested soldiers for raiding homes in a nearby village to take meat and bread. Upon questioning the stunned soldiers replied that they were merely following orders. Their unit was hungry. Some may have been hungry, but most were thirsty, and not for water. Sergeant 'Malenkov' from the 57th Guards Division ransacked the home of a man in Saxony in search of vodka in July as well. Shouting and threatening him with a knife, the sergeant created such a ruckus that neighbours called the SVAG patrol, which managed to arrest him, but not before the sergeant had stabbed the German and then turned the knife on the patrol officers.[3]

Food requisitioning was better organised for the collection of the 1945 German harvest. Farmers were given foodstuff quotas and allowed to trade their surplus amounts – a privilege Soviet peasants had not enjoyed since the 1920s. But soldiers continued to raid homes for food and goods, with or without orders from above. Requisitioning was accepted army practice across the zone, with some officers considering the violence a necessary consequence. People in Saxony certainly understood this well by July, but luckily for them the raids diminished as the winter approached

[2] GARF – f. r-9401, op. 2, d. 97, ll. 71–2.   [3] GARF – f. r-7212, op. 1, d. 51, l. 94.

and became less violent and more systematic as the army began to organise requisitioning better. Other areas were not so lucky. Oranienburg had
breathed a sigh of relief after the mass repatriation of Soviet and Polish
citizens in September 1945, hoping that violence would cease, or at least
diminish. It did, but not for long. After the mass departure of the dreaded
repatriates, locals began to ready for the winter in October 1945. They
looked to replace the essentials taken from them during the rampages –
coats, boots, linen, and lamps. With black market prices for these basic
items simply too high, many men turned to stealing, women to prostitution. Whatever goods they had managed to replace, they too were soon
taken by soldiers stationed in the city during raids in October. The locals
pleaded with the SVAG head of Oranienburg, Major 'Khasanov', to try
and intervene, but he dismissed their complaints. In 'Sovietspeak' the
offenders were not soldiers, but only German criminals wearing Red
Army uniforms. With no help from 'Khasanov', local officials secured
help from a *komendant* nearby, who allocated six SVAG guards to the
affected villages on the outskirts of the city. The guards scared off the
soldiers, but they were soon removed for fear of typhus spreading to
the area.[4] The attacks resumed and continued until 'Khasanov' was replaced
in December for threatening to beat up complaining German officials.[5]

Upon reflection, perhaps he should have made good on his threat. The
complaints from the German officials helped remove him from office.
Here lies the importance of reading correspondence between SVAG and
German administrators along with broader Soviet sources. German
administrators had their own agendas, but their careful complaints reveal
the dysfunction of the occupation machinery on the lowest levels, and also
allow us a broader perspective in which to understand SVAG's complaints
against the army. 'Khasanov' was not the only 'negligent' SVAG officer in
the area who couldn't have cared less about the rise in troop violence. That
is until he was lambasted by his superiors and would have placed blame for
the violence squarely on troops who were beyond his control. The 'per-
missive' attitude prevalent among army officers was shared by some of
their SVAG counterparts. In some ways, given their wartime experience,
their apathy towards occupation duty and permissiveness towards troop
violence is much more understandable than the ferocity with which their
SVAG comrades fought the army.[6]

[4] GARF – f. r-7077, op.1, d. 178, ll. 30–3.
[5] N. V. Petrov, ed., *SVAG i nemetskie organy samoupravleniia 1945–1949: Sbornik dokumentov*
(Moscow: Rosspen, 2006), 308–12.
[6] See Chapter 5.

Delegating control and avoiding responsibility were central to 'Khasanov's' practice, as it was to any officer who wanted to enjoy the occupation. Before he was replaced, he suggested that the local German police deal with the 'civilian offenders' in Oranienburg. This was useless advice. German police were helpless to intervene with rampaging troops and until SVAG armed them in 1946, they were even unable to deal with rampant local German crime effectively.[7] The few who tried to intervene were often shot or stabbed by soldiers.[8] The luckier ones were beaten or treated to some 'poetic justice' by soldiers with a taste for irony. In Pirna, Saxony, tensions between police and guards at the local camp for Soviet POWs had reached a climax by September 1945. Not only did the guards fail to guard the camp properly, but they had been invading people's homes and accosting well-dressed women on the street for weeks, stripping them of coats and jewellery. They carried the bounty home to their young and eager German girlfriends with whom they lived (illegally). After the police repeatedly warned the guards that robbery was also against the law, the guards arrested and incarcerated them in the POW camp. Days later SVAG eventually freed the police and arrested the guards, while the women were fined for accepting contraband.[9]

The ineffectiveness of the police and rampant indiscipline in the army often made committed SVAG officers the first and last line of defence for the occupied population. But the defence was thin. SVAG could not replace every bad apple immediately or place guards in every village across the zone. SVAG officers on patrol rarely stumbled upon rapes and robberies in progress. More often they were alerted to them by police and were able to

---

[7] Theft was clearly the most prominent form of crime throughout the entire occupation period. In the first half of 1946, 112,295 cases of theft (*krazha*) were recorded by SVAG and security organs operating in the zone, in comparison to 20,349 violent robberies or marauding/pillaging (*grabezh*). In response to the gradual rise of theft and other less common crimes in the first quarter of 1946, 7,848 GSOVG officers and men were arrested in comparison to 6,474 Germans. Zakharov, 'Voennye komendatury SVAG', 49.

[8] There were exceptions. SVAG took measures in early 1946 to arm German police with pistols after it became apparent that unarmed police were unable to defend themselves from attacks. There was nothing to fear according to the NKVD chief in Germany and Zhukov's first deputy on civilian affairs General I. A. Serov, as ever since they had been armed, the police had showed no inclination to use their firearms 'illegally', that is, against occupation forces. Petrov, ed., *SVAG i nemetskie organy samoupravleniia*, 164–9. Serov's assessment, made in a June 1946 report, was generally accurate but failed to take into account exceptional cases of 'illegal' firearm use. On 10 March 1946, German police stopped three soldiers travelling in a car through Chemnitz (Saxony) and shot them. This incident was noted in a general report providing information to the SVAG Propaganda Administration, to which Serov had access in his capacity as Zhukov's deputy on civilian affairs. It seems, however, that he was either unaware of this incident or refused to report it. GARF – f. r-7212, op. 1, d. 188, l. 23.

[9] GARF – f. r-7212, op. 1, d. 13, l. 191.

arrest the suspects if they found them quickly, but usually not without a knife or gunfight. It was as dangerous when they attempted to arrest suspect soldiers days or weeks after the incident had occurred. Many thus spent as much time trying to govern their areas as chasing shadows in Red Army uniforms protected by their officers, especially during 1945.

SVAG officers did much of their chasing in Saxony during the summer. Overwhelmed by the level of violence meted out in regional areas by the troops, they pleaded desperately with the army officers to bring their men to heel. Ignored, SVAG tried to go it alone. Unable to chase up every robbery and beating, SVAG focused on the most serious crimes – two soldiers and their sergeant-major from the 8th Guards Army who invaded the home of a German doctor and raped his wife in front of him and his children on 21 July in Plauen near Zwickau. A week later drunken soldiers opened fire in the town square from their machine guns for no apparent reason, spraying wildly in every direction. A townswoman was shot in the stomach and died the following day. Not knowing which soldiers were responsible, but only the units to which they belonged, SVAG officers interviewed locals, police, even troops. Unable to ignore the case any longer, army officers began to hide the suspects and thwart the SVAG investigators. They were as concerned with maintaining unit cohesion as with avoiding 'unpleasantness', which meant the possibility of facing questions from their own superiors about the laxity of their command.[10] They had some reason to be wary. Colonel General M. E. Katukov, the famous tank commander, had just been appointed the SVAG chief in Saxony. SVAG officers naturally sent their complaints to him.

But so did everyone else, and it is difficult to know if Katukov ever read the report in the chaos of harvest season when collection was highest on everyone's list. SVAG chiefs appointed to each land/province in the zone were less 'hands on' than their deputies who effectively ran them and certainly selected which reports to bring to the attention of superiors. Nothing was done in this case. Army officers won this battle, but the war between SVAG and the army in Saxony was only beginning. SVAG scored some victories, but they were few and far between. At 8:30 pm on 31 June 1945, three soldiers from the Guards Army accosted a German family on a village road about 100 km west of Chemnitz. They pinned down the twenty-three-year-old daughter to rape her, while her mother ran screaming to the village for help – her young son helpless. They shot the mother dead, but the children escaped. By 11:00 pm the SVAG patrol arrested the soldiers in their barracks after being alerted by locals. There was no

[10] GARF – f. r-7212, op. 1, d. 13, l. 36.

reported resistance. The officers had retired to their separate quarters and probably had no idea of what had happened, let alone a chance to protect the soldiers. Two weeks later two of the soldiers were sentenced by the Guards Army's military tribunal to a total of thirteen years imprisonment.[11] This was a normal sentence. Three soldiers of the 2nd Shock Army in Mecklenburg each received five to seven year sentences in a forced labour camp two months later for breaking into an apartment through an upstairs window and raping two of the women who lived there. The Shock Army's military tribunal also stripped two of the soldiers of their war medals.[12]

Other soldiers would have considered them unlucky. The number of prosecutions paled in comparison to offences at this time. 'Protection' accounted for this, but military prosecutors' offices which should have been investigating all the complaints made by SVAG were overworked, severely understaffed, and part of the armies whose soldiers they prosecuted. In some areas there was simply no prosecutor's office at all. SVAG had detained a number of suspect soldiers during the mass operations in July and August 1945 in Luckenwalde, but had no prosecutor to send them to. The *komendant* of Luckenwalde wrote to his superiors for months asking for instructions but received none.[13] As with the venereal drama in Luckenwalde the following year, staff shortages were central to SVAG's difficulties and the locals' torment.

SVAG's increasing capacity to police the zone and arrest soldiers further exposed staff shortages in the military judicial system, which failed to grow at the same pace. SVAG patrols increased over the winter and managed to arrest over 7,000 soldiers during the first quarter of 1946, but it could only prosecute the most serious offenders whom they had caught in the act or had overwhelming evidence against.[14] German testimonies alone were usually not enough to bring soldiers to the tribunals. Under pressure from army officers to release their men, SVAG was forced to give back those arrested for drunkenness and stealing and hoped they would be punished by their officers. In some cases punishment was meted out, perhaps a reduction in pay, demotion, and extra fatigues, but the same soldiers tended to get arrested again and again. SVAG officers knew full well that these drunks were responsible for the worst offences, but could prove little. The situation improved slightly with the development of independent SVAG military tribunals, which only started operating by 1947.

[11] GARF – f. r-7212, op. 1, d. 13, ll. 51–2.   [12] GARF – f. r-7103, op. 1, d. 6, l. 39.
[13] GARF – f. r-7077, op. 1, d. 90, l. 211.
[14] Zakharov, ed., *Deiatel'nost' sovetskikh voennykh komendatur*, 49.

Until then, SVAG could do little to battle 'protection' and better prosecute violent soldiers. Both were symptoms of a broader problem, the lack of clarity between SVAG and army command responsibilities. SVAG exercised control throughout the zone via the hundreds of *komendaturas* that were strategically located across it. Each *komendatura* was responsible for governing a set geographical area and was run by a *komendant*, small staff, and guard. From the beginning of June 1945, SVAG officers had begun to replace *komendants*, who had all been pure army officers. But army units which were positioned in or passed through *komendaturas* remained under the direct authority of their own officers. It often proved difficult for *komendants* to deal with the large number of troops in their areas without establishing a good relationship with the army officer in question – seldom done. The central issue between them became who had the right to deal with violent soldiers. Many officers did not bother to act on SVAG complaints regarding the behaviour of their men because many felt that they were an encroachment onto their authority that needed to be guarded against. *Komendants* thus found themselves in an intractable situation, where the more they tried to clean up their areas by complaining to army officers about violence and even arresting their men, the greater resistance they faced.

It was not surprising that army officers would relax their disciplinary attitudes towards their men with no more war to fight. As one historian has noted, after enduring the horrors of the war together, the relative strictness of the officer–soldier wartime relationship 'gave way to a cosy familiarity' in Germany, with the officers 'condoning crimes if that helped everyone to thrive'.[15] After all, despite the shift in the Soviet propaganda campaign, most still considered the Germans an 'enemy people'. But this culture of hatred alone or even the allure of booty fails to explain why these officers condoned, ignored, or dealt with offenders only leniently when there was a serious crackdown on such behaviour by the military authorities from mid 1945. It certainly does not explain why the violence continued for so long. What is missing is an acknowledgement that this cosy post-war relationship between officers and men, the strong unit loyalties that bound them together, may have been born of war and hatred, but was now maintained by post-war necessity and cold-hard logic. If officers were to keep control of their men after the war, they needed to condone and punish – a balance attainable only within a loyal unit.

Perhaps some army officials in Moscow with a long memory may have hoped that mass demobilisation would help tackle the problem of

---

[15] Merridale, *Ivan's War*, 348.

'protection' by removing masses of men and thus breaking down these unit loyalties. In the early 1930s it was exactly short service periods and the high turnaround of soldiers that made it most difficult for unit loyalties to emerge in the Red Army.[16] Although discipline was low for a number of reasons, 'protection' was less of a cause in the 1930s than during the war when the men could fight together in the same company or at least battalion for years, especially from 1942 onward. The demobilisation waves launched from June 1945 may have broken down loyalties, but did nothing to improve discipline or cooperation between *komendants* and army officers. They had the opposite effect.

The problem lay in the composition of the Red Army and the method of demobilisation. In 1945 Red Army soldiers looked quite unlike the young, clean-shaven soldiers who abounded in propaganda posters. From the beginning of the war Soviet authorities drafted 'able-bodied' men aged seventeen to fifty years. 'Able-bodied' was a broad term, as many of the older recruits found it most difficult to meet the extreme physical demands of modern military service. But most of those who were in their forties and fifties had seen action in the First World War, the Civil War, or both and brought a wealth of military experience to the Red Army. Many of these older men quickly became NCOs, helping to fill the massive staff gaps caused by the egregious casualties in the first months of the war, some 4.5 million by the end of 1941.[17] If officers needed to walk a tightrope between protecting their soldiers from outside prosecution and punishing them internally for indiscipline, then such frontline NCOs were their balance pole. They generally commanded respect and did their job of meting out punishment to maintain discipline in the ranks extremely well.

By the end of the war many of these NCOs were in their late forties, the breadwinners in the families, and needed to be sent home after years at the front. The first wave of demobilisation was launched in June 1945 and released the oldest soldiers, those aged between forty and fifty-two. The second wave initiated in September released those aged between thirty and forty but was more problematic because it targeted sergeants' ranks specifically for removal as well as educated soldiers who had completed secondary school and were thus essential to the reconstruction effort back home.[18] Some of these men may have relaxed their disciplinary streak

[16] R. R. Reese, *Stalin's Reluctant Soldiers: A Social History of the Red Army, 1925–1941* (Lawrence, Kans.: University Press of Kansas, 1996), 58.

[17] W. S. Dunn, *Hitler's Nemesis: The Red Army, 1930–1945* (Westport, Conn.: Praeger, 1994), 57.

[18] M. Edele, 'A "Generation of Victors?" Soviet Second World War Veterans from Demobilisation to Organisation 1941–1956', unpublished PhD thesis (The University of Chicago, 2004), 63–4.

after the war, but nonetheless the Red Army was still losing its most experienced disciplinarians, its non-commissioned intellectual backbone, and leaving officers stumbling along the tightrope.

The younger NCOs who took their place generally failed to wield the same sort of authority as their predecessors. Even those officers committed to punishing soldiers for attacking locals found it most difficult to do so without capable NCOs. The lack of good NCOs further exposed the weakness of some of the younger officers, especially the junior lieutenants (*mladshie leitenanty*) who had been unduly thrust into positions such as company commander due to staff shortages. The majority of soldiers who were not caught in the act of raping or robbing but only accused of it could thus usually rely on these and even the more experienced officers to protect them. Officers would provide alibis for their men and frustrate investigations, driving *komendants* mad. The heart of the matter was that the haunting spectre of SVAG and especially the prospect of investigations into the quality of their command gave both good and bad officers a greater impetus towards protection than old loyalties ever could. At least initially, there was thus no way for military authorities to facilitate the demobilisation of forces in Germany without contributing to the post-war violence among those forces who remained. Demobilisation gradually worked to reduce the violence, quite simply because fewer soldiers remained to commit it.

But this was not the worst situation that *komendants* faced in the summer of 1945. At least in most cases they knew which officers were responsible for not punishing their men and were able to lodge complaints against them to superiors. In others, they had no idea who was responsible. Many officers rarely tracked the whereabouts of their men or sought to identify and detain other soldiers located in their areas without proper authorisation. Soldiers were supposed to stay with their units and not leave their designated area unless authorised, yet many simply travelled about eastern and sometimes western Germany as they pleased. With the mixing of soldiers across different units it became more difficult for *komendants* to establish the identity of offenders. Unless they arrested the armed offenders, a most dangerous proposition, they could no longer assume that rapes or robberies committed in this or that area were committed by soldiers belonging to the unit situated there.

This problem was compounded when offenders wore masks, as victims were even more reluctant to report rapes when they couldn't identify the rapists. SVAG only learnt of the crimes from their mail censors who pored over German mail in search of fascist conspiracies and other criminal plots, but more often came across secret revelations of rape and murder. A Schwerin woman wrote in November 1945:

We have had another experience. The Russians visited us 'nicely' during the night. The dog howled but the door was closed. Horrible unrest broke out. The men entered Paul's apartment and locked a woman in there. No one could enter. Around the house sentries had been posted so no one could call for help. Around eight Russians were wearing masks and were dressed in military uniform. They mainly stole things. One woman was raped over and over again.[19]

SVAG officers in Schwerin knew who the woman was, but could hardly expect military prosecutors to allocate scarce resources to investigate. Prosecutors had enough bare-faced offenders to deal with. In any case, they would have suspected that the rapists were not soldiers, but deserters and repatriates who were more concerned about hiding their identities. There were even cases of German criminals posing as Soviet soldiers when robbing and raping, often muttering broken Russian commands for effect.[20] 'Khasanov's 'Sovietspeak' was not total nonsense.

The laxity in command and especially the tension between *komendants* and officers should have been easy to address given that SVAG was born of the Red Army and the highest command structures between them were closely integrated. Zhukov was commander-in-chief of GSOVG and SVAG and his leading officers occupied positions in both organs. Even the commanders of the main armies which occupied each state in the zone were appointed as SVAG heads, such as Katukov in Saxony. Their orders were binding on both organs. They issued reams of them to increase discipline in the ranks and punishments for violent offenders, but to little avail. There was a gap between them and the army officer corps that could not be bridged in 1945.

Over the summer Zhukov grew more and more frustrated at his inability to stop the violence and weary at the prospect of mass demobilisation. Troop transfers had already proved a trigger for mass violence, with troops evicting Germans from their homes to stay the night en route to their destinations. Many strayed or even deserted from their units during transfers as well, wreaking havoc on locals. These problems would multiply with hundreds of thousands of armed troops moving across the country to departure points for dispatch back home unless Zhukov could do something about it. He was renowned for his 'iron fist' approach during the war when his staff acted as a mobile execution squad, shooting officers and men for breaches of discipline, desertion, and even incompetence. This uncompromising attitude was central to his success as a wartime commander, and there was no sign of change now. On the eve of the

[19] GARF – f. r-7103, op. 1, d. 10, l. 122.
[20] For cases in Thuringia see GARF – f. r-7184, op. 1, d. 10, l. 45, for Mecklenburg GARF – f. r-7103, op. 1, d. 24, ll. 29–31, for Saxony GARF – f. r-7212, op. 1, d. 185, l. 121.

demobilisation transfers at the beginning of July, he issued orders prohibiting evictions and establishing numerous army and NKVD patrols in each of the cities and towns through which the troops were to pass. The armed patrols would keep order, pick up any stragglers, and prosecute them. This was all normal protocol. Zhukov's draconian innovation was to order that officers of the units to which the stragglers belonged would also be punished regardless of their service records. Men who had fought bravely for years now faced demotion and even prosecution for the actions of their men.[21]

These measures reduced the expected number of stragglers and scale of violence, but were only in effect during the demobilisation transfers. The problems thus soon reappeared. Nonetheless, Zhukov felt he had found the bridge between the army command and officer corps – collective responsibility. The only difficulty now was to make it permanent. On 9 September Zhukov signed an order drafted by the Military Council which codified collective responsibility and laid a framework for its implementation. Officers would now live in the soldiers' barracks with their men, from NCOs to company commanders. They would monitor them much like a sentry guard and stop them from taking unauthorised leave, a root problem that gave soldiers the opportunity to rape and rob. Not even the officers were allowed to leave without permission from their superiors. If anyone did, they would have most likely been arrested by the new beefed-up 24-hour patrols or shot if they resisted. The officers who remained would be punished while the surviving escapees found guilty of serious offences would be sent to special penal areas in the Soviet Union to stop them from travelling abroad. According to Zhukov, this would ensure that these people would never again be able to 'dishonour our Soviet people and Red Army in the opinion of our Allies and the German people'.[22]

If this order had been implemented for more than a few days it may have reduced the violence, if only because it turned soldiers into prisoners and the army into a chain gang. For Zhukov, this was the only way forward. Stalin disagreed. On 20 September he 'asked' the Council to rescind the order. He felt it was unfair to punish good officers for the crimes of a few bad apples after the war. Zhukov may have expected this. He understood Stalin's attitude to troop violence. During the war Stalin had been reluctant to see good fighting officers punished for rape. He pardoned a major who had been sentenced to death by a military tribunal for shooting a fellow officer who tried to stop him from raping a German woman, sent

[21] GARF – f. r-7317, op. 1, d. 1, l. 15.
[22] An extract of the order is available in Petrov, *Pervyi predsedatel' KGB Ivan Serov*, 54.

him back to the front, and boasted that he had become a Hero of the Soviet Union for his bravery in battle.[23] Stalin's order to his troops in April 1945 during the drive on Berlin to treat German civilians and POWs better was born of military necessity rather than humanitarian concerns. The order accelerated the push towards pro-German propaganda and like policies in the army. However, like the soldiers' attitude, Stalin's remained unchanged. This may have been a reason why Zhukov did not follow protocol and send the 9 September order to the *Stavka* (General Staff) in Moscow. More probably, he felt that this order was not substantially different from his others which he also did not communicate to Moscow. The to and fro with the bureaucrats would only cause further complications. Stalin only found out about the order from SMERSH (an acronym for Death to Spies) – one of his security agencies which kept an eye on the army and SVAG in Germany. He made sure to remind Zhukov of this in his reply to the Council and, as usual, the boss' tone was politely menacing:

I happened to find out from SMERSH that the Military Council ... issued an order on 9 September 1945 ... I request of you to quickly change that order. Find a way in which to change it that does not cast a shadow on the command of the military. I am not writing you a formal order in the name of *Stavka* ... so as not to put you in an embarrassing position.[24]

Stalin had more practical concerns about the order as well. He feared that officers would be discredited in the eyes of their men if they were forced to live together and even prosecuted together. This fear was not ungrounded. Officers walked a tightrope between punishing soldiers for indiscipline and protecting them from outsiders to maintain unit cohesion. If they had been stripped of this discretion and turned into harsh jailers, rates of desertion and insubordination may have increased, especially during troop transfers. Zhukov's implied logic may have been that the order would have stopped the violence and thus the necessity of protection, but Stalin was unconvinced. He also reminded Zhukov of the damage that the order would do to the image of the Red Army if it were to become widely known. The Soviets were already scrambling to deny recent western press reports about mass rape, so the last thing that they needed was an order which implied that the Red Army was out of control.[25] It would have worsened the Soviet negotiating position with the

[23] Djilas, *Conversations with Stalin*, 110.
[24] Zakharov, ed., *Deiatel'nost' sovetskikh voennykh komendatur*, 457–8.
[25] RGASPI – f. 17, op. 125, d. 316, l. 131.

Allies as well at a time when they were still speaking about unifying their separate occupation zones.

Stalin did not specify it in his reply to the Council, but he may have been concerned to maintain military cohesiveness because the army still had work to do. The army was heavily involved in the demilitarisation of Germany, destroying or dismantling weapons factories and military installations. 'Trophy battalions' established for dismantling non-military factories also operated under the jurisdiction of the Commissariat of Defence (NKO). Most *komendants* were already opposed to the dismantling of non-military factories, let alone to the brutal manner in which some of these battalions operated. They forced some German workers to dismantle their own factories for twelve to fifteen hours a day, beating those who failed to keep up the hectic work pace and sometimes denying them pay.[26] That most of this activity was taking place in working-class districts was especially painful to SVAG. Its political departments fought tooth and nail to encourage grass-roots proletarian support for the Soviet-sponsored German Communist Party (KPD) and, from April 1946 onward, the Socialist Unity Party (SED).[27] One could only imagine how SVAG-led arrests and prosecutions could have stunted demilitarisation and dismantling work. Would these units now require special authorisation to leave their barracks to do their job along with army units working on demilitarisation? If soldiers beat German workers for slackness, would their officers now be punished? Demilitarisation and dismantling were the dual foundations of Soviet occupation strategy in 1945 and 1946. It is little wonder that Stalin acted so quickly to rescind the order and put Zhukov and the Council in their place. They would have to submit all further 'serious' orders to the *Stavka* for approval by Moscow bureaucrats whose knowledge of conditions in Germany was sketchy at best. After all, Stalin was never comfortable with the idea of popular military heroes taking charge.

Stalin may have denied Zhukov, but some historians argue that Stalin realised something needed to be done about troop violence even by late 1945.[28] It was making it difficult for SVAG to achieve some of the tasks that he had set them, to run the country, and position Soviet-friendly political parties at the apex of political power. In November 1945 the Soviet Supreme Court dramatically increased punishments for offences committed by occupation troops. This was a public acknowledgement

---

[26] GARF – f. r-7212, op. 1, d. 188 l. 6.

[27] In April 1946 the two major leftist parties in Germany, the KPD and Social Democrats (SPD) united under Soviet pressure to form the SED. See Chapter 9.

[28] Petrov, 'Formirovanie organov nemetskogo samoupravleniia', 35.

that something needed to be done.[29] The law borrowed from Zhukov's theory, as now even minor transgressions that had been dealt with on a unit level were to be transferred to military tribunals. But despite the harshness of the new law, it did not establish a new mechanism for its enforcement. This was the real problem. Zhukov's September order outlined this point by suggesting that the army itself was incapable of enforcing disciplinary measures according to 'normal' procedures. As such, there was no use in affording military prosecutors and tribunals greater power to punish soldiers for violence against the occupied population if their superiors refused to bring the indiscretions to the attention of the military prosecutors in the first place. The unwillingness of officers to do this or even to cooperate with investigations once they were launched was apparent to Berlin and Moscow before November 1945.

The Supreme Court order was a half-measure, perhaps meant to intimidate would-be offenders but not to prosecute more of them and deal with the core problem. That would require 'collective responsibility' and the significant changes in the occupation regime that it entailed. Stalin was wary of these changes when he denied Zhukov his 'collective responsibility' reform in September, and was as wary of them now when appeasing him. Without this reform, the system of military discipline remained flawed, and, not unexpectedly, the effect of the court order was limited. When officers did report according to the new law, it was often numerous cases of very minor offences such as tardiness that the overworked, understaffed, and now angry prosecutors did not follow up. When SVAG officers tried to report more serious offences, protection again often stifled the investigations and elicited more resistance from army officers. There was no silver bullet to solve the violence problem in 1945.

This very complex problem was restricted to Germany, where SVAG and the army pursued conflicting aims, or at least many army officers cared little for how their behaviour hindered SVAG from achieving theirs. In the German–Polish borderlands, where their policy aims of removing factories and natural resources coalesced, officers cooperated well. Perhaps the greatest symptom of this cooperation was that army officers were strict in restraining their men from attacking German civilians and also prepared to protect them from attacks by Polish civilians and military forces. Some historians have noted this tendency to protect Germans, usually refugees expelled from Poland en route to Germany, yet there has

---

[29] Order no. 13/14/V of the Plenum of the Soviet Supreme Court, 'On the responsibility of servicemen of occupation armies for the crimes committed according to wartime laws'.

been little attention paid to the various factors that account for this behaviour, let alone a focus on SVAG–army relations.[30]

Soviet forces were in the process of handing over authority of eastern German border areas to Polish authorities after the war, but retained enough control to strip these areas of factories and natural resources for shipment back to the USSR.[31] The violent conduct of Polish civilians and military forces towards Germans, their tendency to plunder Soviet supplies and reparations loads, and the tolerant attitude of the new Polish authorities towards this conduct threatened Soviet control and altered the dynamics of the old conflict between SVAG and the army. Sensing an encroachment on their shared jurisdictional authority by the 'wild' Poles, a common enemy who failed to heed the warnings given to them, the army cooperated with SVAG to retain that control required to do their job, of which protecting civilians/factories from violent mobs was an integral part. Their relationship in the borderlands was thus a microcosm of successful interaction that could simply not be reproduced in the zone.[32]

In many ways, the borderlands were a much simpler place than Germany for the Soviets. There was no talk of feeding Germans there or reconstruction, or at least any reconstruction that the Soviets would need to perform. The Poles were supposed to do both with the crumbs of industry and natural resources that the Soviets left them – both SVAG and the army.[33] Moscow was well aware of these comparative complexities. Even after the September debacle Zhukov was able to gain some leverage to reduce tensions between SVAG, the army, and other occupation organs.

---

[30] Naimark's short discussion of the expulsions is a most useful introduction to the topic, N. Naimark, *Fires of Hatred: Ethnic Cleansing in Twentieth-Century Europe* (Cambridge, Mass.: Harvard University Press, 2001), 122–38. Although a number of insightful chapters regarding the expulsion of ethnic German refugees from Poland during the final stages of the Second World War and thereafter can be found in a recent work by Siljak and Ther, little attention is paid to the Soviet protection of Germans, A. Siljak and P. Ther, eds., *Redrawing Nations: Ethnic Cleansing in East–Central Europe, 1944–1948*, Harvard Cold War Studies Book Series (Lanham, Md.: Rowman & Littlefield, 2001).

[31] At the Potsdam Conference the major powers agreed that the Oder–Neisse line would form the new provisional border between Germany and Poland. Poland was thus awarded a large swathe of eastern Germany consisting of approximately 21,600 km². Although the Soviets gradually handed over administrative authority of the territory to the emerging Polish government, they still maintained a presence there throughout 1945 and for much of 1946 and retained control over some aspects of governance. For a broader discussion of the Oder–Neisse division see D. J. Allen, *The Oder–Neisse Line: The United States, Poland, and Germany in the Cold War* (Westport, Conn.: Praeger 2003).

[32] For a further discussion of this point see F. Slaveski, 'Competing Occupiers: Bloody Conflicts between Soviet and Polish Authorities in the Borderlands of Post-War Germany and Poland, 1945–46', *New Zealand Slavonic Journal* 42 (2008).

[33] GARF – f. r-7103, op. 1, d. 22, l. 49.

But fundamental contradictions remained. Zhukov was charged with hoisting the KPD to political prominence in the zone, but was stopped from tackling the biggest obstacle to its popularity – mass troop violence. Given the close ties between the KPD and the Soviets, many considered the party complicit in the crimes of the occupier. Zhukov was charged with reconstructing the country, but also with assisting other organs dismantling Germany's military-industrial base and sending it back to the Soviet Union. So Zhukov received complaints from his *komendants* about the removal of this or that power station from their cities and on the same day received orders from Soviet commissariats to deliver more German power stations to the Soviet Union. In some cases he fought for his *komendants* and succeeded. But these were exceptions. The commissariats needed to be satisfied in 1945 when 'smash and grab' occupation policy was dominant in Moscow and Berlin.[34] This policy anticipated only a short occupation period in which they should extract as many riches as possible from Germany, forcing Zhukov to rebuild the country only with the crumbs that fell off the commissariats' tables. Until a new long-term occupation policy was adopted in late 1946 aimed at seriously rebuilding the country, Zhukov and his successor would battle in the mire of these contradictions and the occupied population suffer them without recourse.[35]

---

[34] Kynin's document collection contains a number of valuable Soviet documents relevant to the leadership's planning for post-war Germany. G. P. Kynin, *SSSR i germanskii vopros 1941–1949: Dokumenty iz arkhiva vneshnei politiki MID Rossiiskoi Federatsii* (Moscow: Mezhdunarodnye Otnosheniia, 1996). Filitov assumes a broader chronological approach in dealing with the topic. A. M. Filitov, *Germanskii vopros: Ot raskola k ob"edineniiu: Novoe prochtenie* (Moscow: Mezhdunarodnye Otnosheniia, 1993).

[35] See Chapter 10 for the change in occupation strategy.

4   SVAG–army conflicts in 'peacetime'

On 25 March 1946, a SVAG military patrol arrested Senior Lieutenant Sychkov for public drunkenness in Bergen auf Rügen. The patrolmen beat him unconscious before locking him in the local guardhouse, but not without some difficulty. They too were drunk, having already knocked back a litre of *samogon* that day, the foul-smelling moonshine they mixed with methylated spirits and paint thinner. It often made them sick and sometimes blind. When they awoke from their drunken slumber the next morning, they found Sychkov in the same prostrate position in which they had left him, now dead.

Twice had Sychkov's comrades begged for his release at the guardhouse on the 25th, and twice had they been denied it by the Bergen *komendant* himself, Lieutenant Colonel 'Grekov'. He and his deputy, Major 'Bychkov', had for months been arresting soldiers in their area for the most minor 'offences'. All were fair game, drunken soldiers out late, those who shouted in public, and especially those who tried to woo pretty German girls that the Bergen crew had their eyes on. 'Bychkov' was especially keen to remove the competition when dancing and drinking with his band of German girlfriends at local nightspots.

Being crammed into the back of a patrol car was just the beginning of the ordeal for any soldier arrested in Bergen. 'Grekov' and 'Bychkov' taunted the soldiers with insults and beat them at the guardhouse in open view (sometimes in front of German visitors). They set precedents of behaviour for their men, most of whom revelled in the freedom to arrest and beat without censure. Like their leaders, they were drunk most of the time. Only a few men in the Bergen crew tried to avoid the cycle of drink and violence, or at least tried to pretend that they had before the military prosecutors who investigated Sychkov's death and numerous other complaints filed against the Bergen *komendatura*. The entire crew fell like a house of cards under investigation. Privates blamed their NCOs for setting a bad example and NCOs blamed their officers for doing the same. Their squealing paid off. In the end, the prosecutors only recommended the *komendant* and his deputy for court martials. All that 'Bychkov' could muster in response was that he thought that Sychkov may have been an English spy.

According to the prosecutors, 'Grekov' and 'Bychkov' had been simply unable to establish order in the area according to the legal powers available to them. The prosecutors did not address the reasons why they had failed to do so, but they are clear.[1] Like many other SVAG officers, they were sick and tired of having to send back troublesome soldiers to their detachments a day after their arrests, knowing full well that their officers would simply not punish them sufficiently, or at all. Prosecutions were not working. Eventually, they responded by trying to intimidate the soldiers into submission, hoping that arresting them at will and beating them senseless would send a message to stop rampaging in Bergen. They made sure to send the soldiers back to their detachments with fresh bruises on their faces. But these 'noble intentions', if they were ever prevalent or, indeed, shared among most in the Bergen crew, were soon overwhelmed by sadism.

The sadism of the Bergen crewmen was an aberration in SVAG. But the mixture of alcohol and violence was not. Nor was the decline from *komendants* trying to work with army officers in the summer of 1945 to refusing to speak to them by the winter. If the officers would not cooperate with them to stop the violence, they would do it alone. But this bravado only increased tensions with commanders, reducing whatever slim chance there was of adopting a joint approach to the violence problem. Many *komendants* and officers began to see each other as enemies, and that's exactly what they became.

It is the preponderance of these conflicts between *komendants* and army officers that encourages a reassessment of the predominant understanding of why troop violence endured so long after the war. In his groundbreaking study of the occupation, *The Russians in Germany*, Norman Naimark argues that each set of troop replacements marked their arrival in Germany with rape and plunder, a result of 'the ignitable combination of aggressiveness and defensiveness that was associated with first time occupation duty'.[2] Similarly, any time the troops were moved from one place to another, violence was sure to follow. The mobility of forces is thus central to explaining why troop violence remained a serious problem well into the occupation. The evidence presented here suggests the opposite. Conflicts between the same *komendants* and commanders and their respective subordinates which developed over long periods allowed the violence to continue. The ostensible contradiction between these

---

[1] For the entire report see GARF – f. r-7103, op. 1, d. 26, ll. 167–71.
[2] Naimark, *The Russians in Germany*, 90.

explanations, however, dissolves upon further analysis. In fact, both are important in arriving at a more comprehensive understanding of troop violence.

The influx of raw recruits into the army was important in fuelling troop violence. As already discussed, demobilisation's removal of experienced NCOs who would have been able to handle the troops better was also a factor. What is important to note, however, is that the violent behaviour of the raw recruits towards the occupied population and their dismissive attitude towards SVAG were not only a symptom of their 'psychological engagement' with first-time occupation duty. Both were reflective of existing and accepted behavioural norms in the army. The young soldiers' violent behaviour was not unique, nor was the apathetic attitude of their officers towards it. The lack of effective disciplinary measures that could be taken against army officers also allowed this behaviour to continue beyond the first days of occupation duty and assume a habitual character. The habitual nature of the violence provoked the ire of the *komendant* of the area in which the detachment was located, while his arrest of the violent soldiers provoked the same from their officers. If conflicts between *komendants* and officers thus raged for months, usually until the detachment was relocated, then it should come as no surprise that after its relocation the detachment continued to attack civilians in its new surroundings. Nor is it surprising that the relevant *komendant* would complain to high heaven about the 'steep rise' in violence that accompanied its arrival. In this sense, evidence that testifies to the connection between first-time occupation duty, troop movements, and outbreaks of violence is congruent with the role played by SVAG–army conflicts in allowing the violence to continue.

SVAG–army relations were worst in Saxony during the first summer of the occupation. From the July shootings and public rape in Plauen it was clear to SVAG that the 8th Guards Army commanders were not interested in cooperating to find the perpetrators and stop the violence. Soldiers from this and the 1st Guards Tank Army stepped on SVAG toes all across Saxony over the next few weeks, rampaging in Zwickau, Meissen, Radebeul, Dresden, and all the major cities in the state.[3] By August, SVAG officers in Meissen had come to the end of their tether. On

---

[3] Although the 8th Guards Army headquarters were located in Weimar (Thuringia), approximately 100 kms from Zwickau, it was only to be expected that 8th Guards Army detachments would frequent places such as Zwickau. Divisions between lands and provinces were fluid and armies traversed and operated across them as a matter of course.

the night of the 17th several tank officers visited a local cinema where Soviet films were usually screened for troops and locals alike, although always at different times. It seems that the officers arrived early and joined the German crowd, and not for the first time. Upon noticing the officers, a group of ten men headed by a junior officer from the Meissen *komendatura* tried to arrest them. When the tank officers resisted, NCOs from the *komendatura* group attacked them, shooting their machine guns erratically inside the theatre as German cinemagoers ran for their lives.

The next morning the Meissen *komendant*, Major Strokov, refused to accept a delegation of tank officers who came to settle the dispute. Strokov was insulted that the head of the delegation was a mere captain, a subordinate officer instead of a major like himself or, better still, the commander of the tank army. One may have hoped that Strokov would thus understand the indignity felt by the tank officers after they were attacked by NCOs. Clearly, he didn't. That morning Strokov ordered the same *komendatura* group responsible for the shooting to go out and try to arrest the tank officers who had fled, which meant that any officer in Meissen with a tank insignia on his uniform was fair game. Strokov effectively cut all links with the tank army, electing to treat its soldiers as criminals to be arrested on sight.[4] This did not intimidate them into staying within their barracks, but encouraged them to keep their weapons loaded and return fire, and not only in Meissen.

On 28 October they did return fire, shooting to kill when another SVAG patrol tried to apprehend them in Zwickau, some 100 km south-east of Meissen. Soldiers from the tank army had opened fire on a local storefront and entered to take what they wanted before being set upon by the patrol, which succeeded in arresting one of the men within an hour, while the others fled. Unperturbed by the patrol's presence in the area, the soldiers committed a similar robbery later in the day. When another patrol attempted to reapprehend them that night, the gunfight began. Again, officers from the tank army were uninterested in helping SVAG to identify the culprits.[5]

Strokov thus not only intensified the battle with the tank army, but made it all the more difficult for those tank officers committed to improving relations with SVAG, not least the head of the 'peace delegation'

---

[4] GARF – f. r-7212, op. 1, d. 57, ll. 100–1.
[5] GARF – f. r-7212, op. 1, d. 55, l. 50. There are numerous other reports of gunfights and shootings between patrols and soldiers during late 1945 in Saxony. In October, for instance, an unfortunate Captain 'M', a dismantler, was shot by a patrol after he refused to heed repeated calls from the patrol to pull his car to the side of the road. The patrol was concerned about the captain's drunken state and the identity of the two repatriate girls in the car with him. GARF – f. 7212, op. 1, d. 51, l. 93.

Captain Khinevich. He was a political officer attached to the 1st Guards Tank Army who witnessed the cinema drama. That is why he had come. Moscow handed SVAG political officers a pitiful lot, charging them with winning the hearts and minds of the German people and increasing support for socialism in the most unpropitious conditions. But those who didn't transfer to SVAG and remained in the army like Khinevich in some ways had it worse, having to juggle their unit loyalties and difficult relationships with army officers with their instinct towards building socialism. Each count of rape, murder, and robbery made socialism and especially the Moscow-backed socialist parties more and more unattractive to the Germans and reflected poorly on their work. Political officers were, after all, responsible for 'educating' the troops. Having all come from the Political Administration of the Red Army,[6] both army and SVAG political officers enjoyed a network of former comrades and familiar procedures which they used to work together. But they needed to convince their *komendants* or officers that cooperation was worth it. Khinevich could hardly convince his commanding officer to cooperate with the Meissen *komendatura* when Strokov refused to see him. The more extreme the positions of *komendants* and officers became, the less middle ground remained for well-meaning political officers.

It is little wonder then that by October 1945 the army was also in no mood to cooperate or even listen to the nearby Zwickau *komendatura* when it complained its troops were shooting out the windows of houses and attacking people on the street in broad daylight. The army's relationship with SVAG in the area had already been severed.[7] Such aggressive SVAG behaviour culminating in denunciations and the arrests of soldiers may have removed them from the street for a day or two. But it only angered their officers and hardened the resolve to protect them in future. SVAG's harsh methods thus exacerbated the inter-organ tension that gave rise to them in the first place.

This is the problem that 'official Russian' histories of the occupation fail to address when lauding the good work of SVAG patrols in arresting greater and greater numbers of violent soldiers. There is no doubt that patrols were effective in picking up repatriates who evaded broader operations, as well as violent soldiers. For the first three weeks of September 1945, for instance, patrols in Dresden arrested 194 soldiers, 360 Soviet repatriates, 75 former Red Army soldiers, and 1,554 Germans.[8] As SVAG policing capabilities increased, over 7,000 soldiers were arrested during

---

[6] Officially the 'Main Political Administration of the Workers' and Peasants' Red Army' (GlavPURKKA).
[7] GARF – f. r-7212, op. 1, d. 13, ll. 36–8.   [8] GARF – f. r-7212, op. 1, d. 13, l. 413.

the first quarter of 1946.[9] The subsequent deportation of repatriates greatly contributed to the gradual stabilisation of conditions, while the arrest of violent soldiers was effective in the short term. The essential problem with the 'official histories', however, is the failure to address the reasons why, despite the volume of arrests made by patrols, arrest was not a clearly effective method in protecting the occupied population from troop violence in the long term.

The reasons are clear. The Zwickau example cited above is one of many which demonstrate that patrols were sometimes ineffective in physically stopping soldiers from offending, but certainly ineffective in intimidating others into following military laws. Soldiers knew that, unless there was significant evidence to charge them, they would be released to their detachments. And even if there was, they would have been unlucky to be prosecuted by the understaffed prosecutors' offices. No military police force or military justice system can operate effectively without a capacity to discourage criminal activity.

But what about the consequences of the arrests for relations between SVAG and army officers? Army officers demanded the release of their men from SVAG detainment and naturally tried to protect them from the growing and dangerous threat of SVAG patrols and prosecution. Generally, a most combative atmosphere developed that discouraged cooperation and fostered that behaviour which was most counterproductive to addressing the violence problem. Political officers became less well meaning in this atmosphere, especially by the winter of 1945. Those who transferred to SVAG and their *komendants* developed a habit of blaming everything that went wrong in their *komendaturas* on violent troops stationed there and especially on their officers. Troop violence was then the reason why they couldn't boost fledgling support for local socialist forces, reduce high worker absenteeism, and speed up reconstruction work. To some extent this was true, but they came to blame the army for all of their own shortcomings. Some of them even exaggerated reports of army violence and 'protection' to do so.[10] The problem was that this soon became clear to army officers, who were understandably angry and chomping at the bit to get their hands on the 'liars'.

---

[9] Zakharov, ed., *Deiatel'nost' sovetskikh voennykh komendatur*, 49.

[10] Political officers in some areas of the zone received instructions from their departments on how to format their reports. Report writing, however, was not regulated by the political departments. In fact, the instructions were quite basic and referred mostly to the themes that were to be covered in the reports and the order in which they were to be dealt with. The report-writing techniques employed by political officers were very much a bureaucratic skill used to increase their jurisdictional authority. See the instructions given out to political officers in Brandenburg during late 1945, GARF – f. r-7077, op. 1, d. 178, l. 55.

This tendency to divert blame to others and exaggerate the violence makes understanding the conflict between SVAG and the army all the more difficult. In the chaos of mid 1945, SVAG officers were overawed by the monumental tasks assigned to them. By late 1945 they had tackled some of them and managed to significantly reduce the violence by facilitating the mass removal of repatriates, with the beginnings of demobilisation also helping. As much as the removal of experienced NCOs allowed the violence to continue, there were hundreds of thousands fewer soldiers in the zone and thus less violence. But apart from the limited and sporadic impact of Zhukov's disciplinary orders, there was little indication of violence decreasing significantly among those who remained. As occupation conditions stabilised, so did SVAG's tolerance for troop violence. Now it placed greater pressure on the army to behave to a higher standard by denouncing army officers more freely and pursuing ever more severe punishments for violent troops. An October 1945 report best indicates this tendency at the time. During the first twenty days of the month alone, 14 rapes and 104 cases of marauding against locals were recorded in Mecklenburg (approximate population 2.5 million). In response to this 'insignificant amount of excesses', to use his term, the SVAG officer ordered that the harshest measures be taken against soldiers and others responsible for these and similar acts, not to mention their officers who did little to stop them.[11]

SVAG officers smelt blood. If denunciations of their army counterparts were serious enough, they could travel up the chain of command to the SVAG–army integrated command structures and result, theoretically, in the disciplining, demotion, or even removal of the officer in question. This happened less in practice, as army officers wrote counter-complaints and staff shortages in the officer corps made removals costly. But denunciations, replete with gruesome details of troop violence, did help officers to secure favourable decisions from superiors and achieve greater control, thus becoming part of the broader arsenal in the SVAG–army conflict. Read alone, these 'complaint reports' give the impression of SVAG machine working well if it were not buckled by the army. Luckily, they are only part of a much broader source base in the archives that allows us to cross-reference information and understand this seeming paralysis as both an indication of occupation conditions stabilising and tensions growing between the protagonists. They also reveal much about the internal problems within SVAG and how its conflict with the army was not as

---

[11] Zakharov, ed., *Deiatel'nost' sovetskikh voennykh komendatur*, 458–9.

clear-cut as the SVAG officers sought to impress upon their superiors in their denunciations.

Strokov and his fellow *komendants* in Saxony were certainly guilty of denouncing too freely, but ran into less trouble than *komendants* in Mecklenburg. Some of the army officers that they tarred with a broad brush were harsh disciplinarians committed to establishing law and order both in their garrisons and the cities in which they were located. Activist officers came to pose more of a threat to the authority of some *komendants* than their negligent comrades. Activist officers read complaints against them with incredulity and responded by writing their own, filled with witness testimonies, to superior authorities. The culture of denunciation thus not only discouraged negligent officers from cooperating with SVAG, but also scuttled possible cooperation with those notoriously hard-nosed officers committed to discipline in war and peace.

Major I. V. Sakunenko, the *komendant* of Ludwigslust, fell into trouble when he wrote to his boss, Colonel Nemkov, in April 1946 trying to blame problems in his *komendatura* on violent troops housed in the Ludwigslust garrison and their intransigent officers. This came as an unwelcome surprise to one of the alleged intransigents, Hero of the Soviet Union Lieutenant General Zherebin. He had just worked with Sakunenko to investigate a shoot-out between a SVAG patrol and a soldier from the Ludwigslust garrison. After the investigation Zherebin sentenced the soldier to five days of strict arrest (*strogovyi arest*), a harsh form of solitary confinement where soldiers slept on the floor and were given only meagre rations. Zherebin's report to his superior on *komendatura*–army relations in Ludwigslust goes some way to explaining Sakunenko's duplicity.[12]

SVAG men in Ludwigslust arrested soldiers and officers alike from the garrison, often shooting any who resisted. It seems that one of the reasons Sakunenko exaggerated the extent of crimes committed by men of Ludwigslust garrison was to help explain the growing number of soldiers and officers wounded on his watch. But as with the Bergen crewmen, by 1946 it became difficult to distinguish between the zero-tolerance approach to troop violence and ulterior motives. Not sadism, but the usual mix of personal rivalries and material gain. More often than not, the arrests were made outside nightspots and theatres, with 'disputed cars' involved. In January 1946, Captain Shestakov and his chauffeur drove to their local theatre in Demitz. Before he entered, the *komendant* of the city along with his machine-gun-armed guards approached Shestakov demanding to see his 'car documents'. As Shestakov had none, the

---

[12] GARF – f. r-7103, op. 1, d. 20, ll. 334–6.

komendant ordered his guards to arrest him and his chauffeur and drive them back to the *komendatura* guardhouse. They all crammed into Shestakov's car for the short trip except for the *komendant*. Upon reaching the guardhouse, the captain jumped from the car, dragging the guards out with him. Fighting with both guards and trying to wrest control of their machine guns, he screamed at his chauffeur to take the wheel and drive the car back to his apartment. But before he could flee, one of the guards managed to break free and open fire on the chauffeur, wounding him terribly. General Zherebin added in his report that 'a condition that deserves notice is that the Military *Komendant* of city Demitz knows Captain Shestakov ... very well, he knows where he lives, and actually sold Shestakov ... the car in question only three months ago'.[13] In other words, he wanted the car back without paying for it.

Two months later one of Sakunenko's deputies tried a similar ploy on a couple of soldiers from the garrison. He opened fire on the soldiers and commandeered the disputed car just south of Ludwigslust, but was brought to trial and sentenced. This was a major change. It was one thing for the sadists in the Bergen crew to be court-martialled, it was another for SVAG men at least appearing to be doing their job of checking for car documents and making dangerous arrests to be prosecuted. This was especially surprising because everyone knew that car and fuel shortages were pushing both SVAG and army men to extremes.

That Zherebin and leading officers from the Ludwigslust garrison were able to push this prosecution chilled SVAG men like Sakunenko to their core. That Zherebin started putting together his own patrols to scour the city for both army and SVAG men behaving badly froze them completely. Garrisons set up their own patrols across the zone, but it was less common for these patrols to descend upon the city and subject drunken SVAG men to the same treatment as their own. They were beginning to give their SVAG counterparts a taste of their own medicine. Sakunenko then did the most intelligent thing to protect himself from accusations of allowing his own men to drink in public and do as they wished – he made the same accusations against Zherebin. No wonder he began to avoid the 'conciliation meetings' called by Zherebin, claiming that he was too sick to attend. But it was less intelligent of him not to stay indoors during his fake illness, driving around Ludwigslust in full view of Zherebin's officers instead. This was the way that the Soviet system operated. Unlike Sakunenko, however, Zherebin was less a cog in this system and more a firing piston. He instituted the beefed-up patrols because the SVAG

---

[13] GARF – f. r-7103, op. 1, d. 20, l. 334.

patrols couldn't arrest soldiers without shooting them and were doing little to establish law and order in the city. In fact, according to Zherebin, the patrols and members of the Ludwigslust *komendatura* were fuelling the chaos.

But so were his men. In fact, any patrols were bound to run into public gunfights when trying to arrest armed and drunken soldiers who refused to accept the authority of the jailers. And if army men disregarded SVAG authority, then SVAG men dismissed the army's altogether. On 7 April Major Tyshchenko and his political officer from the Ludwigslust garrison went on patrol to local bars and hotels in the city in search of their soldiers breaking night curfew without authorisation. At about 10:30 on this Sunday night they came across Captain Barashkin from the Ludwigslust *komendatura* in a hotel. Drunk out of his mind, Barashkin ambled over to Tyshchenko from the dance floor and accused him of drinking and dancing illegally, as if to underline that only he had the power to arrest men for offences to which he was immune. Even one of Barashkin's own men, a junior lieutenant, tried to restrain him and send him home. But Barashkin was having none of it. He chased after Tyshchenko, who had left the 'unbecoming' scene as he put it, confronting him on the street in front of the hotel and in view of the remaining German revellers. Barashkin ordered the sentries standing guard outside the hotel to arrest Tyshchenko and his political officer, but was countermanded by his well-meaning junior lieutenant, who assured the sentries that Barashkin was too drunk to give orders. Barashkin then tried to make the arrest, flinging himself at Tyshchenko. Tyshchenko stepped back, but Barashkin managed to strike him across the chest, breaking off his epaulets. Incensed, Tyshchenko then pounced on Barashkin, who tried to pull his gun. The pair wrestled until they were pulled apart, much to the horror of the German bystanders.[14]

Zherebin pushed for Barashkin's prosecution, even though Barashkin claimed to remember nothing of the incident. This was a common and probably honest retort, given the amount of alcohol drunk during the days-long binges. But it was clear that, unlike the Bergen crew, Barashkin's junior lieutenant and the sentries were going to support their captain in any investigation. Thus Zherebin faced the same problem of 'unit loyalty' that had driven his SVAG counterparts mad for months. But at least they were now fighting for the same aim of reducing troop violence, even if they still fought each other to achieve it.

---

[14] GARF – f. r-7103, op. 1, d. 20, l. 335.

There was no such development with the secret police agents of the NKVD and SMERSH. *Komendant*s and army officers could not forget their temporary differences with these agents and reminisce about peace and the motherland over a drink. They were not old comrades. Agents were in Germany to eliminate any slim threats of German resistance, and to this end they often worked with SVAG and the army. But agents were also there to spy on Soviet officers, who the Moscow leadership feared may not have been able to resist the allures of Western Europe. Officers could end up in the Gulags for years if agents made cases against them, sometimes over the most banal of real or fabricated offences. To make matters worse, drunken agents denounced officers who gave them the slightest hint of trouble as traitors and spies.

Lieutenant Colonel V. G. Rolenko, the *komendant* of Neustrelitz, and his crew were some of the first SVAG officers to feel the wrath of the NKVD. Tension between them and the NKVD detachment in the city had been brewing for months, with agents extorting money and foodstuffs from local merchants and farmers who were supposed to be supplying the *komendatura*. Tension over these conflicting business interests had been limited to denunciations to superior authorities and stares on the street until September when it flared up, again in another cinema drama. On Sunday 9 September a film screening had been organised for German locals at a theatre in Neustrelitz. The screening was supposed to end at 9:30 pm, allowing half an hour for them to leave before troops from the local garrison arrived for the 10:00 session. Just before 9:30, Lieutenant Colonel 'Lobov' from the NKVD detachment arrived with his crew, grabbed the theatre manager, and threatened to arrest him if he didn't play his favourite Soviet classic for his men. Rolenko's political officer made the mistake of stepping in and trying to calm 'Lobov' down, which only enraged him further. In front of the German crowd and arriving troops, 'Lobov' berated the political officer, accused him of sabotage, and threatened to gather incriminating evidence against him and bring him and the rest of the Neustrelitz *komendatura* 'to account'.

These were not idle threats. The next day 'Lobov' refused to take calls from the *komendatura* and, as it became clear soon thereafter, was making a case against Rolenko. 'Lobov' did as he pleased in Neustrelitz under the rubric of 'battling fascists'.[15] The problem was that he allowed his men to

---

[15] NKVD reporting that may have exaggerated the threat posed by anti-Soviet elements was largely seen on a local level. General Serov assumed a different position when reporting to his superiors in Moscow throughout 1945 and early 1946. An analysis of his reports that reached Stalin and the central leadership gives the impression that he and the NKVD were firmly in control of the occupied population and were easily dealing with the threat posed by small groups of insurgents that were directing their efforts against the regime. Serov

do the same, dismissing SVAG complaints against them as fabrications. SVAG could secure prosecutions against some army men but not against NKVD agents, leaving 'Lobov' and his men as a law unto themselves. Rolenko could do nothing to stop one of 'Lobov's' henchmen from trying to rape women during October. On one of his drunken binges, Junior Lieutenant 'Veselov' crashed into an apartment block, knocking down the doors to each room in search of more vodka. He found none, but managed to kidnap a German girl, dragging her by the hair from room to room. When he arrived at the room of the girl's relatives, he demanded that they join him in raping her. When they refused and told him that the girl was 'sick of venereal disease', he rose, summed up the situation, and tried to use her mouth for the same purpose. Somehow, the girl escaped, but this was just another night out for 'Veselov'. 'Lobov' was not interested in complaints against his subordinates. Like his comrades, he refused to heed warnings from a 'subordinate' organ' (SVAG).[16] However, he was slightly more restrained than his comrades in Saxony, who in October rebuffed the Oschatz *komendant*'s similar criticisms by making violent telephone calls to his office and threatening him with 'uncensored words', to use the Soviet euphemism.[17]

These public displays drove home the message to the Neustrelitz locals that SVAG was not the final authority in the city. They knew who the NKVD was and this menacing reputation came in handy when 'Veselov' and his crew bashed down doors to local stores and farmhouses, demanding money and supplies. That the shopkeepers and farmers protested that they had already signed supply agreements with SVAG didn't bother them in the least. 'Veselov' arrested one such farmer who tried to blame him for failing to meet his quota of grain to the Neustrelitz *komendatura*.

Wielding authority was just part of the equation. 'Veselov' was not only confiscating goods to make his mark on the town, or even sell on the black

---

spoke less and less about the possibility of widespread anti-Soviet sentiment acting as a catalyst for violent resistance as the occupation continued. Serov's reports generally offer a much calmer impression of Soviet control than those of his local NKVD chiefs, while still indicating a high level of domestic crime among the occupied population. Serov may have been keen to demonstrate to his superiors that he and his forces were capable of dealing with the anti-Soviet threat in post-war Germany. Given that Serov knew full well that the current SMERSH chief, V. S. Abakumov, had been pursuing measures to undermine his authority in Moscow during 1945, it is likely that Serov also did not want to relay to the leadership any evidence that may have called for a greater SMERSH presence in the zone. See Serov's frequent reports to Beria, the head of the NKVD, on the monthly activities of the NKVD in the zone in GARF – f. r-9401, op. 2, d. 93–6.

[16] GARF – f. r-7103, op. 1, d. 9, ll. 105–6.   [17] GARF – f. r-7212, op. 1, d. 148, l. 17.

market and send home. By 1945 the NKVD was as much a business empire built on forced labour as it was a secret police organisation. It worked with dismantling organs in Germany to send back factories and equipment to its network of labour camps back home or to those springing up in occupied Europe. The NKVD thus put so much pressure on farmers to deliver foodstuffs in harvest season because it needed to feed the many thousands of prisoners in their German camps and its food supply arrangements with SVAG were sketchy at best. As in many other cases, the tensions between organs can be traced back to poor planning for the occupation and, in this case, massive food shortages that exacerbated these problems.

Poor planning may not be the best term. Even though some command structures between SVAG and the NKVD were integrated, they were never supposed to fit together and they were certainly never supposed to be equal. One of Zhukov's first deputies, General I. A. Serov, was also the head of the NKVD in Germany and worked closely with him to co-ordinate the mass 'clean up' operations in late 1945 which reaped such impressive results. Serov's deputies in each land and province in the zone were also supposed to work with their SVAG counterparts. But where SVAG pushed to rebuild factories, the NKVD pushed for their removal.[18] Where SVAG encouraged Germans to join local governments, agents arrested them on the slightest whim of past, present, or prospective anti-Soviet activity. And where SVAG fought tooth and nail to curb troop violence by prosecuting the offenders, Serov tried to prosecute the victims. Frustrated by German letters complaining that violence had not ceased by late 1946, Serov ordered the following:

It is necessary to select 2 or 3 provocative letters regarding murder etc. from each province and to prosecute their authors in a military tribunal, the sentences of which should be published in the press of the [relevant] provinces.[19]

This was the way the NKVD dealt with complaints. And if this raised concern among the SVAG brass, then it was much easier for Serov or his successor to hear of it. In fact, one of the points of integration was to allow

---

[18] Beria and Malenkov, head of the Special Committee, were quite close on dismantling matters – so much so that, to streamline the process by which NKVD officers could investigate and request industrial equipment, both agreed that its officers should be attached to Special Committee teams that surveyed dismantling sites. Malenkov's *osobaia papka* (special file) in GARF contains his correspondence with Beria on dismantling matters throughout 1945. GARF – f. r-9401, op. 2, d. 110. For Beria's request to add NKVD officers to Special Committee teams see l. 134.

[19] Cited in Petrov, 'Formirovanie organov nemetskogo samoupravleniia', 35.

agents a closer look at the 'military heroes', making it easier for them to stifle 'incorrect' policy initiatives and gather evidence against the heroes for their 'bourgeois diversions'. The NKVD and SMERSH did this extremely well.

By October 1945, Colonel 'Lobov' had submitted more than enough evidence against Rolenko to his boss, General Gubin. 'Lobov' then secured the support of the deputy head of SVAG in Mecklenburg, Major General M. A. Skosyrev, and together they issued a state-wide communiqué on the 22nd ordering all SVAG and NKVD officers to try to cooperate better with each other and establish friendlier relations.[20] One can imagine Rolenko's incredulity upon reading the order as well his rage when saw his own name listed among the *komendants* known for their intransigent attitude towards NKVD agents, the rapists and murderers whom he had been fighting for months. Rolenko could do nothing but protest his innocence to Skosyrev, pleading that it was impossible to cooperate with the NKVD, who were lying through their teeth about his 'indiscretions'.[21] Not that it made any difference. NKVD accusations and whatever meagre evidence they could muster to support them were often good enough to get things like this done or put good men like Rolenko away. Like Sakunenko, NKVD agents understood the practice of denunciation, but were much better at it.

There was always room for cooperation between SVAG and the army in dealing with violence, even if it was small. The army brass was committed to solving the problem, and outstanding officers like Zherebin set an example for their subordinates. But such cooperation was impossible with the NKVD. Serov shared the same attitude as his agents towards 'German victims'. As long as he and his successors had that attitude, there was simply no way for SVAG to stop violent NKVD agents from doing as they pleased. When the NKVD did speak of cooperation, they really meant the best way for SVAG to keep out of its way. That is why Colonel 'Lobov' targeted Rolenko in his reports to his superiors. Rolenko simply didn't know his place, just like the other SVAG men, who set up their own mail censorship networks to gauge the mood of the population rather than relying on the NKVD's, or detained their own saboteurs.[22] Such initiative only demonstrated their 'ignorance' of the hierarchy and the workings of the broader Stalinist system, whether it be in Germany or back home.

[20] GARF – f. r-7103, op. 1, d. 9, ll. 76–8.   [21] GARF – f. r-7103, op. 1, d. 9, l. 105.
[22] See Chapter 6.

SMERSH agents were fewer in Germany and more concerned with gathering evidence against SVAG and army officers. But some agents lacked the necessary patience to do so and couldn't have cared less about jurisdictional tensions with SVAG. In late 1945 agents in regional areas of Dresden beat up SVAG officers and made their lives a living hell. Personal vendettas were at play here. The agents had previously worked with them before being removed from their posts on counts of indiscipline and drunkenness. Service in the SMERSH detachment was a type of punishment in which they revelled, because it gave them a chance to get back at the SVAG 'traitors' who had informed on them, which meant anyone in SVAG uniform. Their first victim was the unsuspecting Lieutenant Iazikov. They set up a fake roadblock and flagged him down as he drove towards them. They 'asked' him to hand over his papers and get out of the car. Iazikov handed over his papers but refused to get out. They then dragged him out of the car, beat him, and left him to die on the roadside. Now with a car at their disposal as well as bottles of good vodka that they had embezzled from the supply store, the agents were ready for their usual night out. They would walk along Dresden city streets beating up pedestrians and shooting their machine guns erratically around the city centre, or more accurately at ducks swimming in the city pond.[23]

These examples challenge a dominant understanding of SVAG relations with the security services, which draws a distinction between the relative disruptiveness of NKVD and SMERSH activity to SVAG business. Naimark argues that where NKVD agents expressed a desire to work with *komendants*, SMERSH agents were in Germany, predominately, to spy on them.[24] They did have different and, perhaps, relatively more disruptive functions, but drawing a distinction between these agencies misses their commonalities, which were much more troubling for SVAG. It is clear that the NKVD did enjoy a more integrated relationship with SVAG than did SMERSH. NKVD area chiefs would regularly report to SVAG officers about their arrests, while SVAG would habitually deliver suspects more readily to the NKVD than SMERSH if they fell under their jurisdiction, and cooperate in operations and investigations. Yet this type of institutional cooperation, much stronger at the higher levels of

[23] GARF – f. r-7212, op. 1, d. 57, ll. 145–6.
[24] N. Neimark [Naimark], 'Sergei Tiul'panov i Sovetskaia voennaia administratsiia v Germanii', in *Sovetskaia voennaia administratsiia v Germanii: Upravlenie propagandy (informatsii) i S. I. Tiul'panov, 1945–1949 gg. Sbornik dokumentov*, ed. B. Bonvech [Bonwetsch], G. Bordiugov, and N. Neimark [Naimark] (Moscow – Sankt Peterburg: AIRO – Pervaia Publikatsiia, 2006), 12.

command, hardly inhibited local NKVD groups from engaging in violent behaviour against the occupied population or SVAG workers. More importantly, it hardly provided an institutional incentive for NKVD officers to respond to SVAG pleas to put an end to it. In this sense, it seems that it was the superior jurisdictional position of both the NKVD and SMERSH that became more important in allowing for the continuation of their violent behaviour, rather than their different duties or the nature of their working relationship with SVAG.

How widespread were these inter-organ battles? The culture of denunciation forces us to answer this question with another. How do you measure the extent of SVAG–army conflict when the combatants had a vested interest in highlighting the violent and intransigent behaviour of their opponents? As mentioned earlier, a broad range of sources allows us to situate specific battles within their broader context. This approach encourages the conclusion that many such men who roamed about the zone attacking locals and SVAG men who stood in their way during their days-long drinking binges were not engaged in jurisdictional disputes. They were bored and frustrated, the fate of most soldiers stuck in any army without anything much to do. But they were still combatants in a broader conflict, even if they were drunk for most of the fighting. Many of their officers protected them and kept them on the streets because they saw SVAG as an opponent and its 'law and order' agenda as nothing more than an attack on their authority. The more they treated SVAG men like enemies, the more they became them. This attitude not only stifled attempts to curb violence by setting up joint SVAG–army patrols (only established in 1947), but also turned routine meetings on food allocations and other supplies into a battle. For all the day-to-day cooperation on such matters between many *komendants* and officers, there was as much disregard between others during 1945 and 1946.

Stalin understood that cooperation was never the point, and, on some instinctual level, perhaps the combatants did as well. But men like Zherebin and thousands of others committed to doing their job of rebuilding Germany and making it a safe place did not.

They struggled against more powerful men by employing well-meaning, but ultimately flawed, procedures of arrest. That is what makes their meagre achievements so outstanding and, in the end, so important in the eventual shift in policy thinking towards Germany from mid 1946. Now Stalin began to look less on Germany as a vanquished foe ripe for the taking, and gave Zherebin and his SVAG comrades more power to turn it into a strong, loyal ally on his westernmost border. It is only in this context that the violence ceases to be a staple of occupation life. In early 1947 laws were enforced that confined troops to their barracks and required their supervision – a slightly tamer form than Zhukov's September 1945 draconian proposal.[25] And they were much easier to supervise, as mass demobilisation had reduced the close to 1.5 million-man army to 350,000 by mid 1947.[26]

[25] Naimark, *The Russians in Germany*, 92–7.
[26] Naimark estimates that the occupation force at the end of the war consisted of up to 1.5 million Soviet troops. After a series of demobilisation drives, the force had reduced to approximately 700,000 by September 1946, and then to 350,000 by July 1947. Ibid., 17.

5   Suicide, apathy, violence

Millions of Germans evacuated westward ahead of the Red Army's advance in the winter of 1945. Of those who remained, some took their own lives before the Red Army arrived. Fearful of retribution for German crimes in the Soviet Union and terrified by the German propaganda that promised it, they may have considered suicide their best option.[1] Others killed themselves after suffering at the hands of the occupier, particularly women who had been raped. They were not always successful, as Soviet officers noticed women with cuts to their wrists and sometimes to their children's.[2] Not surprisingly, suicide remained a serious problem months later with many still writhing from their losses in war and now under occupation.[3]

Equally unsurprising was that suicide became a serious problem among Soviet occupation forces, particularly among those who remained after the waves of demobilisation had taken their comrades home. In many ways, they had lost more in victory than defeat. Equipped with its vast anti-bourgeois lexicon, the SVAG brass offered simple explanations for the many 'shameful' suicides it investigated. This was especially the case

[1] SMERSH officers attached to the 2nd Guards Tank Army who investigated mass suicides across Brandenburg in March 1945 found that many of the victims were members of fascist organisations who had also killed their families before committing suicide themselves. In one village thirty-five suicides were recorded for the month. The investigators interviewed surviving members of fascist organisations to find out exactly why there was such a high rate of suicide. It seems that local Nazi authorities had promised to evacuate party members ahead of the Soviet advance. When it became apparent to the members that they had been abandoned, they committed suicide believing that they would be executed by the Soviets in any case. GARF – f. r-9401, op. 2, d. 93, ll. 334–5.
[2] An NKVD group operating in Königsberg during February 1945 interviewed three women and twelve children with obvious cuts to their wrists. All of the women claimed they had been raped several times by Soviet soldiers, which the children had witnessed. GARF – f. r-9401, op. 2, d. 94, l. 87.
[3] Richard Bessel argues that suicide was also fuelled by hatred towards fellow Germans and the state inspired by losing the war. R. Bessel, 'Hatred after War: Emotion and the Postwar History of East Germany', *History and Memory* 17, nos. 1–2 (2005). Other historians explore broader causes, e.g. C. Goeschel, 'Suicide at the End of the Third Reich', *Journal of Contemporary History* 41, no. 1 (Jan. 2006).

for the SVAG men who murdered their German lovers in drunken rages before killing themselves, or committed suicide with them, hand in hand.[4] SVAG investigators subsumed the complex path of suffering that led to these violent ends under the Soviet phrases of 'bourgeois infection' and 'moral decay'. They faulted the dead men's commanding officers for allowing them to descend along this path, particularly for allowing them to live with the women (illegally) and continue their alcoholism unchecked. This criticism was most forceful after an investigation into the spike of suicides at the beginning of 1947 of not only SVAG men and their lovers, but also officers' wives who had come to Germany to live with their husbands but couldn't survive their indiscreet philandering:

The long-term relationships between the local German population and our Soviet people slide down the path to complete moral degeneration when not brought to a timely end by the relevant chiefs and political workers. Without a doubt, the majority of cases of suicide may have been prevented . . . in conditions where the morale of the staff is studied and political–educational work is conducted.[5]

As with many complex social problems within Stalinist society, suicide was understood within a Stalinist framework and its 'solution' invariably tied to increasing one's knowledge of and devotion to socialism.[6] Despite the 'Sovietspeak', however, SVAG investigators understood full well that more classes on the history of the October Revolution would do little to stop men on the path to killing themselves and perhaps others. Suicide

[4] In a July 1947 order to all *komendants*, the head of the SVAG staff (*shtab*) M. Dratvin discussed numerous cases of suicide to demonstrate the urgent necessity to improve poor discipline in SVAG. All of the cases from February to May 1947 also concerned German women and were, according to Dratvin, representative of suicide trends in SVAG. Zakharov, ed. *Deiatel'nost' sovetskikh voennykh komendatur*, 464. But the nationality of the women was not decisive. Other murder suicides involved Soviet women, such as that on 8 December 1945, when Sergeant 'P' visited the apartment of a Soviet repatriate. Upon arriving, he shot the woman and then himself. It was revealed that the two were former lovers and that the woman had begun to see another man, which could have led to the shooting. GARF – f. r-7317, op. 7, d. 124, l. 41.
[5] This was part of Dratvin's conclusion in his order above. Zakharov, ed. *Deiatel'nost' sovetskikh voennykh komendatur*, 464. The wives who stayed at home were no less angered and dismayed by their husbands' reported philandering with German women. Many wrote to military authorities and even to Stalin in search of their husbands who had ceased correspondence and stopped sending part of their pay checks home. This was part of a broader problem during the war of 'unofficial marriages' concluded between troops on the move and women in the rear, which allowed some men to claim they were single and thus take more than one wife and father numerous children. They were then liable, if the 'unofficial marriages' could be proven, to hefty alimony payments. See the letters and SVAG's investigations into the women's claims in GARF – f. r-7317, op. 10, d. 8.
[6] Pinnow's study of the revolutionary state's response to suicide in the 1920s is most instructive in this respect. K. M. Pinnow, *Lost to the Collective: Suicide and the Promise of Soviet Socialism, 1921–1929* (Ithaca, NY: Cornell University Press, 2010).

was only one consequence of root problems with the 'moral state' of SVAG personnel and broader institutional problems within the organ. The other consequences were more devastating for occupiers and occupied alike.

SVAG became the occupied population's first and last line of defence from rampaging troops because many of its officers considered the safety of the Germans central to achieving their occupation aims. But this defence, as we have seen, was thin. And even when there was cooperation between SVAG and army officers in defending locals and prosecuting soldiers, it failed to touch the deeper, human source of the violence. SVAG was born of the Red Army and its men shared similar experiences of war and occupation with army officers. The apathy towards fulfilling occupation duties, antipathy towards the occupied population, and general melancholy prevalent in the army were thus also present in SVAG all along the chain of command. For all of the *komendants* who fought tooth and nail to protect their locals from rampaging troops to administer their *komendaturas* better, others couldn't have cared less. Given their wartime experience, their behaviour seems more understandable than the bellicosity of their more enthusiastic comrades.

The line between apathy and the continuation of violence, however, was not always straight. The puritanical SVAG brass constantly complained about the 'amoral' behaviour of 'certain elements', noting their black market dealings, daytime drunkenness, cohabitation with German women, and, often as a result, workplace absenteeism. But some of these officers still guarded their jurisdictional authority jealously from opponents, if only to continue their 'amoral' behaviour unchecked. In this sense, protecting locals from rampaging military detachments was more a function of maintaining control and demonstrating authority. This distinction helps to explain why some SVAG officers were willing to stop other violent soldiers from attacking locals, but unwilling to stop their own. In a few cases SVAG officers even led the violence against Germans in their own or other *komendaturas*.

The most common problem, however, was that some SVAG officers simply failed to report cases of troop violence or protect locals from attacks. As much as reporting these attacks or attempting to stop them contributed to hostile relations with the army, at least superior authorities became aware of them and could try and do something about it. When these cases were not reported, especially in regional areas far away from other *komendaturas*, superior authorities had little way of gauging the severity of troop violence there. The complaints from German civil administrators or party functionaries about the violence were simply not always taken seriously. Neither the enthusiasm of the bellicose nor the apathy of the melancholic could solve the troop violence problem in 1945 and 1946.

The SVAG brass was always concerned about the 'moral state' of its men, launching periodic investigations into 'troublesome' *komendaturas* across the zone. The puritanical criteria by which the men were evaluated left few untarnished by charges of succumbing to the bourgeois pleasures that Germany had to offer, from wearing designer suits instead of their uniforms to fleeing to the West with their German lovers. The general impression from these exhaustive investigations is that some *komendaturas* were barely functioning. 'Certain elements' were still stumbling from the psychological toll of the war, with many seeking solace in the greater amount of alcohol available in Germany and some, eventually, in suicide. Alcohol abuse had a long history in the Red Army, but the daily and even workplace binge drinking had now become a similar problem to that before the war, especially among officers who enjoyed better access to spirits in Germany.[7] Some of the senior SVAG officers who investigated the *komendaturas* understood this as a natural degeneration of the post-war period, claiming that 'war breeds its own discipline, but now we have to do it ourselves'.[8] The difficulty lay in convincing some of the men who had lost so much from war and German occupation that it was worthwhile maintaining wartime discipline to administer the country better, and protect the Germans, whom they deemed responsible for their loss, from their violent comrades in SVAG or the army.

It was worth trying to convince them, as staff shortages and demobilisation limited SVAG's capacity to replace 'bad apples' at will. Thus, even though hundreds of other *komendaturas* across the zone were functioning relatively well, it was still important for the SVAG brass to investigate 'troublesome' *komendaturas*, catch officers on the downward spiral, and 'rehabilitate' them. Some officers, however, were beyond rehabilitation. Investigators from the *Komendant*'s Service (KS), SVAG's chief department,[9] were scathing of the apathetic attitude of 'certain elements' towards following, let alone enforcing, military laws. These elements were 'infecting' the rest of the organisation and stunting SVAG's capacity

---

[7] Reese discusses alcoholism in the 1930s peacetime army as part of a broader disciplinary problem, especially among officers. R. R. Reese, *The Soviet Military Experience: A History of the Soviet Army, 1917–1991* (London: Routledge, 2000), 82–3.

[8] GARF – f. r-7317, op. 7, d. 124 (v), l. 20 (October, 1945).

[9] The KS was the most powerful administration within SVAG with subordinate departments in each land and province in eastern Germany. It was charged with fulfilling a range of different and most challenging occupation tasks, from organising German central administrations to reparations.

to achieve its occupation aims.[10] Perhaps the most scathing investigator was the head of the KS in Saxony, Colonel General N. I. Trufanov, who reviewed twenty Saxon *komendaturas* during late 1945. Trufanov was shocked by the poor state of some *komendaturas* located in Leipzig, Chemnitz, and Bautzen. Many officers and NCOs were avoiding their duties such as conducting weapons searches among locals because they were drunk or too busy cohabitating with German women. They left their weapons lying about and didn't even post sentries around their *komendaturas* or keep any detailed records of the arrests they had made or the amount of property they had sequestered. Trufanov's chief criticism, however, was the most damming:

> The officers of the *komendaturas* are feebly waging the battle for military discipline and order. There are severe perversions in the implementation of military discipline in nearly all *komendaturas* in the region – educational measures are only being applied by the *Komendants* and their assistants – almost no one gives any encouragement for carrying out the dominant form of punishment, mainly arrest. The *Komendant*'s platoons and the sergeant ranks do not take any part in disciplinary practice.[11]

The lack of disciplinary practice was not only due to 'amoral' behaviour. As we have seen, the second wave of mass demobilisation in September 1945 removed SVAG's elder, educated NCOs and reduced the pool of potential army recruits from which it could draw to replenish its ranks.[12] The majority of NCOs in these areas were only twenty-one or twenty-two years of age in 1946.[13] Just as in the army, apathy in the ranks, disciplinary problems, and slack soldiering were thus no big surprise, given that NCOs were traditionally responsible for punishing their subordinates for breaches of discipline.[14] Moreover, many of the young NCOs had no idea how to properly clean or operate their weapons, which surely indicates the extent to which even militarily inexperienced young soldiers were unfairly thrust into positions of authority before they were prepared to deal with the responsibilities attendant on them. This is to say nothing of the large number of accidental soldier deaths that resulted from inexperienced weapons usage, or from using weapons when inebriated.[15]

---

[10] See a report on the political morale of SVAG personnel from October 1945, GARF – f. r-7317, op. 7, d. 124 (v), ll.17–20.

[11] GARF – f. r-7212, op. 1, d. 13, ll. 327–30.

[12] Some SVAG commanders simply refused to follow SVAG order no. 059 of August 1945 that required the demobilisation of all men born in 1900 for fear that they would be left without capable staff. GARF – f. r-7103, op. 1, d. 26, l. 65.

[13] GARF – f. r-7133, op. 1, d. 117, ll. 1–2.   [14] GARF – f. r-7133, op. 1, d. 117, l. 101.

[15] GARF – f. r-7317, op. 7, d. 124, ll. 16, 23.

Again, it by no means follows that 'amoral' officers did not seek to protect their jurisdictional authority from opponents if they deemed their behaviour a threat. Officers from some of the *komendaturas* cited in the investigation, such as Dresden and Meissen, were engaged in violent disputes with military detachments which attacked locals within their jurisdictions. But it is also clear that it was less likely for officers from the more dysfunctional *komendaturas* to consider troop violence a threat if they were committing it themselves. Trufanov was painfully aware of this fact from his earlier experience as *komendant* of Leipzig.[16] Exerting control over regional and district areas was one of the greatest difficulties faced by Trufanov and other city *komendants*, particularly when regional *komendants* resisted interference from central authorities. The *komendant* of the Leipzig district area, Colonel Litvin, was notorious for this, and for failing to discipline his subordinate officers for their riotous behaviour within the city limits. According to Trufanov, Litvin and his men often descended onto the city, stole goods from stores, lodged illegally in German houses, and refused to follow work orders requiring them to clean up public places. Litvin's men assumed such capricious airs because, much like their army counterparts, they knew that their *komendant* would not punish them for their behaviour. Trufanov was especially irate over this point in his correspondence with Litvin in August 1945:

Officers of the Leipzig district Military *komendatura*, not without your protection, destroy the internal order of the city, and not taking note of their own behaviour, cause disorganisation and do not fulfil my orders. I remind you for the final time. I am the head of the garrison and you and your administration have no right to do anything within the city boundaries without my approval.[17]

Komendants acquired rights by successfully petitioning superior authorities to intervene on their behalf in jurisdictional disputes and, in some cases, by force of arms. Reminding people of their jurisdictional limitations and paper warnings such as Trufanov's achieved little. The deputy SVAG head in Thuringia, Major General I. S. Kolesnichenko, was reminded of this painful fact during mid 1946. In an attempt to stamp out troop violence in Thuringia with a view to the upcoming elections in September and October, Kolesnichenko issued a 'discipline strengthening' order to all of his *komendants* in July 1946. He echoed Trufanov's complaints that many *komendants* were simply uninterested in arresting

---

[16] Trufanov filled this post until 29 October 1945, when he was promoted to the head of the Saxon KS.

[17] GARF – f. r-7212, op. 1, d. 1, l. 39.

soldiers from the army or their own subordinates for infringements against military discipline, particularly in regional areas:

Many officers and Military *Komendants* do not understand that similar arbitrary acts [and] lawlessness ... toward the local population denigrate our position and may result in undesirable consequences in our election campaign.[18]

The arbitrary acts to which Kolesnichenko referred took place in Heiligenstadt during mid May 1946. The *komendatura* received a distress call from nearby villagers alerting them to a rape being committed by Soviet troops. The *komendatura* group did nothing, claiming they lacked fuel to drive to the village. This may have been true given that fuel shortage was a serious problem, particularly in regional areas. However, the group's response to the local German police's repeated requests for them to come and arrest the suspected soldiers suggests that they were not particularly concerned about the negative consequences which troop violence posed to their sponsored party's electoral popularity.[19] Kolesnichenko continued:

The Hegen police established the whereabouts of the rapists and once again telephoned the *komendatura* asking that they come and collect the aforementioned persons. The answer to this request from the *komendatura* was, 'All of our soldiers are home, and we have no business with the others.'[20]

---

[18] Petrov, ed., *SVAG i nemetskie organy samoupravleniia*, 181. As with many Soviet-era military memoirs, Kolesnichenko's work provides a rather dry account of life in post-war Germany, offering nothing of the excitement and complexities evident in his correspondence with other SVAG officers found in the archives. I. S. Kolesnichenko, *Bitva posle voiny: O poslevoennoi zhizni v Germanii* (Moscow: Voenizdat, 1987).

[19] The dismissive attitude towards the concerns of German police was not uncommon among SVAG officers. In fact, Skosyrev issued an order prohibiting SVAG officers from using German police as their personal assistants on 19 September 1946 (no. 170). The order had a limited effect. The military prosecutor of Mecklenburg, Capitan Mikhailovskii, reported to Skosyrev in late September 1946 that the problem was continuing. He cited instances where the *komendant* of Waren threatened to arrest the entire German police force in his *komendatura* if they failed to deliver a motorcycle to him within five days; also, how the police chief in Plau was detained by the local *komendatura* for refusing to follow orders to find a soccer ball and deliver it to them. The chief protested that this was not the function of the local police, yet finally acquiesced by agreeing to deliver a ball of some sort. Mikhailovskii's report contains many other such examples. GARF – f. r-7103, op. 1, d. 26, ll. 193–201.

[20] Petrov, 'Formirovanie organov nemetskogo samoupravleniia', 181. Kolesnichenko took measures to remedy this situation. As an example to other officers, he sentenced the *komendant* of Heiligenstadt to three days' house arrest and reduced pay for failing to report the above rape incident. He also ordered that for the remainder of the election campaign, *komendants* must completely eradicate troop violence against the occupied population by educating the troops as to the importance of the elections, increasing patrols, and reacting to any call from the police for help (and thus making sure that there was enough fuel in the staff cars for this purpose).

'We have no business with the others.' Few phrases capture better the apathetic attitude of some SVAG men towards dealing with the troop violence problem. As the rapists were not members of the Heiligenstadt *komendatura* but most probably members of a local military detachment, this response is more understandable. The physical dangers attendant on apprehending armed soldiers were significant, and by 1946 the group may well have seen that arrests were doing little to stunt the continuation of troop violence in any case. But their inaction was worse. Local German police couldn't arrest members of the occupation force and given that Soviet soldiers and even some repatriates were well armed, few tried to do so. Without SVAG intervention, there was no way that the rapists could be stopped. The final part of the Oranienburg communists' appeal to SVAG to protect them from rampaging troops in August 1945 quoted in Chapter 2 highlights the police problem:

> The majority of our complaints to the *Komendant* of Oranienburg have been ignored on the basis that those who committed these crimes are [German] civilians (in red army uniforms) ... we requested the assistance of the military police but were refused on the pretext that this was a matter for the local German police. Can you imagine five unarmed German police fighting against armed soldiers?[21]

To complicate matters further, the *komendants* of both Heiligenstadt and Oranienburg failed to report these incidents, suggesting that other *komendants* sharing similar attitudes towards the violence problem did the same, leaving superior authorities to find out about them second hand and often far too late to do anything about it.

SVAG recognised the severity of this problem in January 1946, as the level of troop violence evident in the reports from German civil administrations and KPD men squared poorly with the lack of information received by the public prosecutors to whom *komendants* were supposed to report such matters. This was especially evident in Mecklenburg. In response, Skosyrev reissued orders to all of his *komendants* to report every instance of troop indiscipline in the area to the prosecutor, and, in cases of extreme violence such as rape and murder, express telegrams were to be sent to his office immediately.[22] These attempts were not as successful as he had hoped. The prosecutor wrote back to Skosyrev in March 1946 complaining that some *komendants* were still not reporting on the majority of violent cases taking place in their *komendaturas* and that he was still finding out about most of them from other sources.[23] Skosyrev had little choice but to reissue his order again, another paper threat, and urge his

[21] GARF – f. r-7077, op. 1, d. 178, ll. 30–3.   [22] GARF – f. r-7103, op. 1, d. 21, l. 28.
[23] GARF – f. r-7103, op. 1, d. 20, l. 242.

komendants to intensify their efforts in arresting offending soldiers and delivering them to prosecutors.[24]

One cannot help sympathising with the well-intentioned SVAG officers who followed the order, largely because it encouraged them to try to exert some control over the army by applying procedures that were fundamentally flawed. For the enthusiastic among them who considered the safety of the occupied population central to the success of their occupation tasks, their vigilant responses to troop violence, namely arrest, contributed to the problem. On the other hand, for those SVAG officers who had crossed the dead zones left by the Wehrmacht in 1944, the small-scale erratic spikes of violence throughout late 1945 and for much of 1946 could have done little to stir them to defend the Germans. Neither enthusiasm nor passivity could stop the violence. It would not cease to be a major feature of the occupation until late 1947 when the heavily reduced occupation force was confined largely to military barracks, making it easier for SVAG to maintain law and order and much easier for apathetic *komendants* who remained in Germany to enjoy the relative peace.

However, until 1947 putting a halt to the violence was an unrealistic aim in any case. This was part of a broader problem in the transition from war to peace across Eastern Europe, where authorities struggled to manage the violence unleashed by war and consign wartime brutalisation to the past, to the space of war. Within this difficult transition, one could not have expected the army most brutalised by its wartime experience to transform itself from a fighting mass battling the threat of genocide into a benign occupation force overnight.[25] That enthusiastic SVAG men crawled across the chaotic webs of Soviet bureaucracy to quicken this transformation makes their initial success more impressive – doubly so given that some of their SVAG comrades couldn't make the transformation themselves. It is easy to forget that the massive waves of troop violence seen in the first half of the year had receded by the latter months of 1945

[24] GARF – f. r-7103, op. 1, d. 24, ll. 30–1.

[25] The difficulty of this transition from war to peace is part of an emerging and most important literature on the question of how Europeans got themselves out of war (as opposed to how they got themselves into it). Much of this literature, however, is focused on the impact of war on historical memory and identity in post-war Europe and less on the political significance of different forms of violence discussed here. On the concept of 'post-war', see T. Judt, *Postwar: A History of Europe since 1945* (London: Pimlico, 2007). On memory and identity, see R. Bessel and D. Schumann, eds., *Life after Death: Approaches to a Cultural and Social History During the 1940s and 1950s* (New York: Cambridge University Press, 2003) and F. Biess and R. G. Moeller, eds., *Histories of the Aftermath: The Legacies of the Second World War in Europe* (New York: Berghahn Books, 2010).

with the mass removal of repatriates. The erratic spikes of violence that followed them thus occurred in a more stable environment.

Yet this chronology of lessening violence meant little to the occupied population. Even the relatively lower level of violence served to maintain a state of fear and apprehension that first became apparent during the closing stages of the war. These conditions convinced much of the occupied population that there were hardly any measures they could pursue to protect themselves from the Soviet threat. As many came to understand that it was pointless to try to resist armed Soviet soldiers, more and more people chose to protect themselves by cooperating with the regime or fleeing from it – physically and mentally.

6   The muted German response to violence

> As soon as our units occupy one or another city district, the locals gradually begin to come out onto the street, with nearly all of them holding a white flag in their hands. Upon meeting our soldiers, many women throw up their hands, cry, and shake with terror. But as soon as they become convinced that the soldiers and officers of the Red Army are not at all like those people depicted by fascist propaganda, the terror fades away, and more and more people go out onto the street and offer their services to the Red Army.[1]

If only the terror had faded away so quickly. Reams of similar reports from the front flooded army headquarters during the Soviet advance into Germany, promising a new dawn for Soviet–German relations. These reports are filled with lengthy quotations from locals who were meeting the 'Russian beasts' for the first time. Goebbels' Propaganda Ministry had promised them that Soviet victory would bring physical annihilation, mass rape, and the Siberian gulags, and news from further east seemed only to confirm these fears.[2] The locals quoted encountered none of these fates, at least initially, and found the Red Army establishing ad hoc food kitchens to feed them. For them, especially the Berliner quoted below, the end of the war was a new beginning:

> Those horrible weeks are in the past. The Nazis frightened us into thinking that the Russians would send all Germans to perpetual slavery in cold Siberia. Now we see that this was a blatant lie. The measures taken by the Soviet *Komendant* demonstrate that the Russians are not planning to insult and exterminate us. Once again, I have gained a perspective on life.[3]

These responses were not manufactured, but genuine outbursts of astonishment and gratitude from those who managed to speak to their

[1] RGASPI – f. 17, op. 125, d. 321, ll. 10–12.
[2] E. K. Bramsted, *Goebbels and National Socialist Propaganda, 1925–1945* (Michigan: Cresset Press, 1965), 329.
[3] G. N. Sevost'ianov and V. A. Zolotarev, eds., *Velikaia Otechestvennaia voina 1941–1945*, vol. IV (Moscow: Nauka, 1999), 276.

occupiers through the scarce translators or, less articulately, through broken Russian and hand gestures. These responses are so prominent in the positive reports on army relations with locals in April and May 1945 that even an 'official' Russian history of the Great Patriotic War claims that the 'new perspective' of the Berliner cited above was prevalent among most Germans under Soviet occupation by mid 1945:

The concern of Soviet forces for the German populace produced a definite calm; as people adjusted to the new conditions they gained some hope for the future.[4]

Perhaps Germans did hold some hope for the future, born of the end of the war and trying to forget about it as best they could. Germans spoke of the total defeat in 1945 as the 'zero hour' (*Stunde Null*) and 'appeared to draw a line neatly between themselves and what had occurred (and, by extension, what they had been involved in) during the years of Nazi rule'.[5] But lines between war and peace were more crooked in the chaos of 1945, in which there was little calm. The German-Jewish diarist Victor Klemperer spoke for so many of his countrymen when recording his entry of 23 June 1945 in Dresden:

Every couple of minutes, every couple of lines, no matter where I start I end up with the same sentence: everything is uncertain, everything is in suspense, there is nothing solid under one's feet, in one's hands.[6]

Klemperer's fears are found in German mail and other Soviet reports, which investigated the 'mood of the population' through informant networks and thus relied less on the confessions of enthusiastic Germans to provide assessments of public opinion. These other sources detail the terror felt by much of the occupied population in the face of mass troop violence and its aftermath. The end of the war brought little respite to them, with fears of Siberian deportation, rape, robbery, and murder still widespread months, if not years, afterwards when deportations ceased and levels of troop violence fell. The impact of mass violence, then, was felt long after it subsided, distorting the chronological boundary between wartime fear and post-war calm espoused by 'official' narratives. German responses to the occupier within this undefined and frightening space were varied, though muted, hindering and helping SVAG's attempt to establish control over the zone.

White, not red, was the colour of the Soviet advance. The Red Army was met by an abundance of white flags or, more accurately, any piece of light

[4] Ibid.
[5] R. Bessel, *Germany 1945: From War to Peace* (New York: HarperCollins, 2009), 395–6.
[6] Cited ibid., 320.

fabric or paper hung on a stick. It encountered hardly any armed civilian resistance during or after the advance, even at the height of the violence. There weren't many civilians left capable of serious resistance as boys too young and men too old for service in the Wehrmacht had been quickly drafted into ramshackle national militia (*Volkssturm*) units, most of which were quickly dispersed by the Red Army or by their own volition. Some of them took to the woods and found others who continued to fight the Red Army by guerrilla means, sniping here and there and trying to blow up bridges, but their numbers and impact were negligible.[7] In cities, towns, and villages there are only a handful of cases where resistance was reported, with some committed by women, children, and old men shooting erratically out of their windows at approaching soldiers.[8] Much to the surprise of the Red Army and especially the NKVD, which was in charge of eliminating resistance, the resistance failed to emerge once the war was over. By the summer of 1945 there was no insurgency to speak of.[9] Most Germans were simply tired of war and, with the dissolution of the Nazi state and its promises, had nothing left to fight for. The daily battle for

[7] Beria ostentatiously reported to Stalin in October 1945 that his men had arrested 3,336 'werewolves' (German resistance fighters) in the course of massive security operations launched in the rear of the advancing Red Army during the final stages and immediate aftermath of the war. This is certainly an impressive number that may also account for the lack of resistance activity, but these figures must be assessed cautiously due to the NKVD's wide definition of who constituted a werewolf. Some of these werewolf groups were actually criminal bands dealing in the black market, formed by POWs and repatriates of all nationalities. Armed and dangerous, these groups resisted Soviet attempts to liquidate them, sometimes killing Soviet soldiers in the process. Also, in some cases 'guilt by association' was a sufficient cause to arrest suspects, who in most cases were teenagers. Furthermore, it is most likely that a large number of werewolves arrested may have also been charged with specific crimes such as 'spying'. As such, their arrests could be listed under both categories, leading to a duplication of arrest numbers and a heightened impression of anti-Soviet activity and NKVD efficiency. For Beria's report to Stalin see GARF – f. r-9401, op. 2, d. 100, ll. 91–7.

[8] In the absence of military-aged men in those areas occupied by the Soviets during the advance, women, children, and elderly men sometimes committed acts of violent resistance against Soviet forces. Such incidents occurred on the Second Belorussian Front and were reported to Moscow. Throughout January 1945, four German women were arrested for murdering four Red Army soldiers in Askerau, a thirteen-year-old boy was apprehended for attempting to kill a Soviet intelligence officer, and an elderly man and two women opened fire at soldiers from their home. RGASPI – f. 17, op. 125, d. 321, ll. 5–9. Similar incidents are reported in RGASPI – f. 17, op. 125, d. 320, l. 37.

[9] The conclusion drawn by a recent study on 'werewolf' activity during the closing stages of the war that, 'although there had been scattered sniping, arson attacks, and guerrilla warfare, there had been no major outbreak of insurgency' is thus supported by Soviet sources that indicate the low level of such activity during this period. P. Biddiscombe, *Werwolf! The History of the National Socialist Guerrilla Movement, 1944–1946* (Toronto: University of Toronto Press, 1998), 272.

food, health, and one's safety was all-encompassing.[10] Some of the Soviet officers who complained that troop violence would certainly spark a partisan war gradually realised that the Germans would not wage one, no matter how violent the provocations of the troops or the harshness of occupation policy.

The harshest of these policies was also the shortest-lived. In December 1944 the Soviets began to round up Germans nationals from areas they had occupied in Eastern/Central Europe for forced labour in the Soviet Union. By the end of January 1945, 61,375 able-bodied German men had been transported as well as some of the 138,500 Germans arrested by the NKVD in Eastern/Central Europe and Germany itself.[11] Despite the fact that deportations from Germany were relatively small and all had ceased by April, news of them quickly spread further west with the mass exodus of Germans fleeing the Soviet advance, and confirmed Goebbels' promise.[12] Even after the Soviets made it clear after the war that they were not deporting anyone anywhere, mass fear of deportations continued. In Mecklenburg rumours that the Soviets were preparing to send a new batch of young and healthy German workers to Siberia spread like wildfire during the summer of 1945. When the mayor of Bad Kleinen attempted to solve the area's unemployment problem by calling on all healthy men aged from sixteen to sixty, and women from eighteen to fifty, to report to the local administration for work, many people arrived with their families

[10] Gary Bruce argues that the majority of Germans did not engage in any sort of resistance against the regime during the first year of the occupation because daily life was 'characterised to a much greater degree by eking out an existence and contending with the brutality of the Soviet occupation ... merely surviving the post-war conditions was a feat unto itself'. G. Bruce, *Resistance with the People: Repression and Resistance in Eastern Germany 1945–55* (Lanham: Rowman & Littlefield, 2003), 46. As for defining resistance, the unique occupation conditions which emerged in eastern Germany encourage one to question the profitability of using a precise definition, or even placing this definition within the broader scholarship of anti-Nazi or GDR resistance. In the absence of any violent resistance, we may consider as 'resistance' other responses which upset the stability of the power relationships that emerged between occupiers and occupied. The following chapter looks at these responses and the introduction to Bruce's work contains a succinct discussion of the historical debate on this point.
[11] German men from seventeen to forty-five and women from eighteen to thirty years of age were considered able-bodied by the order issued by GKO (no. 7161) in December 1944. RGASPI – f. 644, op. 1, d. 345, l. 8. Most were interned from Hungary, Czechoslovakia, Romania, Bulgaria, and Yugoslavia. GARF – f. r-9401, op. 2, d. 93, ll. 26–45.
[12] Transportation of labourers to the Soviet Union quickly dried up, though the dispatch of detainees caught in the NKVD operations continued until April 1945 under NKVD order no. 0016. Given the logistical difficulties associated with the practice, Beria asked Stalin on 17 April 1945 to allow him to keep people in NKVD camps in Germany and parts of Central Europe who were not of 'operational interest' to the Soviet Union, to which Stalin agreed. Mironenko, ed., *Spetsial'nye lageria NKVD/MVD*, 16.

under the impression that they were being sent to Siberia for forced labour. The Soviet officer on the scene reported that families parted with emotional goodbyes, clutching at one another in fear of imminent deportation. They only realised later that they were being called to gather the local harvest.[13]

This sense of relief did not spread beyond Bad Kleinen. Fears of forced labour deportation remained prevalent in Thuringia during August 1945 and severely hindered SVAG's attempts to bring venereal disease under control. The Soviets could treat their own men as discussed in Chapter 2, but it was incredibly difficult for SVAG to do the same for German women and thus reduce the spread of the disease. The rampaging presence of communicable diseases in hospitals threatened infection, and the brutal history of Nazi medical policy towards venereal-diseased women along with social stigma encouraged them to avoid hospitals and suffer in private.[14] To address this problem, the head of SVAG in Thuringia, the famous Marshal V. I. Chuikov, ordered the construction of women's medical help centres in August 1945. He called on all women to come in for free examinations to improve their health, not mentioning venereal disease.[15]

But still, hardly anyone came. The problem was that local authorities had only begun issuing newspapers in Thuringia on 8 August, partially to counter the widespread belief that the help centres were being established so that SVAG could register all healthy women in the area and send them to Siberia, leaving only the sick and elderly in Germany.[16] The propaganda campaign in the press calling on women to attend the centres could

---

[13] GARF – f. r-7103, op. 1, d. 5, ll. 154–7. Skosyrev's report to Lieutenant General F. I. Bokov is extremely important in understanding conditions in Mecklenburg during August 1945.

[14] For a broader analysis of Nazi policy see A. F. Timm, 'The Legacy of "Bevölkerungspolitik": Venereal Disease Control and Marriage Counselling in Post-WWII Berlin', *Canadian Journal of History* 33, no. 2 (1998): 181–2. For the presence of typhus, see Naimark, *The Russians in Germany*, 123.

[15] The local drive to eradicate venereal disease in Thuringia was launched in response to SVAG order no. 25 of 7 August 1945. GARF – f. r-7317, op. 8, d. 1, ll. 76–7.

[16] GARF – f. r-7317, op. 7, d. 14, ll. 190–5. Although SVAG began to print a zone-wide newspaper on 29 June 1945, it took SVAG some time to begin large-scale newspaper production and circulation in the major cities and even longer in regional areas. Similar delays inhibited the wide circulation of KPD material and Soviet attempts to set up central radio squares in city areas. By September 1945, however, provisions were made to establish radio squares in towns and factories across the zone and to lift the ban on Germans owning personal radio transmitters. N. P. Timofeeva, 'Germaniia mezhdu proshlym i budushchim: Politika SVAG v oblasti kul'tury, nauki i obrazovaniia v 1945–1949 gg.', in *Politika SVAG v oblasti kul'tury, nauki i obrazovaniia: Tseli, metody, rezul'taty 1945–1949. Sbornik dokumentov*, ed. J. Foitzik and N. P. Timofeeva (Moscow: Rosspen, 2006), 34.

hardly dispel this deep-seated fear, which continued to discourage women from seeking treatment. Nonetheless, it is doubtful that most women would have started seeking treatment if they had known the truth of SVAG's intentions, which became apparent months later. Women working in health and food industries were obliged to undertake monthly check-ups at the centres. Once found, those infected with venereal disease would lose their jobs, be placed on a register of infected women, and made largely unemployable. If they or other infected women were deemed prostitutes, a loose definition in 1945 'Sovietspeak', they would be forced into treatment. Uninfected prostitutes who continued to work after their brothels had been shut down were detained and assigned to forced labour (in Germany).[17] The treatment may have been worse than the disease.

Mecklenburg farmers and women in Thuringia had little reason to believe Soviet assurances that they would not send them to Siberia, at least any longer. How many of them had seen Soviet slave labourers harvest crops during the war, or even enlisted them? How many had seen men like Koch, 'the Russian killer' from Chapter 2, humiliate the labourers under his control? Slave labour was a right of the 'war of annihilation' that Germany had waged on the Soviet Union, so why wouldn't it remain a right of the victors in occupation as Goebbels had promised? This fear that what German forces had done in the Soviet Union and perhaps what ordinary Germans had done themselves would now be visited on them is palpable in the sources, particularly mail.

The Soviets confiscated German letters speaking of troop violence to identify their authors and limit the spread of 'anti-Soviet' sentiment among the population. Now available in Soviet archives, these letters have provided later generations with an insight into the depths of the problem. The Soviets considered mail censorship essential to their capacity to administer Germany and, indeed, the Soviet Union. However, this by no means meant that censorship was conducted efficiently. The NKGB was officially in charge of mail censorship, but only a few hundred of its agents operated in Germany at any time during 1945 and 1946.[18] Mail censorship became a widespread and haphazard

---

[17] Petrov, ed., *SVAG i nemetskie organy samoupravleniia*, 624. According to SVAG, prostitutes were mainly responsible for spreading sexually transmitted diseases among the ranks. Despite these measures, prostitution and venereal disease remained a central problem in Thuringia throughout the winter of 1945–6. While ordering much harsher penalties for prostitution in February 1946, the brass in Thuringia conceded that until then many of their officers were simply not interested in dealing with the problem. GARF – f. r-7184, op. 2, d. 3, l. 149.

[18] Most NKGB activity in Germany seems to have been focused on mail censorship. In fact, most of the 339 NKGB agents working in the zone by January 1946 worked in the military

practice beyond the reach of the security services because SVAG officers in Saxony and Mecklenburg took it upon themselves to organise their own mail censorship operations, much to the chagrin of the NKGB and NKVD. Largely unskilled in the art of surveillance, they simply delegated censorship duties en masse to the local German administration, which employed 'anti-fascist' postal workers to censor mail. These workers randomly opened as many letters as they could, searching for information on a variety of topics. Once the letters were removed, the censors forwarded the mail to their local KPD representative, who then took it to the relevant Soviet office.[19] Yet even with Soviet and German censors overworked, there were never enough to read, let alone remove the majority of 'dangerous' letters in circulation.[20] The distribution of German mail is thus key to understanding how news of violence spread beyond its victims and witnesses, helping to maintain this fear long after forced deportations ended and the waves of mass violence subsided – as if the enduring shock of them wasn't enough.

The following selection of letters was removed from circulation in Mecklenburg during November–December 1945. As always, letters addressed to people in the western zones attracted greatest attention from the censors, seeking to identify potential border-crossers and limit the spread of anti-Soviet sentiment in the West. A Schwerin man wrote to his daughters living in the western zone of Berlin:

censorship department, monitoring mail activity among the occupied population and among SVAG and the army as well. GARF – f. r-9401, op. 2, d. 134, ll. 231–2. After the shake-up in the security services in March 1946, mail censorship expanded, with 798 personnel working in the military censorship department of the Ministry of State Security (MGB). For a very short discussion of this department see N. V. Petrov, 'Otdel voennoi tsenzury MGB v Germanii (Otdel 'VTS' MGB)', in *Sovetskaia voennaia administratsiia v Germanii*, ed. Doronin, Foitzik, and Tsarevskaia-Diakina.

[19] The NKGB was outraged at this trespass of jurisdictional authority and complained of it to leading SVAG officers. In fact, both the NKGB and NKVD appealed to senior SVAG officers to put an end to this practice. In their appeals they claimed that only the NKGB was sufficiently equipped to conduct these operations secretly, which was essential in maintaining the effectiveness of mail censorship. The delegation of censorship duties to German local administrations, which according to the very evidence provided by mail censors were still dotted with fascist or at least anti-Soviet elements, compromised the secrecy and thus effectiveness of the operation. For Saxony, see the appeal of NKGB Captain Kutuzov to Lieutenant General Dubrovskii in early December 1945, GARF – f. r-7212, op. 1, d. 13, l. 374. For Mecklenburg see the appeal of the NKVD on behalf of the NKGB in March 1946. GARF – f. r-7103, op. 1, d. 20, l. 152. Other complaints are found in GARF – f. r-7103, op. 1, d. 10, l. 285.

[20] In one Mecklenburg town, for instance, two such anti-fascists reported that they looked at approximately 800–1,000 letters a day and from that total removed 5–10 that contained 'anti-Soviet' or KPD sentiments. However, it may be important to note that this answer was given under questioning from SVAG officers. GARF – f. r-7103. op. 1, d. 20, l. 152.

Here they rob us all night and everything is wild. Generally, all of the refugees are going over to the British zone, as the living conditions there are better. We want to see out the New Year and if the living conditions stay the same, then I would like to cross over alone and then bring your mother, as here one lives through the entire night in fear.[21]

A Schwerin woman expressed similar sentiments in early December 1945, somewhat annoyed with her friend for complaining of conditions in the western zones:

My dear grumbler! In all aspects of life we find ourselves in a much worse position living here with the Russians. It is impossible to even put it into words. We must endure it all. Of course, the communists take an active part in all of this. When can we expect peace?[22]

Recent scholarship highlighting the violent behaviour of Allied troops towards German civilians in the western zones, particularly rape, certainly suggests that the complaints made by the 'grumbler' were not ostentatious.[23] Nonetheless, the final question posed by the Schwerin woman best highlights the blurred distinction between war and post-war worlds. The sense of chaos, the continuation of troop violence, and levels of material deprivation encouraged many other women to ask the same question and to answer it in the most despondent tones. A Güstrow woman wrote to her aunt at the end of November 1945:

My dear auntie Mari . . . In the middle of the night three Red Army soldiers broke into our apartment and robbed us completely. My children and I have been left without any clothes. Out fate and future are even darker.[24]

Letter writers convey trauma by drawing on personal experiences or discussing prevailing fears of troop violence. In this sense, letters were written by victims and observers, although the distinction between the two was not fixed. One such letter written at the end of 1945 is most instructive in this respect, because it echoes the common desire to leave born out of observing rather than experiencing violence:

It is not easy to live under the Russians here. The rape and frequent murder of women occur everyday in the city. How about me coming to live with you?[25]

[21] GARF – f. r-7103, op. 1, d. 10, l. 285.   [22] GARF – f. r-7103, op. 1, d. 10, ll. 291–2.
[23] Western historians have generally accepted that rape and other forms of troop violence were committed primarily by the Red Army and that Allied soldiers were much better behaved in the western zones. A recent work, however, illustrates the extent to which troop violence was also a problem in the western zones. G. MacDonogh, *After the Reich: The Brutal History of the Allied Occupation* (New York: Basic Books, 2007), 124.
[24] GARF – f. r-7103, op. 1, d. 10, l. 121.   [25] GARF – f. r-7103, op. 1, d. 10, l. 285.

The intimate confessions in these letters were thus not restricted to those who wrote or read them. They speak for others who were caught in those areas beset by erratic spikes of violence and for those who only heard of them by word of mouth. That such letters addressed within the zone attracted less attention from the censors than those addressed to the West ensured that more fell through their surveillance net, taking news of continuing violence to those areas which were lucky enough to avoid them or believe that it had passed. The spectre of troop violence remained not only because the violence continued, but also because news of it spread via mail much wider than the narrow and sporadic outbreaks of late 1945 would otherwise have allowed.

It is clear that violence cemented hostile German attitudes towards the Soviets, making it most difficult for SVAG to administer the zone and nigh impossible for the Soviet-sponsored political parties to sell a now tarnished socialist message to an angry electorate. But how did mass violence and the 'atmosphere of fear' it engendered long after it subsided influence German attitudes towards the occupier beyond the palpable hatred and resentment? Most historians would agree with Richard Bessel's answer to this question:

The exercise of revenge against Germans in 1945 thus performed a key role in the profound change of mentalities that occurred as Germans constructed a post-Nazi identity as innocent victims in an unfair world.[26]

The change of mentality in the Soviet zone was more dramatic than in the western. These 'avengers' had long been painted by Nazi propaganda as 'subhuman beasts' who needed to be exterminated lest they destroy Germany. For many Germans, mass troop violence strengthened the subhuman images and hysterical fears of the Soviets deeply rooted in racial prejudice which survived the demise of National Socialism, the Nazi state, and its armies.[27] Now there was nothing left to protect Germans from this elemental force, making them not only 'innocent',

---

[26] Bessel, *Germany 1945: From War to Peace*, 167.

[27] Anti-Soviet and remaining racist attitudes in Germany were not restricted to the Soviet zone. Surveys conducted by the Opinions Survey Section of the Office of Military Government, United States (OMGUS) during April 1946 enlisted 1,470 Germans from a range of different age and social groups around the American zone as participants. The survey asked whether or not 'the extermination of the Jews and Poles and other non-Aryans was ... necessary for the security of the Germans', and whether or not 'territories such as Danzig, Sudetenland, and Austria should be part of Germany proper'. Of the 1,400 respondents, 37 per cent answered yes to the first question while over 50 per cent answered yes to the second. The idea that it was necessary to 'remove' substantial elements of an 'enemy' population inhabiting areas that were fit for German colonial expansion was a political manifestation of the racially determinate thinking prevalent throughout Germany during the Nazi period. Even in the American zone, these results

but powerless victims as well. In the zone then, it wasn't merely fear of the occupier, his violent rampages (and news of them), arbitrary arrests, and furious countermeasures to the slightest hint of resistance which encouraged mass docility towards him. Within this seemingly simplistic and, indeed, primal process, complex links between the 'victimhood' mentality and German behaviour emerged to help maintain docility as its dominant expression long after the waves of mass violence which initially inspired it had subsided.

Some historians have noted similar links in their study of the zone. Based on her study of rape in post-war Germany, Atina Grossman demonstrates how xenophobic attitudes towards the Soviets significantly influenced how victims both interpreted and responded to rape:

The narrative of the Russian primitive or exotic curiously absolved him of guilt, as it also absolved women themselves. Such child-like, primitive, animal-like creatures could not be expected to control themselves – especially when tanked up with alcohol – or adhere to rules of civilised behaviour. Nor could women be expected to defend themselves against such an elemental force, backed up in many cases, of course, by rifle and revolver. In the end, German women ... managed to maintain the conviction of their own superiority.[28]

The evidence presented here suggests that this ability to justify one's docility was not restricted to victims of rape. Others with no such experience were able to justify their inability to respond to the violence of the occupier based on their understanding of 'Soviet barbarity'. It seems that mass violence and the xenophobic ideas it confirmed helped to further discourage resistance and, at least in the following case, it did so by encouraging hopes of it emerging.

Germans took heart from the growing tension between the Soviets and the Allies which promised, somehow, to liberate them from the 'Russian beast'. Many had hoped that a separate peace could be concluded with the

corresponded well to later polls seeking to determine levels of 'anti-Soviet racism' and anti-Semitism in Germany that yielded similarly troubling outcomes, as did the realisation that such attitudes were more prevalent among younger Germans. The surveys' results are found in R. L. Merritt, *Democracy Imposed: U.S. Occupation Policy and the German Public, 1945–1949* (New Haven and London: Yale University Press, 1995), 95–6, 130–6. American officers who served in the Opinions Survey Section also offer valuable insights into the topic. See A. D. Kahn, *Experiment in Occupation: Witness to the Turnabout. Anti-Nazi War to Cold War, 1944–6* (University Park, Pa.: Pennsylvania State University Press, 2004).

[28] A. Grossman, 'A Question of Silence', 60–1. James Mark arrives at a similar conclusion in his study of the post-war occupation of Hungary. Based on his interviews with Hungarian rape victims conducted decades after the event, Mark also found that many victims remained sympathetic to the Soviet rapists. J. Mark, 'Remembering Rape: Divided Social Memory and the Red Army in Hungary 1944–1945', *Past and Present* 188 (2005): 146.

western powers in the closing stages of the war, allowing all German forces
to move eastward and halt the Soviet advance. These hopes were quickly
dashed in April 1945, as Soviet and American forces met on Elbe River
and continued their advance into Germany. But faith in an impending
conflict between the Soviets and the West also re-emerged in the post-war
period, as it did in some other areas of Europe. Many Germans agreed
that a new war between the Soviets and the West was the only way in which
the Red Army could be ejected from Germany. Even with little public
indication of problems within the Grand Alliance to support such gran-
diose claims, much of the occupied population seems to have interpreted
local and international events in such a way. The 'war myth' allowed many
to rationalise that it was unnecessary to react violently towards occupation
forces or resist SVAG orders in view of impending liberation. The inability of many Germans to resist the Soviet occupier thus encouraged the
widespread nature of this desperate belief, which itself only bred an
attitude of passive anticipation.

The 'war myth' was one of the most widespread rumours across the
Soviet zone, of which there were many in mid to late 1945 before the
broad circulation of newspapers, especially in regional areas. Rumours
became very important in carrying information within this context, spread
by word of mouth and propaganda leaflets.[29] In fact, even after official
Soviet and KPD newspapers were established, people were often cautious
about believing what was printed in them. Understandably, the myth was
discussed at length in reports written by security officers concerned about
the spread of such rumours and interested in exaggerating them. But it
also appeared in many reports written by other officers simply discussing
'the mood of population' under their control, in censored mail, and
eventually in memoir literature.[30] A former soldier from Saxony wrote
to his mother in December 1945:

---

[29] The importance of rumours and gossip during times of crisis has been well noted by Sheila
Fitzpatrick in her work on the Soviet Union in the 1930s. She argues that '[R]umours
disseminate information ... on public matters to those who hunger for it. But they also
express popular hopes and fears and attempts to explain puzzling events.' Fitzpatrick thus
understands rumours regarding the imminent outbreak of war between the Soviet Union and
the West during the late 1930s as an expression of disaffection towards the Soviet regime
widespread in the Soviet Union, and as a hope for change. The parallels with the 'war myth' in
the Soviet zone are clear. S. Fitzpatrick, *Everyday Stalinism: Ordinary Life in Extraordinary
Times. Soviet Russia in the 1930s* (New York: Oxford University Press 1999), 183.

[30] NKVD officers sent reports to deputy SVAG heads in each state on a fortnightly basis (or
were supposed to), and frequently discussed the prominence of the 'war myth'. This helps
to explain why the myth was reported across different organs. But the myth was also
widely discussed at the lowest level of reporting, which did not have access to security
service information, further suggesting that the myth was widespread. For SVAG

Yesterday I had a desire to leave, but I think it will be better for all of us if I stay, as sooner or later something has to happen: I will be able to fight against the Russians.[31]

Just what would happen was open to conjecture which many were willing to offer. Most popular was the idea that the Alliance would quickly falter on disagreements over the treatment of Germany at Potsdam, creating an Allied–German alliance against Bolshevism. American and British occupation forces were already primed to invade the Soviet zone and would do so at the eventual breakdown. This belief was based on the notion, which turned out to be partly accurate in the British case, that German POWs interned in camps in the western zones were actually being retrained and rearmed in preparation for possible engagement with Soviet forces. POWs who were released from western captivity saw fit to spread this rumour upon their return to the zone, causing significant alarm in Soviet ranks and forcing them to launch their own covert investigation into these and other so-called camps.[32] Addressing a group of listeners, a local of the Anklam district in Mecklenburg cried:

Only a new war can save the Germans from the Red Army. German soldiers, armed [and] uniformed . . . are at the border and are awaiting the beginning of the war with Russia.[33]

complaints on the NKVD not reporting to it on security matters in Mecklenburg see GARF – f. r-7103, op. 1, d. 22, ll. 257–8, and in Saxony GARF – f. r-7212, op. 1, d. 13, l. 245. For memoir literature see Kahn, *Experiment in Occupation*, 62–3.

[31] GARF – f. r-7212, op. 1, d. 137, l. 177.

[32] For the spread of these rumours in the zone see GARF – f. r-9401, op. 2, d. 102, l. 38, GARF – f. r-7212, op. 1, d. 186, ll. 60–1, 88–9. For the relevant NKVD report regarding the investigation see GARF – f. r-9401, op. 2, d. 134, ll. 208–12. It is important to note that the spread of rumours regarding the retraining of Allied forces was not restricted to the zone. A Czech commissar working in a border *komendatura* informed SVAG in October 1945 that German soldiers released from US captivity as well as civilian Czechs who had returned from the American zone firmly believed that the Americans had trained and armed an SS force of over 75,000 men. They were spreading the rumour that this army had been created with the intention of deploying it in a possible conflict with the Soviet Union. GARF – f. r-7212, op. 1, d. 55, l. 45. In the American zone much of the visible training of former German troops could be explained by the OMGUS push to create a German border police force during the winter of 1945–6. Nonetheless, this push caused SVAG similar anxieties. SVAG complained to OMGUS in April 1946 that German border police had been seen firing into the zone and feared that they might act as weapons smugglers. GARF – f. r-7317, op. 7, d. 37, ll. 16–18. With regard to similar developments in the British zone, however, Rzheshevskii's work on this topic has revealed Churchill's secret plans for a possible military engagement with the Soviets in 1945, in which the use of retrained German troops on the Allied side was envisaged. O. A. Rzheshevskii, 'Sekretnye voennye plany U. Cherchullia protiv SSSR v mae 1945 g.', *Novaia i Noveishaia Istoriia* (1999), no. 3.

[33] GARF – f. r-7103, op. 1, d. 10, l. 98.

This belief encouraged strange incidents in areas of Mecklenburg in the wake of the Potsdam Conference. People began to prepare for a British invasion of Mecklenburg as they misinterpreted the end of the conference as a signal that the Alliance had broken down and that British soldiers had already advanced as far as Schwerin. SVAG's failure to organise the timely printing of the Potsdam Declaration was partly to blame for this misinterpretation, especially in rural areas. But even when it was printed, the official declaration had to compete with counterfeit declarations that were being distributed around the zone by anti-Soviet propagandists. These counterfeit declarations promised much harsher terms than the original and were intended to increase German dissatisfaction with their treatment at the hands of the Allies. According to these declarations, alcohol and marriage were to be forbidden and many Germans were to be forced to work and live in the Soviet Union. As it turned out, these harsher terms were hardly necessary as the original declaration shattered many Germans hopes in any case. Soviet observers reported that upon having the actual declaration read out to them, a deathly silence fell over city crowds.[34]

The 'war myth' thus may have faded for them, but not for others. In fact, the skewed interpretation of the declaration strengthened belief in the myth, as many believed the declaration to be a new platform on which Soviet–Allied tensions could mount. Gossip was widespread that the war between the Allies and the Soviets had already begun or would begin at any moment because the Soviets had broken provisions of the declaration relevant to the treatment of the occupied population.[35] Addressing a group of listeners in November, one man shouted:

The Russians have to leave here soon. All signs point to an impending war. The Americans, for example, ordered that all refugees from the western regions must return to their former places of residence. The Russians stopped this passage, but the Americans have insisted on it, so this already suggests an impending war. I welcome the fact that the Russians will no longer be here.[36]

The situation began to change as Soviet–Allied tensions grew and the myth threatened to turn into reality.[37] Yet even if these developments encouraged belief in the myth, they did not necessarily encourage believers to behave differently. If anything, passive anticipation remained prevalent. Even at the relative height of Soviet–American tension in late 1946, electoral disobedience rather than violence became the dominant

---

[34] GARF – f. r-7103, op. 1, d. 22, l. 155.   [35] GARF – f. r-7133, op. 1, d. 271, l. 74.
[36] GARF – f. r-7103, op. 1, d. 10, l. 98.
[37] Some reports certainly pointed to Churchill's Fulton speech of March 1946 as a contributing factor to the rise of the 'war myth' in the zone. GARF – f. r-7212, op. 1, d. 187, ll. 20–2.

expression of anti-Soviet sentiment among believers and non-believers alike. Standing among local residents in Treptow during October 1946, a voter signalled his intentions to onlookers:

I am going to vote for the CDU ... The English and the Americans are anti-Bolshevik and do not want Germans to become bolshevised. They will only help us when we demonstrate through our votes at the election that we are also anti-Bolshevik.[38]

It is little wonder that the few anti-Soviet elements committed to inspiring a violent reaction against the occupier failed to attract a following. Not only did Soviet security forces haunt these would-be resisters every step of the way, but their message of violent resistance made little sense to a frightened people in the habit of justifying their docility in one way or another.

The 'war myth' flourished alongside similar beliefs in the zone born of desperation and the hope that somehow the occupation would be over-thrown – impossible by German hands alone.[39] These beliefs may have been strongest where violence and the threat of it were most severe, but certainly emerged within a broader sense of victimhood among a people who had drawn a line between themselves and a past they wanted to forget and certainly not fight for. The complex relationship between violence, victimhood, myth, and docility could only develop within this thoroughly German context. In other areas of Soviet-occupied Europe where the myth was prevalent it did not promote docility, but breathed life into the violent resistance movements which endured for years after the war. In Ukraine the myth became a central piece of propaganda used to attract elements of the population to join the guerrilla war against Soviet forces and energised the guerrilla base as the Cold War intensified.[40] In Germany the Soviets found nothing of the violent resistance that they expected. Instead, they encountered more complex German responses that required new, more refined responses to establish control over the zone. These form the subject of the following chapters.

---

[38] GARF – f. r-7103, op. 1, d. 26, l. 222 (CDU – Christian Democratic Union).

[39] In some areas of the zone, particularly those that had been initially occupied by American or British troops and then handed over to the Soviets in July 1945, Soviet officers consistently reported that much of the population considered the territorial exchange temporary, and expected that Allied troops would return to take control of their area once again under one pretence or another. The fact that officers usually refused to answer questions regarding long-term Soviet policy plans in Germany (in many cases, they too were unaware of them) only fuelled speculation. This was especially the case during the Potsdam Conference. Petrov, ed., *SVAG i nemetskie organy samoupravleniia*, 115.

[40] The following monograph is most useful to contrast elements of Ukraine's post-war situation with those of the zone to determine how it was possible for the myth to exert such diametrically opposed influences on social behaviour: J. Burds, *The Early Cold War in Soviet West Ukraine 1944–1948* (Russian and East European Studies no. 1505, 2001).

Part II

The beginnings of peace and stability

7   The struggle to feed Germany

> Occupation forces must be sustained at the expense of the vanquished
> country. Such is the law of war, such is the law of all post-war agree-
> ments. We are still feeding our occupation forces at the expense of our
> people, our country. This is wrong ... We must release our people, our
> country, from the extra burdens that we have consigned her ... Let the
> Germans feed us ... and let every German understand clearly, that as a
> vanquished country, they are required to do so.[1]

Zhukov had good reason to be concerned about food supplies. The war-
ravaged Soviet agricultural sector was struggling to produce a good harvest in 1945. By August it looked as if the harvest would be as measly as the
previous year's, despite the Red Army's liberation of Ukraine and
Belorussia – the breadbaskets of the Union. The harvest eventually
yielded only 47.3 million tonnes of grain, just less than half of the 1940
level.[2] Soviet agriculture was simply unable to sustain the domestic population and export commitments to devastated European countries, not
to mention the millions of Soviet soldiers serving abroad. Something had
to give. The Soviet leadership stopped feeding most of its soldiers (and
millions of German civilians) in Germany, expecting that the summer
German harvest would feed them instead. Many soldiers had already been
'living off the land', though unsystematically. Now over a million troops,
and almost 20 million German civilians, displaced persons, and refugees,
would share a partially sown German harvest that was proving most
difficult to collect. Zhukov's eloquent justification of the leadership's
August decision to rely on the German harvest failed to relieve the angst

---

[1] Zhukov to SVAG Chiefs, August 1945. Zhukov's remark 'Such is the law of all post-war
   agreements' refers to the Potsdam declaration, which stipulated that Germany would bear
   the costs of the occupation. Zakharov, ed., *Deiatel'nost' sovetskikh voennykh komendatur*, 92.
[2] This was the official figure for the 1945 barn harvest given by Soviet officials at the time, yet
   revised later. This has led to some scholarly debate over the actual harvest figure, the
   contours of which have been articulated by Stephen Wheatcroft, 'The Soviet Famine of
   1946–1947, the Weather and Human Agency in Historical Perspective', *Europe–Asia
   Studies* 64, no. 6 (2012).

this decision had caused his audience of SVAG officers responsible for governing the Soviet zone and feeding its people. As many had feared, their battle with the army over food and resources soon intensified. Not unexpectedly, the army often prevailed, which threatened severe food shortages for everyone else in the approaching winter.

At the same meeting in August 1945 where Zhukov enunciated the harsh laws of war, the NKVD's chief agent in Germany, Serov, ironically, offered a calmer approach to the audience: 'Our government does not allow us to feed the Germans cakes, but that does not mean that the situation should come to starvation.'[3] That the situation did not come to starvation, at least on any mass scale, is an enduring testament to the strength of the rationing and broader agricultural system established by the Soviets under the most difficult circumstances. This was the first step to establishing some sense of order in Germany and, rather quickly, further control over the population.

The Soviet success becomes more apparent when compared to the failures of the other occupiers in establishing their rationing systems, especially the British. In this sense, Gareth Pritchard's call for more comparative studies to deepen our knowledge of the occupation is most warranted.[4] Food shortages were more severe in the British zone for a number of reasons. The British occupied north-western Germany, a food deficit area heavily reliant on food imports to feed its population. Importing such large amounts of food became much more difficult in the midst of the world food crisis in 1946–7. The British occupation government's inexperience in mass-managing agricultural affairs prepared them poorly to exploit domestic food sources to replace the lost imports. Food shortages gave rise to work stoppages and even forms of violent protest which constricted economic growth and only compounded the food shortage problem. This terrible cycle plagued the British zone in the immediate post-war period and tore at the health of the population, especially of children, and thus probably for decades more.

There are substantial similarities between Soviet and British food management in post-war Germany and in the crises they faced, none more so than the wartime devastation of the agricultural system in the Soviet zone which reduced its output capacity to British-like levels. The distinctions between them, however, were far more consequential. The most important distinction was that, unlike the Soviets, the British failed to establish an agricultural system in their zone capable of meeting the post-war food

---

[3] Petrov, *Pervyi predsedatel' KGB Ivan Serov*, 235.
[4] G. Pritchard, 'The Occupation of Germany in 1945 and the Politics of German History', *History Compass* 7/2 (2009): 463.

Table 7.1[a] *Land available per 100 people, 1946 (acres)*

Zone	Agricultural land	Arable land
Soviet	85	67
British	62	37
American	80	47
French	95	50

[a] J. P. Nettl, *The Eastern Zone and Soviet Policy in Germany* (London: Oxford University Press, 1951), 172.

crises with which it was confronted. Why were the Soviets more successful than their British counterparts? This question has not been addressed sufficiently in the literature and not at all since the opening of the Soviet archives. The central difference between Soviet and British officers was the former's superior understanding of the structures required to manage food supply and willingness to build them – a superiority which has been ignored by some of the leading historians of Soviet food management in post-war Germany in their vehement critiques of Soviet incompetence and negligence in food matters.[5]

These rationing systems emerged from very different agricultural bases evident in Table 7.1.

The greater amount of arable land in the Soviet zone did not automatically result in greater food supplies during 1945 and 1946. Military operations in the spring of 1945 had severely disrupted the sowing season, with most large agricultural producers in eastern Germany fleeing the Red Army's advance. Nonetheless, even the meagre expectations of the summer harvest were not realised, as the liberation of slave labourers decimated the agricultural labour force. They would not leave Germany empty handed, however, with many taking farm machinery and livestock – slave severance pay – with them. That is, if they could take them before Soviet requisitioning teams arrived to strip the area bare as part of their reparations programme. The lack of horse and machine power made it extremely difficult for the mostly inexperienced German labourers mobilised by the Soviets to do anything resembling effective harvesting by the late summer. Even then, the lack of fuel made it difficult to transport whatever foodstuffs were harvested from rural to urban areas.

[5] For example, D. Harsch, *Revenge of the Domestic: Women, the Family, and Communism in the German Democratic Republic* (Princeton, NJ: Princeton University Press, 2007).

Taking all of this into account, on average, how much food was each occupier able to supply to its population on a daily basis from 1945 to 1947? In answering this question we can only speak of approximate amounts which fluctuate significantly according to time and place. Naturally, rural folk who produced the food were expected to feed themselves and the country, but urban dwellers were organised into an entitlement hierarchy where those who worked harder or closer to the regime received more food than those who did not. Miners thus received higher entitlements than office workers, who received more than the unemployed.[6] Also, just as in the Soviet Union, citizens of major and more populous cities were afforded higher entitlement levels than those of smaller ones, with the capitals Berlin/Moscow receiving the highest and smaller cities the lowest.[7] A similar tiered system operated in the British zone. Table 7.2 compares entitlements in the Soviet sector of Berlin and Dresden, a lower-tier city in the zone of approximately half a million inhabitants.

Soviet entitlement levels for most of their working population were higher than the British for much of the occupation period. Normal consumers, the ration category into which 40 per cent of the population in the British zone fell (some 8 million), received from 1,040 to 1,150 calories. By September the level had risen in most major cities to 1,671 calories, but quickly fell with the onset of the world food crisis in March 1946 to 1,015 calories and remained below the 1,671 level until 1949.[8]

However, 'a ration card was a set of possibilities, not a set of assurances', as William Moskoff observes in his analysis of the wartime rationing system in the Soviet Union.[9] Germans rarely received their full ration entitlement, especially in the British zone after March 1946. The nutritional quality of food was also often poorer than stated, reducing the real amount of calories consumed. The problem of determining consumed calories is compounded by the 'unaccountable' food available to some via

---

[6] The exception to this rule was that special classes of people such as infants and pregnant women received other entitlements in the British zone or special food supplements to their diets.

[7] The occupation zone was divided into a 'four-tiered hierarchy', to use Mark Landsman's term. People living in areas of the first tier (Berlin) were given priority in ration allocations, while those living in second-tier cities such as Dresden and Leipzig were given slightly less priority and so on. M. Landsman, *Dictatorship and Demand: The Politics of Consumerism in East Germany* (Cambridge, Mass.: Harvard University Press, 2005), 20.

[8] Entitlements for women, particularly unemployed women, require a separate analysis, offered in the following chapter. See the population breakdown of ration card recipients in J. E. Farquharson, *The Western Allies and the Politics of Food: Agrarian Management in Postwar Germany* (Leamington Spa: Berg, 1985), 259.

[9] W. Moskoff, *The Bread of Affliction: The Food Supply in the USSR during World War II* (New York: Cambridge University Press, 1990), 143.

Table 7.2[a] *Daily ration entitlements for the Soviet sector in Berlin and Dresden, August 1945 (calories)*

Ration category	Bread	Potatoes	Cereals	Meat	Fat	Sugar	Total calories[b]
I Heavy industry labourers							
Berlin	1800	252	80	280	84	97.5	2593.5
Dresden	1350	315	40	140	84	97.5	2026.5
II Light industry labourers							
Berlin	1500	252	60	182	42	78	2114
Dresden	1200	315	30	112	42	58.5	1757.5
III Office workers							
Berlin	1200	252	40	112	28	78	1710
Dresden	900	315	20	98	28	58.5	1419.5
IV Children							
Berlin (0–15 years)	900	252	30	56	56	97.5	1391.5
Dresden (0–16 years)	750	315	20	56	56	97.5	1294.5
V Dependants, unemployed, etc.							
Berlin	900	252	30	56	19.6	58.5	1316.1
Dresden	750	315	15	56	19.6	58.5	1214.1

[a] For Dresden levels see GARF – f. r-7212, op. 1, d. 13, ll. 80–1. For Berlin, Zakharov, ed., *Deiatel'nost' sovetskikh voennykh komendatur*, 299–302. The five-category ration system operated in the larger cities in the zone such as Dresden, whilst the six-category system operated in all other areas. The six-category system included semi-heavy labour as the second category with a slightly smaller amount of rations allocated.

[b] Coffee and tea were also issued on a monthly basis as well as supplements to special categories discussed above. Slightly different totals are given by Donna Harsh, yet the above totals are converted from standard foodstuff issues in grams to calories by using Soviet conversion tables, which afford them a high degree of accuracy for the August 1945 period. See D. Harsch, 'Approach/Avoidance: Communists and Women in East Germany, 1945–9', *Social History* 25, no. 2 (2000): 162.

home garden plots, the black market, or trade with farmers.[10] For our purposes, however, the issue at hand is not only how many calories occupiers supplied to their population, but how they managed to do so in the face of the most severe crises which threatened mass starvation.

[10] Trips to the countryside were most time-consuming and difficult to make for urban dwellers seeking to supplement their rations due to the breakdown of transport services. Even when they reached the countryside, trade with farmers was generally made on unfair terms, especially for workers who had little to trade but the clothes on their backs. Some workers stole crops such as turnips and potatoes when they could not afford them, which only added to city–rural tensions. This happened in the British zone as well, where workers waited for farmers to harvest their crops and then stole them.

The Soviets were in a much better position to deal with these crises because they had rebuilt the devastated agricultural system in eastern Germany to establish a monopoly over food supplies. It was difficult to do so in the British zone because the Nazi-era agricultural system was still intact and, despite the wishes of some British officials, it was clear that the occupation government lacked sufficient personnel to tear down and rebuild anything. Hopes that the existing system would at least provide a basis from which to quickly organise food supply were soon dashed, however, as its lingering evils soon became apparent to the British. Chief among them were the German agricultural managers who staffed the system and quickly developed an inattentiveness to British orders and hostility to their rule. They were supposed to set product quotas for local farmers to fill based on what the area could produce, collect the product, and then send it to urban areas for consumption. The problem was that managers often set quotas much lower than what farmers were capable of producing in the interests of keeping food in regional areas. Managers thus became 'mere instruments of self-supply for their own [rural] community', rather than instruments to ensure supply of urban areas which were in most desperate need of food.[11] As much as the British complained about these managers and the 'localism' inherent to the system, without the bureaucratic machinery to replace managers or the policing apparatus to compel German farmers to produce more food, the British had little choice but to accept the status quo.[12] Threats to introduce heavy fines for such corrupt practices were undermined by their inability to enforce them on a large scale.

Unable to exploit domestic food resources fully to feed their cities, the British became more reliant on food imports at a time when worldwide food shortages constricted export markets. As evident in Table 7.3, by March 1946 the calorific entitlement had dropped dramatically for normal consumers, as well as for special category recipients such as workers engaged in heavy industry. People took to the streets in protest, rioting and ransacking bakeries in search of food, which only exacerbated food shortages, as after March the British struggled to supply even these lower entitlements.

If in 1946 a cycle of food shortage and economic inefficiency was beginning to emerge as the basis for civil unrest, by 1947 it had crystallised

---

[11] This was conceded by Hans Schlange-Schöningen, who, in January 1946, was appointed chief of the German Inter-Regional Food Allocation Committee (Gifac), a body consisting of German food experts established by the British to advise them on agricultural policy. Farquharson, *The Western Allies and the Politics of Food*, 63.

[12] The same problem severely limited the denazification programme in the British zone.

Table 7.3[a]   *Calorific entitlements for normal consumers (NCs) and very heavy workers (VHWs), 1946*

Ration period	NCs	VHWs
Jan.–Feb.	1671 (avg.)	2495 (avg.)
4–31 March	1015	2265
1–28 April	1040	2325
29 April–26 May	1050	2335
27 May–23 June	1050	2335
24 June–21 July	1050	2340
22 July–18 Aug.	1135	2445
19 Aug.–15 Sept.	1335	2645

[a] Office of Military Government for Germany, US, 'Report of the Military Governor: Statistical Annex', no. 34 (April 1948), 18, 25. The VHWs average is calculated from Nettl, *The Eastern Zone and Soviet Policy in Germany*, 182.

into the most salient feature of the broader mismanagement of occupation affairs in the British zone. This was most pronounced in the Ruhr mining regions. Coal miners only received high ration supplements at their work-places, which made it more difficult to provide food for their families. They too, in times of crisis, were forced to miss work and forage for food. Rolling work stoppages wreaked havoc on the British zone's economy, as the British mainly used the proceeds from coal exports to pay for food imports. Less coal meant less imported food and less fuel for food-producing industries, which, in turn, only compounded food shortages that gave rise to low coal production in the first place. As John Farquharson notes in his groundbreaking work in this area, food shortages became self-exacerbating problems.[13]

This coal–food cycle peaked in the first half of 1947, as real ration levels for miners dropped significantly below even their reduced post-March 1946 entitlement. Miners in the Ruhr downed tools in the spring, costing about half a million tonnes of lost coal by April[14] and another million tonnes of hard and 355,000 tonnes of brown coal by the following month.[15] This loss was much steeper than the usual drop in production

[13] Farquharson also discusses the range of diplomatic issues that contributed to the coal–food cycle. Farquharson, *The Western Allies and the Politics of Food*, 121–2.

[14] Great Britain Foreign Office, 'Weekly Political Intelligence Summaries' no. 387 (October 1947).

[15] American Military Government (OMGUS) estimates, Office of the Military Government for Germany, US, 'Report of the Military Governor: Statistical Annex', 24.

Table 7.4^a *The 1947 coal–food cycle (tonnes)*

	March	April	May
Hard coal production	6,119,000	5,094,000	5,192,000
Solid fuel exports from mines	8,420,000	6,800,000	8,370,000
Flour and grain imports	243,200	178,000	302,000

^{a} Office of Military Government for Germany, US, 'Report of the Military Government: Statistical Annex', 19, 25, 28, 29.

during the seasonal transition, further straining the British purse and cutting food imports.

Miners not only downed tools in response to the drop in entitlements, but protested with their countrymen against both the German food administrations and the British occupation government. In their reports to London, British intelligence highlighted the anti-German, rather than anti-British, tone of the protests, but could only do so most disingenuously when reporting on a riot in Düsseldorf at the end of March:

> During a mass food demonstration of 30,000 people . . . unruly elements smashed windows of British offices and overturned into a lake a Volkswagen in the British service.[16]

The confluence of malnutrition and disease worsened the health situation among Germans across the Ruhr and fuelled the riots beyond April. This is most understandable given the rising mortality and particularly infant mortality rates in early 1947 evident in Tables 7.5 and 7.6.[17]

The available data suggest that infant mortality was highest in the Ruhr. Allied scientists studied the impact of malnutrition on infant and child health in Wuppertal, just east of Düsseldorf, during 1946. With the aid of birth records for 22,000 infants from the local hospital, the scientists found that the average birth weight of newborns in the hospital when

---

[16] Great Britain Foreign Office, 'Weekly Political Intelligence Summaries' no. 387. For a more detailed analysis of food protests in western Germany in response to food shortages see G. Trittel, 'Hungerkrise und kollektiver Protest in Westdeutschland 1945–1949', in *Der Kampf um das tägliche Brot: Nahrungsmangel, Versorgungspolitik und Protest 1770–1990*, ed. M. Gailus and H. Volkmann (Opladen: Westdeutscher Verlag, 1994), 377–91.

[17] Subjective factors also contributed greatly to tensions between the Germans and the British. Many Germans expected that they would be well fed by the British, especially in comparison to their countrymen in the Soviet zone. For changing German attitudes towards the British regarding food see B. Marshall, 'German Attitudes to British Military Government 1945–47', *Journal of Contemporary History* 15, no. 4 (1980): 660–2.

Table 7.5[a] *Birth–death cycle in the British zone, 1947*

Period	Number of births per 1,000 inhabitants	Number of deaths per 1,000 inhabitants
January	30.4	14.9
February	27.8	17.4
March	30.2	13.7

[a] UN, 'Monthly Bulletin of Statistics', vol. II (New York: July 1948), 16. February also saw the lowest conception rates for the year, further suggesting that it was the harshest month of the winter (the lowest birth rate for 1947 was recorded in November [14.3], nine months later).

Table 7.6[a] *Infant mortality rates in the British zone, 1946–7*

Period	Number of deaths per 1,000 infants
1946 – 4th quarter	105.0
1947 – 1st quarter	102.0
1947 – 2nd quarter	77.0

[a] Office of Military Government for Germany, US, 'Report of the Military Governor: Statistical Annex', 71.

food availability was high in 1937 was 185 grams heavier than in 1945. It is probable that this disparity was worse in the first half of 1947.[18]

High mortality rates and, indeed, even the coal–food cycle which induced an over-reliance on food imports need not have been so severe. That it was largely the failure to replace corrupt managers and their inefficient practices which caused this over-reliance becomes most apparent when comparison is made with the Soviet case. One could contrast the heavy-handed collection tactics of the Soviets, such as arresting recalcitrant farmers and, in extreme cases, executing them, to the less severe punishments meted out by the British to demonstrate this argument. But this would miss the point. The intelligence of the Soviet system lay not in its punishment of farmers for failing to meet delivery quotas, but in how it discouraged farmers and managers from underestimating the amount they were capable of delivering. A more valuable comparison between Soviet and British collection networks thus concerns how quotas were set.

[18] The Findings are summarised in J. C. Mathers and E. M. Widdowson, eds., *The Contribution of Nutrition to Human and Animal Health* (Cambridge and New York: Cambridge University Press 1992), 297.

In contrast to the British zone, agricultural managers in the Soviet zone were not 'mere instruments of self-supply for their own community'. By setting high grain and other quotas on farmers, they became the opposite – rural instruments of supply for the urban community which could not feed itself. To prepare for the 1945 harvest, SVAG officers established numerous special commissions in rural areas to inspect farmland and work with local German authorities, mostly local KPD or SPD party members and experienced farmers, to determine yield capacity and set production quotas. Despite staff shortages, the Soviets managed to set quotas for most large farmers in the Soviet zone.[19] In most cases where KPD/SED members were involved, according to Soviet tradition, quotas were set beyond realistic levels. They were undoubtedly eager to please their Soviet bosses. Such an arrangement was only possible because, unlike the British, the Soviets had overhauled the agricultural as well as the political system where they pushed party members into positions of local authority who understood their role as providing agricultural goods to feed urban centres, rather then hoarding goods for the sake of the locals.

The best example of unrealistic yet 'effective' quota setting comes from Brandenburg in 1946, where the Soviet-friendly mayor promised SVAG a bumper harvest figure for his region and, much like his comrades across the zone, did so without taking into account the lack of horse and machine power which made the target incredibly difficult to attain.[20] Nonetheless, the farmers' failure to do so attracted fines and, in some cases, imprisonment. On the one hand, setting unrealistic quotas was most problematic as it created a minefield of legal red tape and handfuls of jailed farmers, which stunted collections. But on the other, by setting the higher quotas to which most farmers necessarily aspired, the Soviets ensured that even the lower level of product that was delivered was more commensurate with actual yield capacity.[21] Farquharson's critique of the British system's focus on collections, 'that whatever percentage was surrendered, it was of a demand that was abnormally low in the first place', cannot be levelled at the Soviet.[22]

The weight of punishments in the Soviet system also fell more heavily on offences dealing with establishing yield capacity and setting quotas rather than collections. It was inevitable that some farmers and local officials would conspire to set lower quotas. In the haste to reconstruct

---

[19] For a good example of preparations made for quota setting and harvest collection see a SVAG officer's report on the Annberg region of Saxony at the beginning of August 1945, Zakharov, ed., *Deiatel' nost' sovetskikh voennykh komendatur*, 270–4.

[20] GARF – f. r-7077, op. 1, d. 199, ll. 16–21.

[21] Zakharov, ed., *Deiatel' nost' sovetskikh voennykh komendatur*, 273.

[22] Farquharson, *The Western Allies and the Politics of Food*, 63.

local political and agricultural systems, sometimes officials were appointed by SVAG or local German administrations with little, if any, investigation into the 'trustworthiness' of their characters. Those who engaged in localism were rooted out gradually with sporadic purging. They could only engage in localism because commissions could not inspect all farmland during the 1945 harvest season and thus depended on many farmers and officials to do the work for them. This placed the Soviets in a similar position to the British, who relied on local agricultural mangers to do so. The Soviets, however, conducted systematic inspections of the farmland once manpower became available and found that some farmers, expectedly, were underestimating their yield capacity and underreporting their livestock numbers, while local officials were happy to accept these blatantly false reports and set much lower product quotas than those expected.[23]

Farmers and officials found guilty of these offences were usually imprisoned or fined heavily, but some were punished severely as a warning to others. A Mecklenburg farmer was sentenced to death by the military tribunal of the 2nd Shock Army for incorrectly reporting the size of his farm to local authorities in August 1945.[24] He failed to declare an extra 23 hectares of arable farmland attached to his property and another 4 hectares at the second registration as well, which reduced considerably the amount of grain that the Soviets could demand of him.[25] His sentence was to be made known to the other farmers in the area to make it clear that such misreporting would not be tolerated, especially by large landowners and repeat offenders on the cusp of the land reform programme, which expropriated large farming estates and afforded their smaller plots to poor 'new farmers' free of charge.[26]

[23] See the detailed report on the results of these inspections in Mecklenburg sent to the deputy head of the state, M. A. Skosyrev, in January 1946. Most of the offending farmers were fined. Zakharov, ed., *Deiatel' nost' sovetskikh voennykh komendatur*, 287–91.

[24] The military tribunal also sequestered his farm and property, which was a more common punishment meted out to repeat offenders. GARF – f. r-7103, op. 1, d. 5, l. 275.

[25] The Soviets and the Germans operated from different agricultural traditions and used different measurement systems and terminologies. Confusion over measures and definitions of what constituted arable land were thus to be expected. In some cases where these misunderstandings prevailed, German farmers may have been unduly punished. But in general, such cases were avoided because the Soviets worked together with local German officials and farmers to inspect farmland and establish quotas. In the above case, it seems that confusion was not the problem.

[26] Agricultural producers identified as Junkers, Nazis, and war profiteers were expelled from their land by the Soviets, who broke up large agricultural estates over 100 hectares and divided them up among new farmers as part of their land reform programme. New farmers, mostly German refugees from Eastern Europe without the agricultural experience of those expelled, struggled to harvest crops on their small parcels of land, which

Having failed to establish an effective policing system in the country-side, the British were unable to punish most misreporting farmers and officials, apart from levying fines that were often left unpaid. British government commissions set up to investigate illegal livestock holdings in 1946 conceded as much, stating that it was impossible to enforce punishments when most local officials were related to the farmers they were supposed to punish.[27] And if by some miracle officials had sought to punish their cousins, most farmers would have been imprisoned and the land left without anyone to work it. The Soviets avoided this problematic cycle by allowing the military to try farmers for such misreporting. Military tribunals attached to each army strewn across the zone were thus able to investigate and try farmers for misreporting on a scale more commensurate with the actual number of offences committed. In this sense, it is not that the British were unwilling to be as brutal as the Soviets in dealing with misreporting farmers. If anything, the Soviets exercised much more restraint in punishing German farmers for misre-porting than they ever did with their own.[28] The essential problem is that the British had allowed a system to develop in which misreporting was the dominant feature, so much so that it was impossible to extricate it without abandoning the entire system itself – something they were unwilling to do. This meant that more food stayed in the regional areas, hoarded, sold on the black market, or used as fodder, while the urban centres were left malnourished.

The failure to overhaul the agricultural system in the British zone thus restricted the British from performing one of their primary occupation duties, exploiting the country's resources sufficiently to feed the people under their control. As discussed earlier, this failure gave rise to cycles of economic downturn and civil unrest which climaxed by the time the British zone joined the American to form Bizonia at the beginning of 1947. If not for this union, and the millions of tonnes of American food delivered to British areas (neither of which was a certainty in 1946) the situation certainly would have been much direr than it was.

were simply not as productive as the large estates of which they were originally part. This was most problematic in Mecklenburg and Western Pomerania, where over 60 per cent of farmland in the region was farmed in estates larger than 1,000 hectares. Even though the Soviets allowed some of the more productive estates to remain intact, the implementation of this land reform programme decreased the short-term agricultural output of the entire agricultural sector. Norman Naimark discusses the land reform programme at length, Naimark, *The Russians in Germany*, 142–62.

[27] Farquharson, *The Western Allies and the Politics of Food*, 67.

[28] For a social history of state–peasant relations in the Soviet Union see M. Lewin, *Russian Peasants and Soviet Power: A Study of Collectivization* (London: Allen & Unwin, 1968). For a more recent work see S. Fitzpatrick, *Stalin's Peasants: Resistance and Survival in the Russian Village after Collectivization* (New York: Oxford University Press, 1994).

The system established by the Soviets proved much more resilient to the food crises which confronted it, and well it should have, given that the Soviets had been battling the localism which plagued the British system since the October Revolution in 1917. As we have seen, however, Germany presented new opportunities to eliminate localism without the bloodshed which accompanied it back home. Historians have long focused on the Soviet reconstruction of the entire agricultural system, particularly the introduction of land reform policies in September 1945 and the general reduction in agricultural production which this entailed. But less attention has been paid to how the Soviets drew on their close ties with local regional officials to ensure food supplies to urban areas in Germany and even to the Soviet Union in times of crisis. This was the real strength of the Soviet position in Germany and is most evident in the Soviet response to the food crises approaching in the winter of 1945–6 in Saxony.

Mass starvation was averted in the state's capital, Dresden, but only marginally in its surrounding areas which occupied the lesser rungs on the tiered entitlement system. Donna Harsch argues that shortages emerged when Red Army units stopped protecting food supplies in Dresden, though there is little discussion of this problem in the Soviet sources.[29] Instead, the sources highlight the military's over-consumption as the major cause of continuing food shortage in the wake of the August 1945 decision to feed troops exclusively from the German harvest. SVAG, which had worked so hard with farmers to reconstruct the agricultural system in any such way that would promote the greatest production of foodstuffs, now saw that the military was reaping the fruits of its labour, not to mention creating havoc in the quota system. By the end of August, SVAG officers in Dresden even warned that at the current levels of consumption there would simply not be enough food to feed the military forces situated there as well as the occupied population. Even high-ranking officers such as the deputy head of SVAG in Land Saxony, Lieutenant General D. G. Dubrovskii, pleaded with the military to reduce its consumption levels until the next harvest season when food supplies would be replenished – but to little avail:

If the 8th Guards Army continues its requisitioning in Saxony, it will soon be necessary to begin importing the same amount of foodstuffs from Thuringia and Province Saxony ... An official was sent especially to [the army] to warn against the inefficient use of food resources, only to be rejected by the army's procurements office.[30]

[29] Harsch, *Revenge of the Domestic*, 26.   [30] GARF – f. r-7212, op. 1, d. 13, l. 147.

Much like the British in March 1946, SVAG was thrown into disarray by
the shortage of food imports. It had no choice but to try and make good on
its threat. There was simply not enough food in Dresden for both military
and civilian consumption, even though SVAG had removed millions
of repatriates by the end of September and hundreds of thousands
of soldiers had been demobilised. This significantly reduced SVAG
expenditure and the level of military consumption respectively, but not
by enough. Unlike the British, however, SVAG did not rely on food
imports from other countries, but only from other regional areas of the
zone, to supplement food shortages. By December, SVAG had begun to
organise the supply of grain and other foodstuffs to Dresden in line with
maintaining ration levels indicated earlier in Table 7.2 and had made
allowances for population growth in the city since August.[31]

These measures eventually reduced the incidence of hunger-related
diseases in Dresden, but not in nearby Chemnitz. This city of 200,000
inhabitants occupied a lower tier on the entitlement hierarchy, giving it a
lower nominal, and indeed real, ration level than Dresden. In fact, less
populated cities located lower on the tiered system like Chemnitz were
often in the worst position, reliant on poor rations but unable to draw on
extensive regional resources to supplement them. Reports of malnourish-
ment in Chemnitz were prominent in August, with one hospital complaining that its admissions had doubled in recent days to 360 patients, most of
them children. According to Soviet estimates, 600 of the city's approximately 200,000 inhabitants were dying every month due to malnourish-
ment, with lowly populated areas of the city worst affected. There seems to
have been some improvement by the end of autumn, with hospital admission numbers beginning to recede.[32] Levels of hunger-related disease in
the regional areas in Saxony-Anhalt (Province Saxony) and Thuringia
'bled' white to feed Dresden are more difficult to gauge.

It is easier to gauge the impact of over-requisitioning on the health of
regional populations in those food-producing areas which bordered
Polish or Czech territories, such as Mecklenburg and Saxony. These
areas absorbed the brunt of the massive influx of ethnic German refugees,
who had long been subject to hunger and disease during their arduous
treks from Eastern Europe, and were now exacerbating the former and
spreading the latter among the German 'natives'.

---

[31] Zakharov, ed., *Deiatel'nost' sovetskikh voennykh komendatur*, 325–6.
[32] GARF – f. r-7212, op. 1, d. 13, ll. 40–3. Hospital numbers need to be treated carefully.
Naimark notes that, given the poor sanitary conditions in many hospitals and the rampaging presence of typhus, people were often reluctant to visit hospitals for treatment.
Naimark, *The Russians in Germany*, 123.

Table 7.7[a] *Monthly infections recorded in Mecklenburg, 1945–6*

	December	January	% increase[b]
Typhus	199	609	300%
Typhoid	4796	5718	19.4%
Diphtheria	2048	2232	10%

[a] Zakharov, ed., *Deiatel'nost' sovetskikh voennykh komendatur*, 355.
[b] Percentages are as given in the source.

Soviet authorities traced the jump in typhus infections during January to an outbreak in a refugee echelon from Poland, which was not detained in a transit camp upon its arrival (as it should have been), but allowed to settle in a local village in the eastern Mecklenburg district. After two months the typhus had spread to eighteen nearby villages. But the 'proper practice' of detaining refugees in transit camps proved little better in limiting the spread of disease. Camps were breeding grounds for all sorts of diseases, as they were often overcrowded, unsanitary, and poorly supplied with food and medical care. With treatment lacking and the camp populations unsustainable and slowly starving, Soviet officers had little choice but to release refugees into the population, particularly when another 142,854 entered Mecklenburg from 1 November to 20 December 1945. Officers compounded this problem, however, by failing to check if areas further west to which they were directing the refugees (often by rail) were willing to accept them. In some cases overcrowded areas experiencing food shortage received refugee trains while those in need of refugee labour did not, which further strained rationing systems and essential services exactly in those areas where they were weakest.[33] This is to say nothing of the millions of repatriates who poured over the Soviet zone's western border requiring food and housing, and medical assistance for a range of health conditions.

SVAG got much better at dealing with food and health crises as occupation continued, markedly so with its food supply preparations over the winter of 1945–6. Now SVAG began to develop long-term and intelligent zone-wide food supply strategies, focusing on the establishment of food reserves and improving food transport and storage facilities.[34] But these strategies only stood a chance of success because SVAG had established

[33] Ibid., 202.
[34] Serov had instructed leading SVAG officers to take these measures in August 1945, as part of his speech quoted at the beginning of this chapter. Petrov, *Pervyi predsedatel' KGB Ivan Serov*, 235.

an agricultural and political system staffed by a network of officials who could enforce the high quotas on rural food producers to feed starving cities with the might of the Soviet occupation machine behind them.

Political considerations were as important as population numbers and certainly health concerns in determining where a city, starving or not, would be placed on the tiered system. And even then cities could be afforded greater priority without official reference to the system. Dresden, for instance, was a 'red city' where working-class support of Soviet-sponsored political parties was supposed to be strongest. SVAG was thus most concerned with ensuring supplies of food to the city, even at the expense of Saxon and Thuringian farmers. Such preferential treatment exacerbated existing urban–rural tensions and hardened pro- and anti-Soviet positions among the population. However, protests which emerged in response to food shortages in the Soviet zone never turned violent or contributed to severe economic downturns as in the British zone. The more repressive atmosphere in the Soviet zone and the greater fear felt by the population towards the Soviet occupier help to explain this discrepancy. But fear was only part of the equation. The politics of rationing spurred the development of complex relations between occupiers and occupied, where both learned how to live with each other more peaceably around the metaphorical dinner table.

8   The politics of food and peaceful protest

The Soviets were always very concerned with the 'political mood' of their people and of any other which they came to rule. They established extensive networks of German informants and mail censorship operations to uncover anti-Soviet elements in society, but also to adjust policies in line with popular expectations. For all of the terror and chaos that marked the occupation, the Soviets developed forms of predominantly civil governance to establish control over and reconstruct the zone. The establishment of a rationing system under the most difficult circumstances was one of the first and undoubtedly the most important of these forms. But the social and political dimensions of rationing were far broader than merely its function of feeding the Germans. Even being fed by the 'Russian beast' was far beyond the expectations of most Germans at the end of the war. Goebbels had promised them that, in the event of a Soviet victory, they could only expect physical annihilation or mass rape and the Siberian gulags. Many did expect one or another of these fates, but the Soviets obliged only half-heartedly. There were no mass deportations from Germany proper or any mass murder of civilians.

The spectre of mass rape and the general warlike conditions which endured into post-war Germany, however, gave some credence to Goebbels' self-fulfilling prophecy. So Berliners responded with awe to the announcement of ration levels in Berlin on 13 May 1945. Some approached Soviet officers for the first time, tentatively, and commented on the unique humanitarianism of the 'Russian'. With the help of bad translators who scurried from one conversation to another, Berliners thanked these officers 'who now gave food to a beaten people whose army caused so much unhappiness in Russia'.[1]

Notwithstanding the Soviets' humanitarian tendencies in feeding their erstwhile enemies, they were well aware that 'probably no other

---

[1] Lieutenant General F. E. Bokov provided a number of these quotations in his report to Lieutenant General K. F. Telegin, a member of the Military Council on the First Belorussian Front, on 15 May 1945. RGASPI – f. 17, op. 125, d. 321, ll. 20–2.

operation . . . is so effective in proving to an anxious and disturbed people that the powers that be are good and have their welfare at heart'.[2] Such was the anthropologist Margaret Mead's advice to American policy makers in planning the post-war occupation of Germany in 1943. To be sure, the Soviets had their own long history of rationing and understood its importance better as an important social control measure. So much so that they diverted foodstuffs from the Red Army's stocks to fund the rationing system in Berlin.[3]

The problem was that the Soviet soldiers found it much more difficult to 'prove that they were good' than the Americans, with their bountiful chocolates and cigarettes. This initial euphoria in Berlin would turn to disappointment and anger when real ration levels did not meet those promised on the ration cards. The Wehrmacht's pillaging of the Soviet Union had helped afford Germans relatively rich wartime diets, which fed such unrealistic post-war expectations. Notwithstanding SVAG's Herculean efforts to provide higher rations in the Soviet zone than in the British or French, most Germans remained dissatisfied. Had they been aware that their levels were quite similar to the average Soviet citizen's, it would have hardly tempered their outrage.[4] Most still felt that the Russians were subhumans undeserving of the same standard of living as 'civilised Europeans' like themselves.

Soviet officers who cited their euphoric meetings with thankful Germans in their reports also noted that elements of this obnoxious attitude were still present and threatened to undermine the goodwill established by the rationing system.[5] Perhaps the most prominent graffiti slogan in 1945 was 'Give us more food or we will not forget Adolf Hitler.'[6] While some locals voluntarily scrubbed these latent threats off city walls, others attempted to better their material situation by making Soviet officers feel guilty about their inability to improve the rationing situation. One officer reported that people often said to him that 'if the *komendant* had

---

[2] A. Grossman, 'Grams, Calories, and Food: Languages of Victimization, Entitlement, and Human Rights in Occupied Germany, 1945–1949', *Central European History* 44 (2011): 118–19.

[3] Zakharov, ed., *Deiatel' nost' sovetskikh voennykh komendatur*, 299.

[4] Elena Zubkova conducts a short, yet informative, comparative analysis of post-war ration levels in the Soviet Union and eastern Germany. E. Iu. Zubkova, 'Obshchestvo, vyshedshee iz voiny: Russkie i nemtsy v 1945 godu', *Otechestvennaia Istoriia* 3 (1995): 96–7.

[5] RGASPI – f. 17, op. 125, d. 321, ll. 20–2.

[6] The Hitler graffiti slogans are evident in many political and security reports dealing with food and material issues. For Mecklenburg complaints during August and September 1945 see GARF – f. r-7103, op. 1, d. 7, ll. 150, 246–7. For complaints in Saxony during early 1946 see *delo* 186 in GARF – f. r-7212, op. 1. Grossman also notes that such graffiti were widespread in the US zone, Grossman, 'Grams, Calories, and Food', 126.

given us more foodstuffs, then we would have seen that the Russians care about the German people'. This situation led another officer to conclude that the 'democratic temperament of the occupied population could be measured by the level of their food rations'.[7] There was a growing sense among some political officers that feeding the Germans 'insufficiently' would cause just as many problems as not feeding them at all.

The question then, is: how did the Soviets use food so effectively to control the population when they simply did not have enough to feed everyone in need? In short, they understood that you didn't need to address every criticism or, indeed, satisfy everyone's stomachs to establish control. You just had to feed the right people well and keep the rest breathing. As evident in the Berlin/Dresden ration table recorded in the previous chapter, the Soviet rationing system established a new form of social stratification as the scale by which people received differentiated pay and ration cards depended on their new employment. It also depended on their new social position. Those whom the Soviets deemed central to the reconstruction of the country, such as party members, police, and administrators received better pay and rations. On the other hand, those expendable or, indeed, harmful to the reconstruction – the unemployed or people with a tainted past, millions of them – could at best hope for lesser pay and an inferior ration card. German police in Dresden, who received category I-like rations, were often the butt of the harshest criticism from those below them on the ration hierarchy, as were KPD/SED members, who received more. Women quipped that 'it is clear that those who must maintain a starving population in a state of fear must be well fed'.[8] There was widespread antipathy towards the groups who had joined the Soviets in developing a new and 'democratic' German society and were benefiting as a result.[9]

---

[7] GARF – f. r-7077, op. 1, d. 199, l. 6. The deputy head of SVAB, Major General Sharov, claimed that talk of new ration levels occupied the central focus of many Germans in Brandenburg during late 1945. Many Germans, especially women, were ready to complain openly to Soviet officers on this issue. One woman echoed other complaints when she said to a Soviet officer 'You give us ration cards but not any food . . . even during the last days of the war we received sufficient food . . . They tell me that people eat much better than us in the western zones.' GARF – f. r-7077, op. 1, d. 179, ll. 66–7. Barbara Marshall notes that people living in the British zone levelled similar complaints against the British occupation government, particularly during the food crisis of 1946–7. Marshall, 'German Attitudes to British Military Government 1945–47', 660–2.

[8] GARF – f. r-7212, op. 1, d. 186, l. 8. Examples of these attitudes throughout Saxony are also found in GARF – f. r-7212, op. 1, d. 187, ll. 87, 121–4 and GARF – f. r-7212, op. 1, d. 186, ll. 8, 87.

[9] Pritchard discusses the tensions between 'anti-fascists' and other sections of the German population, often exacerbated by the higher rations received or taken by the former. G. Pritchard, 'Schwarzenberg 1945: Antifascists and the "Third Way" in German Politics', *European History Quarterly* 35 (2005): 513–14.

Whereas the atmosphere of fear established by troop violence and Soviet repression firmly cemented the simple occupier vs occupied division, this growing stratification of society was one of many features of daily life that complicated it.[10] In fact, what began as a simple and direct relationship between a Soviet food provider and a German recipient quickly evolved into a highly developed system of social relationships which both Germans and Soviets exploited for their own ends – none more so than SVAG officers and those stuck at the bottom of the ration hierarchy: women. As most German women living in urban areas did not work for wages in 1945, or only worked part time, many of them received III and V category ration cards (the III category included cleaners and washerwomen). Faced with the prospect of a low calorie diet, many housewives and mothers receiving the V category ration card complained openly that the system discriminated against them because it failed to recognise that their domestic duties constituted a form of heavy labour, especially in light of the breakdown of essential services in Germany after the war. Mothers were especially vocal in the criticism of category IV, which provided that all children up to the age of sixteen should receive the same amount of rations. One Brandenburg mother of three young teenagers complained they had become malnourished due to the meagre 'infant' rations they were receiving. To make matters worse, she was unable to find work and improve their situation given that she now had to take care of them.[11]

The Soviets didn't need their German informants to tell them how angry women were about rations – the women told Soviet officers themselves. Unlike the scars of the occupation such as rape, hunger was freely discussed with the occupiers, often heatedly. But there was no chance in 1945 or even for much of 1946 of changing the rationing system to meet their expectations. Quite simply, those who worked harder or closer to the regime ate more than those who did not.[12] Political officers reminded their superiors incessantly that perhaps they should listen to the women and get them 'on side' for the upcoming elections. As the largest voting block in the zone, they could prove invaluable to the SED's electoral

---

[10] Richard Bessel argues further that the KPD/SED fostered a political 'discourse of hatred' in order to legitimate their dominant political position. Bessel, 'Hatred after War'.

[11] GARF – f. r-7077, op. 1, d. 179, l. 67.

[12] For a broader critique of this 'production-orientated' rationing system see A. Bauerkämper, 'Nahrungsmittelangebot und Strukturumbruch – Probleme der produktionsorientierten Ernährungspolitik in der Sowjetischen Besatzungszone und der frühen DDR', in *Hunger, Ernährung und Rationierungssysteme unter dem Staatssozialismus (1917–2006)*, ed. M. Widdell and F. Wemheuer (Frankfurt am Main: Peter Lang, 2011).

success.[13] But the Soviets were not ready to make such concessions in the name of electoral politics until late 1946 and early 1947, and even then some were only made on paper.

Historians have argued that women's protests over food shortages during the bitterly cold winter of 1946–7 encouraged these 'official' concessions.[14] They may well have, but the Soviets' intransigence towards policy change until that time did not mean that they failed to address women's ration concerns. Despite their vehement complaints about low and unfair rations, most urban women appreciated the fact that they could not survive without the rations provided to them. The most pressing problem with the rationing system, then, was not that it was 'unfair', but that sometimes it failed to deliver. Complaints turned to protests when women failed to receive any rations from the local German administrations that SVAG had made immediately responsible for administering them. In these cases, the women often protested against their countrymen. The women's exclusively German targets and, indeed, their gender, encouraged the Soviets not to obstruct, but to meet their requests. This 'unofficial' practice not only deflected anger and responsibility away from SVAG, but also allowed women a 'safer' public space in which to influence the political process without troubling the regime. In fact, by appealing to the Soviets in such a manner the women were clearly recognising the power balance established in the zone.[15] These 'unofficial' relationships between occupiers and occupied were central to daily life in the zone and as important as the 'official' policy changes which have long been the focus of historians.

Protests began during the first days of the occupation and were concentrated in regional areas which were often 'bled' white to feed urban centres during food shortages. In Überkmünde (Mecklenburg) 200 women marched to the mayor's office in mid July 1945 and demanded

[13] An incomplete census taken in Dresden and its surrounding area in August 1945 affirms Mike Dennis' estimate of a female–male ratio of 125:100. M. Dennis, *The Rise and Fall of the German Democratic Republic, 1945–1990* (Harlow: Longman, 2000), 7. For the Dresden census see GARF – f. r-7212, op. 1, d. 13, ll. 80–1.

[14] Harsch, *Revenge of the Domestic*, 34.

[15] There are some parallels between food marches and spontaneous protests against 'Nazis'. In both cases the Soviets were reluctant to interfere with protestors. Extreme anti-Nazi protests, however, necessitated a SVAG response. For instance, the KPD leadership in Plauen complained to SVAG that its local members were out of control, arresting and interning suspected Nazis in a makeshift prison set up in a hotel. Upon being notified of this development, the local Soviet *komendant* intervened and arranged for the release of the prisoners. G. Pritchard, *The Making of the GDR, 1945–53: From Antifascism to Stalinism* (Manchester: Manchester University Press, 2000), 85. Such examples encouraged SVAG to exert greater control over 'political activism' in eastern Germany. Mecklenburg was particularly troublesome in late 1945. See GARF – f. r-7103, op. 1, d. 7, l. 133 and GARF – f. r-7103, op. 1, d. 27, ll. 319–20.

the bread ration that they had not received for weeks. In response, the Soviets arrested the mayor for misappropriating flour stocks and then eventually provided the women with the bread.[16] In March 1946, ten mothers with large families of small children in the town of Techentin (Mecklenburg) demonstrated against the local mayor with complaints that they had not received bread or potatoes for some time.[17] Two months later, forty women marched to the office of their regional president in a regional area of Saxony and demanded their ration entitlement of butter, which had not been delivered for weeks. Again, according to the Soviet investigation launched in response to the protest,

[t]he incompetence of a local German supply administrator was responsible for this problem. Provisions were quickly made to supply the women and over 200 of them eventually marched to the *komendatura* to pick up their butter.[18]

Food shortages may not have been primarily the fault of the German administrators in these cases, but this was not a sufficient defence for the officials in their attempt to keep their jobs.

The Soviets were masters at this type of 'scapegoating' behaviour which was only possible because most German administrators were expendable, particularly those without a clear allegiance to the socialist parties.[19] More importantly, the protesting women understood that they would not be punished for their actions. Soviet reports discussing the protests do not suggest any punitive measures against the women. Report writers often expressed sympathy with their plight and the actions of local SVAG officials who met their requests, redoubling the protestors' criticisms towards the German officials.

Naimark argues, however, that SVAG officers became concerned about the prospect of protests developing into a mass movement in times of severe food shortage and asked NKVD officers to focus special attention on protest organisers during 1946. This was easier said than done, as the

---

[16] GARF – f. r-7103, op. 1, d. 22, l. 208.

[17] According to the Soviet investigation, the inefficient local administration had failed to provide the women with these foods for almost two weeks. GARF – f. r-7103, op. 1, d. 20, ll. 220–1.

[18] GARF – f. r-7212, op. 1, d. 188, l. 23.

[19] During the collectivisation drives and the Great Purges of the 1930s, for instance, central Soviet authorities ordered local organs to implement unpopular policies, be it grain requisitioning or mass arrests. When local authorities encountered significant resistance to these policies, central Soviet authorities sometimes reacted by blaming local officials for exceeding their authority and prosecuted the officials in an attempt to evade responsibility for ordering them to implement the policies in the first place. Sheila Fitzpatrick's analysis of the regional show trials of local Soviet officials during 1937 demonstrates this process well. S. Fitzpatrick, 'How the Mice Buried the Cat: Scenes from the Great Purges of 1937 in the Russian Provinces', *Russian Review* 52, no. 3 (1993).

NKVD was reluctant to deal with hungry mothers. For instance, the chief of the NKVD Operational Sector in Mecklenburg, Lieutenant General D. M. Nikitin, wrote to the deputy head of the state Skosyrev on 8 March 1946 in response to the Techentin protest. Nikitin revealed that the marching women were correct in their criticism of the local official and did not suggest that any measures should be taken against them. Apart from noting that one of the protesters, possibly a protest organiser, was married to a former Nazi party member, of whom there were millions in the zone, there was nothing to report.[20]

Complex relationships of mutual dependence between SVAG and German women thus began to develop as soon as SVAG was established in June 1945. These 'unofficial' relationships are clearly examples of both parties 'minimising risk' in the countryside. This wasn't the first time that the Soviets had been involved in this practice. There are striking parallels between the ways in which they responded to women's protests in Germany and to similar forms of women's peasant resistance in the Soviet Union. Russian peasant women resisted 'dekulakisation' and collectivisation policies during the 1930s by conducting protest marches against local authorities. In some cases, these marches turned into violent pogroms in which the women would beat up local Soviet officials and retake the grain, livestock, and even their husbands who had been taken from them.

Soviet women protested in the knowledge that they would not usually be punished for their behaviour, as did German women protesting in the Soviet zone years later. In fact, in both cases the Soviet authorities usually acquiesced in the women's demands, at least in the short term. This encourages us to ask why the authorities generally failed to take legal measures against women, when there was no question of not taking measures against men who offered similar resistance.

With regard to the Soviet Union, Lynne Viola argues that authorities understood the protests and women's resistance to collectivisation within a particular cultural discourse, which enabled them to depoliticise the resistance and thus reduce its insurrectionary quality.[21] The authorities reasoned that there was little need to react to the protests, as the women's resistance was merely a reflection of their gender limitations, political

---

[20] According to Naimark, the spontaneous nature of the protests, however, 'stymied ... attempts to deal with the organizers'. Naimark, *The Russians in Germany*, 385. Other factors besides spontaneity may also have been at play. The extent to which the NKVD/ MGB's mild approach towards protesting women seen throughout 1945–6 continued into 1947 and accounted for the 'failures' to stop the protests requires further research.

[21] L. Viola, *Peasant Rebels under Stalin: Collectivization and the Culture of Peasant Resistance* (New York: Oxford University Press, 1996), 181.

backwardness, and low cultural level. They were too stupid to understand that they were protecting the archaic structures of peasant life such as the church, which constituted the main source of their oppression. It was even more difficult for them to understand that the male 'kulak' agitators who were encouraging them to resist collectivisation were merely exploiting their simple nature for counter-revolutionary ends. They were classless actors without agency, thus incapable of political protest, which can emerge only from class membership.

To be sure, the Soviet secret police[22] was well aware that not all of the protesting women were so simple-minded. In fact, police reports accurately trace how many village women clearly understood that their protests, as wild and violent as they were, could not exceed recognised limits. The main limit was gender. Women discouraged their menfolk from participating in the protests, as this would have given the authorities cause to break them up. When the men did take part in these protests, 'the business ended in murder'.[23] When gender limits were observed, local authorities drew on this official discourse and refused to break up these protests or prosecute the women involved. 'Looking the other way' was a most politically expedient tactic for the Soviets because it minimised 'the nature and extent of the opposition engendered by collectivisation'.[24]

The Soviets also refused to clamp down on food protests in Germany, yet the situation there encouraged more advanced responses. The crux of the matter was that many Soviet officers did not view German women as simple-minded and classless *baby* (peasant women). They were the beneficiaries of their husbands' rampages across Europe and thus archetypal bourgeois whores. Their protests, therefore, were always political in nature, no matter what the grievance. Norman Naimark describes one caricature in the Soviet magazine *Krokodil*, in which a

plump bourgeois Hausfrau is confronted by a strong, lean Russian woman who had worked for her as forced labour. 'Now you'll see, Frau', she says sternly, 'I've come to collect.'[25]

These images were most important in influencing Soviet attitudes towards German women. Similarly important were the testimonies of liberated slave labourers, such as young Russian girls who had worked as domestic servants in Germany. They recounted to their Red Army liberators during the advance how twenty or thirty of them would regularly

---

[22] The main Soviet secret police organ until 1934 was the Joint State Political Administration (OGPU).
[23] Viola, *Peasant Rebels under Stalin*, 204.   [24] Ibid., 203.
[25] Naimark, *The Russians in Germany*, 108.

be lined in front of a 'plump German *Hausfrau*' in search of a domestic servant. While inspecting them, she would poke and prod each girl with a stick as one would do to cattle in search of the healthiest candidate.[26] The widespread dissemination of such stories throughout the ranks by word of mouth and newspapers was certainly one of many important factors which fuelled sexual violence during the Soviet advance. Since German 'bourgeois' women possessed a clear class membership, it was impossible to 'depoliticise' their protests as in the Soviet Union. Instead, the Soviets decided to try and manipulate the women's opposition to their advantage rather than simply nullify it.

The impetus to begin manipulating opposition over food shortages was the lacklustre performance of the SED at the September 1946 local elections. SVAG did its best to boost support for the party beforehand, announcing ration increases in the event of a SED victory and in August its 'equal pay for equal work' policy to entice women voters. These 'official policies' helped the party to secure a slight majority, and some historians have focused on them in their studies of food politics in the zone.[27] But the major provincial elections set for the following month promised to be more difficult and required 'unofficial' policies to really boost party support. Now the head of the SVAG Propaganda Administration, Colonel S. I. Tiul′panov, planned to announce reductions in the supply of raw materials to those areas governed by non-SED officials.[28] Hopefully, this would encourage voter anger towards those officials (and perhaps even protests). At the same time, the administration would announce increases to the supply of raw materials to adjacent areas under the control of SED officials to encourage recalcitrant voters to rethink their anti-SED electoral disposition at the October elections.[29]

---

[26] This information is gleaned from a most useful report citing interviews with liberated slave labourers and describes the initial contact between the Red Army and German civilians who remained in East Prussia. RGASPI – f. 17, op. 125, d. 318, ll. 18–25.

[27] Harsch, *Revenge of the Domestic*, 34–6.

[28] Naimark notes that from its establishment in October 1946 by Sovnarkom order, the Propaganda Administration began to assume most of the responsibilities for political/propaganda work in the zone. In fact, the administration assumed many of the functions that were officially set for more superior organs such as the SVAG/GSOVG Military Council and, by extension, the political administration. By spring 1946, the Propaganda Administration 'practically formulated policy in the Soviet zone', particularly in relation to German political parties, civil administrations, education, and denazification. Tiul′panov's connections in Moscow (Zhdanov) were central to allowing the Propaganda Administration to exercise such policy-making power. However, it was unable to exert control over dismantling organs or significant pressure on GSOVG officers to curb the level of troop violence until the Soviet leadership itself shifted away from dismantling and began to express more concern over the consequences of troop violence for the long-term Soviet position in the zone. Neimark [Naimark], 'Sergei Tiul′panov', 14.

[29] Bonvech [Bonwetsch], Bordiugov, and Neimark [Naimark], eds., *Sovetskaia voennaia administratsiia v Germanii*, 223.

Some evidence suggests that the policy was effective in increasing support for the SED in the month between the two elections, particularly when the administration promised increases in food supply as well as raw materials as Naimark notes in his discussion of the policy.[30] Support for the SED in the Eberswalde region in Brandenburg was probably based less on faith in the party than on the SED's pre-election promise to increase rations for dependants and the belief that all inhabitants of those districts which elected SED candidates would receive better ration cards. The good work of the Political Department in Brandenburg was largely responsible for the widespread nature of this belief in the city. The department instituted a wide-ranging propaganda campaign from mid 1946, which aimed to discredit non-SED candidates by accusing them of being former Nazis, price speculators, and, most importantly, supply saboteurs. The head of the department, Colonel F. G. Filinov, was unabashed in his evaluation of the propaganda campaign's contribution to the SED's September electoral victory in Brandenburg (gaining a 64 per cent majority in Eberswalde and a 60 per cent majority across Brandenburg):

There have been cases where ... entire [party] organisations have left Cottbus and Eberswalde and leading candidates have left the LDP and CDU. The uncovering of CDU supporters as supply saboteurs has attracted great attention from the Potsdam population.[31]

Filinov and his subordinates had already begun to define the Liberal Democratic Party (LDP) and Christian Democratic Union (CDU) as corrupt parties before the September elections, a vote for which would only result in further material deprivation for the good people of Brandenburg. Now only a short time before the October elections, they began to define the SED as the opposite – the party capable of directly increasing material supplies of raw materials and even foodstuffs. Tiul'panov's policy thus completed a dichotomy of material deprivation–abundance that should have greatly assisted the SED at the October elections in Brandenburg and wherever else similar campaigns were launched.

Determining the extent of this assistance, however, is most difficult. For all the reports that indicate the success of the policy, a range of other reports suggests its failure. After all, much of the occupied population considered the SED complicit in the policies and behaviour of the occupier, and many voted against one in protest to the other, especially

[30] Naimark, *The Russians in Germany*, 333–4.
[31] Petrov, ed., *SVAG i nemetskie organy samoupravleniia*, 189.

women. A woman from the Cottbus region in Brandenburg articulated their rationale:

Many say that we women did not vote for the SED. I tell you that this is correct. For us women, politics is not the goal, but the means by which goals can be attained. We women today have still not forgotten how they raped us and what kind of shame we suffered in the recent past. Apart from this, now all burdens fall on the shoulders of women. The farmers supply sufficient bread to be eaten by the workers so that they do not starve. But the bread leaves the farmers and does not reach the workers. They take it to Russia! That is why so few women voted for the SED.[32]

This quotation reminds us of the backdrop of mass antipathy against which political officers who sought to boost support for the SED were forced to operate. Even the most intelligent among them, such as Tiul'panov, capable of traversing the webs of the Soviet bureaucracy to implement 'pro-German' policies, could do little to erase the memory of rape or force the leadership to put an end to the troop violence problem before the elections. Similarly devastating to Tiul'panov's aims was the leadership's failure to discontinue the dismantling programme before the elections. Despite the fact that Tiul'panov had secured an agreement from SVAG for a temporary halt to the programme in the lead up to the elections, dismantling continued.[33]

All of these factors may certainly have accounted for the 'poorer' showing at the October elections, with the SED claiming only 48.89 per cent of the total vote and only 44.75 per cent in Brandenburg.[34] Yet these figures are much more impressive than they seem. The Soviets found it much more difficult to 'rig' these elections. At those held in the previous month, they refused to register a large number of opposition parties in many electoral districts. Only SED candidates were allowed to run in these areas, meaning voters could only choose between them. In Brandenburg alone, opposition parties were unable to nominate candidates in 33 per cent of all electoral districts – a fact that Colonel Filinov left out in his assessment of his contribution to the SED's September electoral victory.[35] Tiul'panov lamented that it was impossible to do the same at the October elections. As a result, he expected that the SED would find it

---

[32] GARF – f. r-7077, op. 1, d. 199, l. 5.   [33] See Chapter 10.

[34] Petrov, ed., *SVAG i nemetskie organy samoupravleniia*, 211.

[35] The Soviets still harassed and intimidated CDU and LDP candidates and members to inhibit or dissuade them from taking part in the October elections. Unable to restrict them from contesting the elections in all districts, however, Tiul'panov expected the SED to gain only 40 per cent of the vote. It was up to the Propaganda Administration to work out how to gain the other 10 per cent. Bonvech [Bonwetsch], Bordiugov, and Neimark [Naimark], eds., *Sovetskaia voennaia administratsiia v Germanii*, 221–2.

difficult to gain a majority of the vote. Taking this into account, the reduced figures of 48.89 per cent across the zone and 44.75 per cent in Brandenburg are most impressive.[36] They suggest that manipulating food supplies and raw materials, or at least promising to do so, was one of a few important policies aimed at highlighting the positive aspects of the Soviet–SED relationship that increased the party's electability.

However, the popularity of the party soon diminished after the elections as SVAG struggled to deliver its promise of higher rations to its supporters. Even worse for the party, SVAG too reneged on its policy to increase rations for most cardholders announced in July 1946 – a policy which SVAG admitted publicly was a response to intense SED petitioning. But the SED and even SVAG were hardly to blame for their failures. The prospect of severe famine appeared in the drought-ravaged western parts of the Soviet Union in mid 1946.[37] To prepare for the famine, the Soviet leadership decided to clear the zone's 'surplus' grain reserves in November to export them to the Soviet Union. Moscow was advised that clearing the surpluses would not reduce rations for Germans, but only stunt any increases for the rest of 1946.[38] SVAG's promise to German voters in July was thus unrealisable.

For those members of the occupation government who were never content with the 'coddling' of the German electorate, particularly Serov, the threat of famine provided ample opportunity to deal with the 'soft men' in SVAG. After hearing of plans to clear the surpluses in Germany, Serov wrote to Beria criticising Zhukov's successor, Marshal Sokolovskii, for acceding to the SED's request for increasing ration levels in July. Serov considered the SED's request improper as it sought 'to win the authority of the people by pursuing measures at the expense of SVAG, rather than by virtue of its own work'. This was most disingenuous, as Serov had spent a great deal of time arresting and harassing the SED's political opponents. But he had his way. Beria forwarded Serov's report to

---

[36] Petrov, ed., *SVAG i nemetskie organy samoupravleniia*, 211.

[37] In Moscow, B. A. Dvinskii, the minister for agricultural supply, wrote to A. I. Mikoyan, the minister for foreign trade, that food surpluses in Germany should be exported to the Soviet Union to deal with the drought and eventual food crisis as early as July 1946. Mikoyan delayed, forcing Dvinskii to write directly to Stalin, twice in September, with the same suggestion. In October, Stalin established a commission to investigate the possibility of clearing surpluses in Germany and other occupied areas. For Dvinskii's reports to Mikoyan see GARF – f. r-5446, op. 49. d. 1614. ll. 54–7. For Dvinskii's reports to Stalin see O. Khlevniuk, ed., *Politbiuro Tsk VKP(b) i Sovet Ministrov SSSR 1945–1953* (Moscow: Rosspen, 2002), 221–2.

[38] Serov's advice to Beria was based on the discussions with the deputy head of the SVAG Department of Trade, Colonel Shumilov. Petrov, *Pervyi predsedatel' KGB Ivan Serov*, 254–5.

Stalin on 20 October 1946 and made a point of highlighting those SVAG officers (Sokolovskii and Bokov) who supported the SED request. Holidaying in Sochi, Stalin informed the Politburo of the soundness of Serov's arguments on 3 November and 'asked' that his plan for the removal of surpluses be approved. Stalin further requested in his telegram that Sokolovskii be brought to Moscow and asked the Politburo to 'convey my request to him in the spirit of the aforementioned demands' and to 'convey my personal thanks to Serov for his note'.[39]

Serov's suggestion of removing 100,000 tonnes of grain, 150,000 tonnes of sugar, and 250,000 tonnes of potatoes was accepted, as was his plan to reduce ration levels and pay for high-ranking SVAG officers who, much to his disgust, were living 'in luxury' with their families while Soviet citizens were threatened with famine. But these removals did little to alleviate the famine that eventually hit the western parts of the Soviet Union hard in late 1946. These amounts would have been only sufficient to feed the wave of soldiers demobilised from Germany, who compounded food pressures once they returned to famine-affected areas.[40] Although Stalin suggested that further surplus removals should be made in line with the further reduction of forces, SVAG sources do not mention other mass removal operations.[41] The operation was thus more a routine adjustment of food levels to population size rather than a famine relief measure. Given Stalin's rapacious attitude towards Germany's resources and that the famine probably resulted in almost 5 million deaths,[42] the question remains: why on earth were no such measures taken in Germany?

Perhaps this is a naïve question, given Stalin's ambivalent attitude towards relieving famine-affected areas in the Soviet Union during the early 1930s when he refused even to accept that famine was occurring until it was too late to do much about it. Now he continued to export grain

---

[39] Ibid., 77.
[40] Of the approximately 700,000 troops remaining in Germany from September 1946, 350,000 were demobilised by July 1947. Given that the 350,000 troops would have been supplied with an annual average of 75,000 tonnes of grain had they remained in Germany, the removal of 100,000 tonnes seems roughly commensurate with the population drop. The same can be said of the other staples. For demobilisation figures see Naimark, *The Russians in Germany*, 17.
[41] Petrov, *Pervyi predsedatel' KGB Ivan Serov*, 256.
[42] Mortality is difficult to gauge. Probably 1 million died directly from the famine, and about 4 million deaths resulted from related diseases, though this distinction is by no means fixed. E. G. Bellinger and N. M. Dronin, *Climate Dependence and Food Problems in Russia 1900–1990: The Interaction of Climate and Agricultural Policy and Their Effect on Food Problems* (New York: Central European University Press, 2005), 168–9.

to Europe, reducing exports only at the height of the famine in 1947.[43] But removing food en masse from Germany was less feasible than it had been earlier. Anti-German attitudes may have remained in the leadership, but Soviet occupation policy was changing from the 'smash and grab' approach aimed at stripping the country of its economic might, to now rebuilding it into a strong ally. Sokolovskii's 'soft' policy approach, for which he was roundly ridiculed by the 'hard men', was becoming central to the emerging shift in Soviet policy towards Germany.

This shift, however, meant little to disaffected and hungry voters in the cold winter of 1946–7. Women's food protests increased, as did the level of anger among all Germans. SVAG's policies of 'minimising risk' in the countryside and Tiul'panov's inventions were no longer sufficient to deal with this backlash. In contrast to the July promise, SVAG was able now to push through the abolition of the lowest two categories of the rationing system that had plagued unemployed women and mothers for so long. It would take time for their real ration levels actually to increase, but they did increase this time because SVAG was becoming more than just an occupation regime struggling against a backdrop of mass violence. It was beginning to assume more control in the peacetime environment that it had fought so hard to create and to become more confident in delegating power to its creation, the SED, to help it cope with these new and broader responsibilities. The leadership's new long-term plans for Germany, which rose to prominence quite unexpectedly in mid to late 1946, could only be realised because this process was already under way. During 1947 the Soviets could scale down their occupation and rely on a 'trustworthy' and reasonably popular party to implement their, and eventually its own, directives. These final major steps or stumbles in the occupation period form the remainder of this book.

---

[43] Exports increased from 339,600 tonnes in 1945 to 1,265,600 tonnes in 1946. RGAE – f. 1562, op. 329. d. 1922, l. 2.

9   Building the SED

Stalin went to great lengths to dissuade some of the gun-ho European communist leaders, especially the Germans, from simply following the bloody Soviet model of revolution in their own countries.[1] He urged them to ride the wave of popular support for socialism in Europe and assume power via elections, even in coalition with other political parties. There was never any doubt that the socialist parties should rule the country and limit the influence of the others, but Stalin understood that the realities of cooperation with the Allies and, indeed of the post-war world, required more refined forms of state-building in some countries than the Soviets had hitherto developed. The weight of this advice squares poorly with Stalin's famous remark to Milovan Djilas, or perhaps more so with its interpretation by historians seeking to demonstrate Stalin's 'clear' post-war plans of communist expansion: 'whoever occupies a territory also imposes on it his own social system'.[2]

The social system which developed in Germany during the violent chaos of the first years of the occupation was not Soviet communism. It was an amalgam of Soviet and German incremental state-building developed 'from below' as much as it was by instructions from above. The instructions from Moscow were intermittent, at times contradictory, and often cloaked as criticisms of the intermittent and contradictory way things were being done. There was little consistency or, indeed, design in the leadership's broad political approach towards Germany. Within this mess and among the contradictory policies of the leadership, however, Soviet officers in Germany developed general tactics to counter political

---

[1] Roberts highlights Stalin's inability simply to dictate political developments in Eastern Europe from Moscow. A primary example remains his failed attempts to urge Tito in 1945 not to proclaim Yugoslavia a communist federation and seek territorial concessions from its neighbours so not to invite British intervention in the Balkans and stifle the Grand Alliance. G. Roberts, *Stalin's Wars: From World War to Cold War, 1939–1953* (New Haven and London: Yale University Press, 2006), 325–6.

[2] Djilas, *Conversations with Stalin*, 114.

threats to basic interests understood among competing organs, namely positioning the SED at the apex of political power in the new Germany.

The reasons for placing the party there, however, had more to do with achieving immediate occupation aims than the eventual result of establishing a one-party dictatorship in a feeble satellite state. Historians have long sparred over whether or not one was supposed to lead to the other, but what will be shown here is how the electoral and political strength of the party fostered by the Soviets made possible the shift from the short-term 'smash and grab' occupation policy towards a long-term and sustainable one in late 1946.[3] The strong 'socialist status' of the party encouraged the Soviets to delegate more and more power to German hands once the shift towards a long-term occupation strategy began. As the number of troops, SVAG men, and even security agents diminished in the zone from 1947 onward, the SED and the state machinery began to assume a more prominent role not only in administration, but also in lower level policy making. The Soviets were thus able to assume a greater advisory role in the zone, as the SED/state mechanisms gradually replaced or in some cases overlapped with the Soviet ones built from mid 1945 onward.

After the war, the real threat to Soviet political interests in Germany came less from outright fascists and more from the 'bourgeois' political forces who battled with the KPD/SED for electoral popularity and political power. The dilemma in mid 1945 was how to limit the impact of these forces without simply eliminating their leaderships, a bloody tactic sure to elicit protests from the Allies and perhaps sympathy or even resistance from supporters. To be sure, the Allies faced a similar conundrum in limiting the support for communist parties in their own occupation zones. Few observers could have appreciated this dilemma in mid 1945. Until the Soviets allowed it, there was little room for political parties other than the KPD and, to a lesser extent, the SPD, to develop in the zone during the immediate wake of the war. There was also little interest in supporting any party from the population angered at the bleak reality of defeat and occupation that the 'politicians' had brought them. The NKVD was still arresting imagined, real, and possible threats to the regime in the most arbitrary fashion, and the daily battle for survival was foremost on most people's minds. It thus came as quite a shock to the zone and even the Allies when SVAG allowed for the re-establishment of the four major political parties (KPD, SPD, LDP, CDU) so quickly in June 1945, and their

---

[3] Loth is most unequivocal in arguing that neither the path to the GDR was clear to the Soviets in 1945, nor was the GDR the outcome most desirable to the Moscow leadership, even on the eve of its creation. Loth, *Stalin's Unwanted Child: The Soviet Union, the German Question and the Founding of the GDR*, trans. R. F. Fogg (London: Macmillan, 1998).

formation into an anti-fascist coalition block the following month. The block would supposedly spearhead the democratic reconstruction of Germany by taking unanimous policy decisions regarding its political development. It thus seemed that the Soviets envisaged running the zone and facilitating the country's unification in alliance with a coalition of various political forces broadly representative of the new German electorate.

Gary Bruce speculates that in establishing the block the Soviets may have sought to endear themselves to the occupied population by demonstrating an appreciation for democratic pluralism, but accepts that we may not know why until we gain greater access to Soviet archives.[4] Based on the greater access that we now have, it is clear that the Soviets were more interested in endearing themselves to the Allies with gestures towards democratic pluralism. More to the point, they encouraged the non-socialist parties to form within the block so as to control their development better. This was the best way to limit their impact without simply eliminating their leaderships. Zhukov was quite clear about this in his meeting with his leading SVAG officers in August 1945:

I am not at all in agreement with the idea that we should maintain an identical and equal relationship towards all parties of the block. We should comprehensively support one party [KPD] and enable it to increase its authority, while we should keep up the others with the aim of neutralising those strata of the population who support the two liberal bourgeois parties.[5]

Just how to 'keep them up' while 'keeping them down' was left to SVAG and NKVD officers to work out.[6] Neither had any experience in operating within a multi-party political system nor much patience for doing so, particularly the NKVD men. The line between political intrigue and outright violence, therefore, was often blurred. It is well known that both made it difficult for the bourgeois parties to call meetings, publish their own newspapers, and thus reach a broader electoral audience with their anti-socialist messages.[7] Entire party branches were disbanded and

---

[4] Bruce, *Resistance with the People*, 25.

[5] Zakharov, ed., *Deiatel'nost' sovetskikh voennykh komendatur*, 93.

[6] For the KPD's role in the formation of the block and 'keeping down' the bourgeois parties, particularly Walter Ulbricht's decisive influence see G. Keiderling, 'Scheinpluralismus und Blockparteien: Die KPD und die Gründung der Parteien in Berlin 1945', *Vierteljahrshefte für Zeitgeschichte* 45, no. 2 (1997).

[7] According to SVAG order no. 19 of 2 August 1945, each printing house required a licence from the local *komendatura* to publish anything, be it party newspapers, journals, or advertising brochures. Even after this initial licence was given, nothing could be published without the express approval of the *komendatura*, encouraging some Soviet officers to refer to the right of printers to publish in quotation marks. According to one Soviet officer, there were few instances where German printers did not follow this law. When it was broken, it tended not to be a serious matter. One printer illegally produced brochures advertising a

their members arrested for suspect political activity and detained for extended periods, such as the Zwickau CDU branch in May 1946. The branch had the gall to call a meeting of industrialists to organise opposition to SVAG's plans to sequester local factories belonging to 'war criminals' (industrialists with 'Nazi links'). The image of bourgeois politicians scheming with rich Nazi industrialists to thwart 'economic justice' was too much for SVAG to handle.[8] Party leaders could also be removed or arrested for refusing to support SVAG policies, as in the case of the CDU leader Andreas Hermes.[9] Tiul'panov referred to Hermes' removal when expanding upon Zhukov's theory of 'neutralisation' in the wake of the September 1946 elections:

I will begin with the CDU. We understand perfectly well that you cannot change the political combination of enemy classes and that you cannot make this party pro-Soviet. But we do pose a problem by dispossessing it of its capacity for anti-Soviet protest, for making ambiguous statements, and by strengthening the democratic elements in this party, which are quite various. Therefore, when this party became a clear threat, when it became a synonym for all reactionary elements, we applied this combination with the dismissal of Hermes and by bringing in Kaiser.[10]

Hermes failed to support SVAG land reform polices during late 1945, which reflected the anti-socialist disposition of many CDU members. As this intransigent position proved unprofitable, the Soviets simply replaced Hermes with an alternative leader who accepted the policy allowing the Soviets to claim that each party within the anti-fascist block had unanimously supported the land reform. The inability of the CDU to defend its core ideals against Soviet pressure within the block alienated the party's

---

theatrical play without approval. He was fined 500 marks and his printing house was closed for two weeks. But brochures aside, this system allowed the Soviets to reject requests to publish non-KPD/SED propaganda in non-political journals and newspapers and also to censor other party journals and newspapers as well. Under these circumstances, it is little wonder that some CDU, LDP, and especially SPD members sought out printing presses in the western zones to publish their pamphlets and then attempted to smuggle them back across the border into the zone for distribution. Many, however, were arrested when attempting to re-enter the zone. These developments are discussed in a report on the work of the propaganda and censor sector of the SVAG Political Department for July and October 1945 in Bonvech [Bonwetsch], Bordiugov, and Neimark [Naimark], eds., *Sovetskaia voennaia administratsiia v Germanii*, 182–5.

[8] GARF – f. r-7212, op. 1, d. 187, l. 80.   [9] Bruce, *Resistance with the People*, 30–1.

[10] Kaiser too was removed from the CDU leadership in December 1947 after proving to be a less docile party leader than the Soviets had hoped. For the relevant section of the inquiry where the concept of 'neutralisation' is discussed see Bonvech [Bonwetsch], Bordiugov, and Neimark [Naimark], eds., *Sovetskaia voennaia administratsiia v Germanii*, 217.

supporters and contributed to its poor electoral performance.[11] As did a range of more refined measures aimed at encouraging conflict between the LDP and CDU. SVAG mobilised church representatives and intellectuals from the LDP to speak out against the CDU and to argue that the church and those who claimed to represent it could not possibly participate in a secular political election. It also allowed a well-known former Nazi party member to lead the LDP branch in Berlin, giving the other parties a better platform from which to criticise it.

The election results suggest that both crude and refined measures had some impact on the popular appeal of the bourgeois parties, not to mention their internal problems.[12] In the election to the municipal bodies at the county level in September (*Kreistags*), the SED gained 361 more seats than the LDP and CDU combined. The shady electoral tactics discussed in the previous chapter were central to the SED's success here, but with only their scattered use at the elections to the five provincial parliaments (*Landtags*) in the following month, the LDP and CDU gained seven more seats than the SED.[13] This loss was offset somewhat, however, by SVAG's ability to pressure other non-party delegates to support the SED and organise the appointment of SED men as presidents and vice-presidents of each provincial government with the exception of Saxony-Anhalt. Some ministerial posts were allocated to the LDP and CDU as well.

The crude and refined measures which comprised Zhukov's tactic of 'neutralisation' could only be really effective within the anti-fascist block. The Soviets were able to arrest party members without evoking further resistance from their party fellows because they had set up a political system in which power could only be gained in cooperation with SVAG. Further resistance only threatened to compromise the very aim towards which these parties were working, namely strengthening their position within the block and ensuring that their members retained their positions in government and civil administrations. Neutralisation thus may have encouraged party members to resist, as some historians have noted,[14] but it stopped their parties from becoming vehicles of resistance and threatening the stability of the regime, at least while the Soviets were still occupying the zone.[15]

---

[11] Naimark discusses this problem at length in 'The Soviets and the Christian Democrats: The Challenge of a "Bourgeois" Party in Eastern Germany, 1945–1949', *East European Politics and Societies* 9, no. 3 (1995).

[12] For internal problems in the CDU see ibid.

[13] Petrov, ed., *SVAG i nemetskie organy samoupravleniia*, 214.

[14] Bruce's study of individual resistors comes to mind, Bruce, *Resistance with the People*.

[15] For the role of the bourgeois parties in the 1953 uprising, particularly the tension between their membership and leaders over the question of joining the resistance or supporting the SED, see L. Haupts, 'Die Blockparteien in der DDR und der 17. Juni 1953', *Vierteljahrshefte für Zeitgeschichte* 40, no. 3 (1992).

Manipulating political parties within a loose coalition was uncharted territory for SVAG, the NKVD, and the Soviet leadership for that matter. The last coalition government the Soviets led lasted a few months and ended in 1918 with its coalition partners attempting to assassinate Lenin and other Bolshevik leaders. Although the idea of a broad-based coalition of parties led by socialists as a means to rule occupied territories was certainly Stalin's, what type of coalition and, indeed, what type of party would lead it was left to SVAG and NKVD officers to figure out. Their greatest challenge was dealing with the SPD, which posed much more of a threat to the KPD than the clearly identifiable bourgeois parties. It was difficult for many officers to come to terms with the SPD's role in the anti-fascist block. It claimed to be a socialist party and enjoyed the highest rates of new membership throughout 1945 in most areas of the zone.[16] It was free from much of the negative association with the occupier that plagued the KPD 'lackeys' and was able to present a 'safer' version of socialism to the occupied population. The problem was that its membership was politically unreliable in comparison with the less popular KPD. In fact, the scale of anti-Soviet sentiment within the SPD was downright alarming.

How did the occupation regime counter the SPD threat? SPD party branches could not simply be closed or members barred from admission to the civil administrations, the police force, or other organs. In fact, given the shortage of cadres and specialists required for administrative work, SVAG relied heavily on the SPD to fill these posts. As such, the regime was unable to threaten a major basis of SPD power in the zone as it could with the CDU and LDP. All it could really do was replace party leaders who were willing to voice anti-Soviet sentiments and arrest the most dangerous. For example, a September 1945 NKVD report to Skosyrev revealed that some leading SPD men had criticised the regime at a public party meeting in Wismar (Mecklenburg). The NKVD agent who attended the meeting claimed that a general consensus emerged, best articulated by one SPD leader who urged his comrades 'not [to] follow Soviet orders, nor allow communists into the leadership of factory organisations, as they would only assist the Soviets in dismantling'.[17] Another SPD leader present at the meeting, comrade 'M', claimed that Soviet incompetence in agricultural matters threatened to starve Germany in the approaching winter. This report was received at SVAG headquarters in

---

[16] In a long report written by Lieutenant General Bokov summarising SVAG's achievements over 1945 and 1946, he listed SED membership in late 1945 at 650,000 compared to 550,000 members for the KPD. GARF – f. r-7317, op. 8, ll. 165–75.

[17] GARF – f. r-7103, op. 1, d. 7, ll. 181–2.

Mecklenburg on 12 September 1945. On the same day HQ issued an order to the *komendant* of Wismar, Colonel Kuzmichev, 'suggesting' that 'M' be immediately removed from the SPD as well as from his position as leader of the city's labour office, and proposing to replace him with a 'trusted communist'.[18] However, some sort of further measure such as closing down the branch was simply unfeasible at this time, even though the report writers highlighted that members shared the same anti-Soviet views as their leaders.[19]

Such forceful measures soon became more feasible. The resounding success of the Austrian Social Democratic Party (SPÖ) at the November 1945 elections helped to confirm Soviet fears that all possible measures needed to be taken to stop the SPD from running as a single party in the zone and trouncing the KPD at the polls. The SPÖ won seventy-six seats to the communist party's (KPÖ) measly four, despite the efforts of Soviet occupation forces in Austria. It became clear to SVAG that some sort of unification of the SPD and KPD was necessary to meld the popularity of the former and discipline of the latter into a 'super party' fit to win the zonal elections and then have some chance at future country-wide German elections upon unification of the zones. There had long been talk in Soviet and German socialist circles about the necessity of unification, as many blamed the division between the parties for allowing Hitler to assume power in 1933 and decimate socialist ranks in the years following. After the Austrian debacle the political landscape in Moscow became more receptive to calls from SVAG for unification, despite the clear dangers that the level of anti-Soviet sentiment within the SPD posed to the regime and the remaining antipathy between SPD and KPD members posed to the union itself. This was especially the case between the KPD and the SPD in the western zones, whose unification was much less feasible. Not unlike the shift in dismantling policy, the broader landscape needed to change before SVAG could successfully lobby Moscow, and Tiul'panov's Administration was at the ready. In the immediate wake of the KPÖ's thrashing, Tiul'panov warned Stalin via the SVAG Military Council that the same electoral fate would befall the KPD if unification in the zone did not proceed. The green light was

---

[18] GARF – f. r-7103, op. 1, d. 7, l. 186.

[19] This sort of behaviour continued across Mecklenburg throughout late 1945. For instance, the NKVD reported that the SPD leader of the Bergen district engaged in the following conversation with an informant in December: 'We are against working together with the KPD (those barbarian bands from the east), and the Russians [who] have always been and will always be our enemies. I, as a German, will never work with the Russians . . . there will come a time when the Americans will come here, and those who worked with the Russians will be punished as traitors.' GARF – f. r-7103, op. 1, d. 6, l. 65.

soon given and the parties were unified into the SED in April 1946 (bar the SPD branch in Berlin).[20]

The child of unification, however, was anything but unified – embodying rather than resolving old ruptures within German socialism which have been a major topic of study for generations of historians.[21] For all of the problems of unification, however, it effectively brought anti-Soviet elements closer to the regime. This gave it better opportunities to identify the most dangerous, prevent them from assuming leading party or administrative positions, and purge them en masse. This stripped SPD members of their former coats of protection and was essential to establishing a command party capable of implementing the policies of their Soviet masters and, eventually, governing on its own. This was by far the most important of the many steps, or, indeed, stumbles that the occupation regime and its German allies made towards establishing a political monopoly in the zone.

Soviet security concerns accelerated in mid 1946 once they began to realise just how much Tiul'panov had underestimated the level of resistance to unification. Some SPD members refused to join the new party and the more fanatical among them took to underground political activity. But most were absorbed into the SED along with their antipathetic attitudes and were now ready to be purged – a process in which the NKVD and even SVAG political officers needed little instruction from Moscow. The number purged was perhaps less important than the nature of purging after unification. It became more pre-emptive, especially in the lead up to the elections. NKVD agents now removed and/or arrested not only anti-Soviet elements within the party that had committed some sort of offence, but also those who they suspected would have trouble implementing Soviet policy without question. Pre-emptive tactics required a greater focus on forceful interrogations, which bore much fruit in Mecklenburg. In a common enough occurrence, NKVD officers arrested a former SPD member in June on a minor suspicion, yet proceeded with a prolonged interrogation. The suspect revealed that he was present at a secret meeting in the apartment of a local SED leader, who outlined his plans to fill candidate lists for the upcoming elections with his former SPD comrades at the expense of former KPD members.[22] The suspect also named the

[20] Bonvech [Bonwetsch], Bordiugov, and Neimark [Naimark], eds., *Sovetskaia voennaia administratsiia v Germanii*, 208.

[21] Tiul'panov did admit that the unification of the parties had occurred in such a way that proper screening of members, social democrats and communists, was not conducted. The security services assumed much of this responsibility upon unification. Ibid., 209.

[22] GARF – f. r-7103, op. 1, d. 26, ll. 217–26. Earlier concerns about the anti-Soviet disposition of many SPD members in December 1945 were voiced in Mecklenburg. GARF – f. r-7103, op. 1, d. 7, ll. 180–2.

attendees to the meeting who were promptly detained, and the NKVD was now even keener to 'adjust' candidate lists in the opposite direction. In this atmosphere of continual purging, much of the information gleaned from such interrogations did not need to be accurate, but only to confirm prevalent suspicions that could be investigated and then eliminated, which was often the same process.

Purging and policing in general, however, were not sufficient to sustain the party. There were over a million SED members upon unification and more had come from the SPD than the KPD. The carrot was needed as much as the stick. Standing at the apex of the emerging political and administrative system of the new Germany, the party offered the faithful and the not so faithful long-term material benefits in a post-war world beset by material shortage. These advantages were not lightly given up for the sake of those removed from the party or concerns about ideological purity. If anything, these purges afforded greater room for upward mobility. The Soviets thus created conditions via unification that might have encouraged some forms of minor resistance but, as with the CDU and LDP, ensured that the parties could not become vehicles of resistance themselves. More to the point, for most party members resistance was simply unprofitable.

As is a rendering here of the gradual delegation of power to the Germans in the zone from 1947 onward, which saw the establishment of new state/party structures that would form the basis of the German Democratic Republic (GDR) in 1949. This process has long attracted the interest of historians.[23] What is important to note is that this process was only possible within a political system characterised by docility towards a dominant and more 'trustworthy' party, for which SVAG and the NKVD were mostly responsible. The SED was not without severe problems which limited its electoral appeal and even capacity for governance, but it was a work in progress.[24] The growing awareness of the independent state-building feats of Soviet officers operating in Germany

---

[23] Among the recent wave of publications, Spilker's work on the SED and the consolidation of the zone into the GDR remains most helpful in tracing the advances in thinking on this topic. D. Spilker, *The East German Leadership and the Division of Germany: Patriotism and Propaganda 1945–1953* (Oxford and New York: Oxford University Press, 2006), 95–142.

[24] Tiul'panov discussed the numerous problems that beset the SED during the election campaign. Most prominent among them was that party members still identified themselves primarily as KPD or SED members. He cited an all too familiar instance where party members would introduce themselves by saying, 'I am a former communist, and member of the SED.' The lack of unity hampered cooperative pre-election work between former KPD and SPD members and gave the impression to many that the party was a body of two halves, rather than a unified entity. Although this complaint is borne out of other sources as well, it should be remembered that, when explaining the October election defeat, Tiul'panov tended to focus more on internal problems within the SED than those of his administration. Tiul'panov's detractors in Karlshorst and Moscow, on the other

in the absence of any concrete plans from Moscow has given rise to new, livelier debates among historians. Among them is the relationship between 'independent actors' and the broader flux of changing Soviet occupation aims and policies in Germany, which is the subject of the following chapter.

hand, argued that the problems within his Political Administration were the primary reason for the lack of the SED's electoral success. Bonvech [Bonwetsch], Bordiugov, and Neimark [Naimark], eds., *Sovetskaia voennaia administratsiia v Germanii*, 210–11.

10   The shift in policy and end of chaos

In the spring of 1944, US Vice-President Henry Wallace headed an American delegation to the Soviet Far East. For almost a month, Wallace and his companions were led across the vast expanses of Siberia and shown manufactured images of Soviet reality by their NKVD hosts. The infamous Magadan forced labour sites and Kolyma's gold fields were hurriedly converted into model work stations and the prisoners into 'volunteer workers'. This subterfuge was most effective, as Wallace wrote of the courage of the 'big, husky' young gold miners who had come from European Russia to the East to seek their fortune, not unlike generations of Americans who had sought theirs in the 'Wild West'.[1] He had no idea that these men with whom he exchanged pleasantries were prisoners, or that the mines were part of the largest complex of prison camps and forced labour sites in the world. Wallace was not the first American to be fooled by the Soviets and chided by later generations of historians for his 'naïveté', but he was one of the most important.

The Soviets masked the bleak realities of their country to convince him of their 'democratic spirit' and thus strengthen the Grand Alliance. A year later they needed to remind the Americans that the Soviet people could not bear the costs of reconstructing their war-ravaged nation alone. No such subterfuge was required for this purpose. They could let the devastated old cities of European Russia speak for themselves. It was clear to the Americans who visited them that this had been a war and occupation like no other, and that their country had been blessed in avoiding the latter. The Germans would have to pay for what they had done to the Soviet Union – if not in marks then in machines and factories to replace what they had destroyed, and in labour to replace the millions of workers they had kidnapped and more whom they had killed. Importantly, not only Germans who would fall under Soviet occupation would pay, but all of them.

---

[1] P. Hollander, *The Survival of the Adversary Culture: Social Criticism and Political Escapism in American Society* (New Brunswick, NJ: Transaction Books, 1988), 188–9.

One of the American visitors was Edwin Pauley, a leading figure in the Lend–Lease programme and then the chief US representative on the Allied Reparations Commission (ARC), the body established to regulate reparations deliveries from Germany to the Allies. Pauley was stunned by the sheer scale of devastation when he visited Stalingrad at his own request. The visit only confirmed Roosevelt's and now seemingly Truman's position of accepting, 'in principle', Soviet reparations demands from Germany. It was during this stage of broad agreement and specific reparations plans worked out by Pauley and the ARC in Moscow that the Soviets pursued the massive dismantling programme during the 'crazy summer' of 1945. Dismantlers worked around the clock to remove German factories and equipment and send them back to the Soviet Union as quickly as possible.

During the Cold War, many western historians refused to accept that post-war Soviet foreign policy making was sensitive to American concerns, let alone to the point of influencing occupation strategy.[2] After all, how serious could Stalin have been about unifying Germany or maintaining the Grand Alliance if he always intended to 'sovietise' Europe? This 'false logic' has survived the opening of the Soviet archives and the revelations of the complexities of foreign policy making in the Soviet Union.[3] In fact, this 'sovietisation thesis' has been developed recently by some Russian historians, such as Nikita Petrov, who argue that sovietisation was not Stalin's primary foreign policy aim, but only the means by which to bind occupied countries to the Soviet Union after the war. In Germany's case, occupation officers may not have been aware of Stalin's grand aims, but their 'Soviet style' reconstruction of the zone such as establishing a single party monopoly on political power served them anyway, as they laid the foundation for sovietisation and, eventually, a Soviet satellite. These satellites would form a 'security belt' in Eastern Europe to help protect the Soviet Union from 'capitalist' attacks.[4] By postulating this connection between sovietisation and security, Petrov attempts to move beyond the old debates over whether or not ideological or security concerns were paramount in Stalin's thinking about Germany after the war. In his words, 'one served the other'.[5]

---

[2] The revisionist strain in cold war historiography was a clear exception to this trend. See W. O. McCagg, *Stalin Embattled 1943–1948* (Detroit, Mich. Wayne State University Press, 1978) and B. Kuklick, *American Policy and the Division of Germany: The Clash with Russia over Reparations* (Ithaca, NY: Cornell University Press, 1972).

[3] Raack is perhaps the clearest exponent of this trend. R. C. Raack, *Stalin's Drive to the West, 1938–1945: The Origins of the Cold War* (Stanford, Calif.: Stanford University Press, 1995).

[4] Petrov, 'Formirovanie organov nemetskogo samoupravleniia', 47.   [5] Ibid.

We can move beyond the old debates as well, though along a different course. The evidence below suggests that the Soviets implemented their 'smash and grab' occupation strategy in Germany after intense consultation with the Allies, which convinced them that their exploitative occupation policies could be pursued within the boundaries of the Grand Alliance. They implemented them in Germany at breakneck speed with little consideration for the long-term consequences – economic and social. After all, both the Soviets and the Americans expected to occupy Germany only for a short period. This is why the breakdown of Soviet–Allied cooperation in Germany during mid to late 1946 posed such a significant problem to the Soviets. They were faced now with the prospect of a long-term occupation of an isolated part of Germany in which the consequences of the 'smash and grab' strategy were materialising. The devastated economic landscape was now less of an assurance of Germany's reduced military threat and more of a hindrance to creating a self-sufficient country. Similarly problematic were the anti-Soviet attitudes of the occupied population. These became more awkward as the new long-term occupation policy devised in the wake of the breakdown of relations with the Allies required the SED to assume a greater role in running the zone. In many ways, the Soviets had burnt their bridges, never expecting to cross back over the river.

This argument is based on a chronology of shifting occupation aims and conditions, whose importance is refuted by historians who promote the 'sovietisation thesis' in its various forms. Yet even those historians who seek to situate a central paradox at the heart of Soviet occupation strategy give little attention to this point. Alfred Rieber's insightful work is important in this respect. He is certainly correct to argue that

[t]here was no way he [Stalin] could reconcile his conflicting aims, that is, to reach agreements with the USA, Britain, and France over the treatment of Germany, exploit the German economy for Soviet needs, keep Germany politically weak, and promote the role of German communists as a guarantee against the revival of fascism.[6]

But Stalin and the leadership only gradually became aware of their incapacity to reconcile these aims. Indeed, in 1945 they had little reason to even consider them contradictory. The present chapter traces this growing realisation among the Soviet leadership during the breakdown of relations with the Allies in 1946. It was this breakdown as much as

[6] A. J. Rieber, 'Stalin as Foreign Policy Maker: Avoiding War, 1927–1953', in *Stalin: A New History*, ed. S. R. Davies and J. R. Harris (New York: Cambridge University Press, 2005), 154.

anything else that brought about the termination of the dismantling programme and the general shift in occupation strategy which sought to
rebuild Germany into a loyal ally. With the completion of this shift, the
crisis years of the occupation were over.

At first glance, the deterioration of Soviet–Allied relations over
Germany was rapid. The Soviets were pleased with the results of the
Yalta Conference in February 1945. Roosevelt agreed 'in principle' to
the satisfaction of Soviet reparations demands of 10 billion dollars from
Germany. He promised the Soviets access to the economic riches of the
Ruhr and massive reparations from other western parts of the country
which would be occupied by Allied forces. All parties agreed that despite
each power occupying a different zone, the German economy should be
treated 'as a whole' and eventually unified into a single economic unit.
Just as importantly, Roosevelt treated Britain as a 'junior partner' in these
negotiations, and their intransigence towards Soviet claims in a similar
vein.[7] At Potsdam some five months later, however, Truman rejected the
Ruhr plan and imposed significant conditions on Soviet access to reparations from western Germany. The Americans considered the Soviets'
failure to meet these conditions a refusal to treat Germany as a 'single
economic unit' and ended economic cooperation in May 1946.

How did agreements over Germany fall apart so quickly? For many
historians, they were subsumed within the broader deterioration of
Soviet–Allied relations marked by Roosevelt's death and Truman's
assumption of the presidency.[8] The two polities were simply too different
to maintain an alliance without a common threat to bind them. The
intensification of the Cold War is thus seen as a logical post-war development. Perhaps, but the Soviets certainly did not think so in 1945. For
them, agreements over Germany were one of the more positive aspects of
their relationship with the Allies in comparison to disputes over Poland
etc. Apart from some chest-beating, there was little indication that
Truman felt differently about Germany than Roosevelt in mid 1945. In
fact, it was exactly the understanding reached at the ARC meetings in
Moscow over reparations with Truman's chief delegate, Pauley, that

[7] J. E. Farquharson, 'Anglo-American Policy on German Reparations from Yalta to Potsdam',
The English Historical Review 112, no. 448 (1997). This personal approach at the expense of the
British reinforced the Soviet assumption that 'after 1945 America would adopt a mediating
role between Britain and the Soviet Union, therefore avoiding any western bloc against the
latter'. According to Farquharson, this assumption also 'exercised a strong influence on US
policy in the period 1945–6'. Ibid., 925.
[8] For a short summary of the major Soviet–Allied tensions in 1946 see C. Kennedy-Pipe,
Stalin's Cold War: Soviet Strategies in Europe, 1943 to 1956 (Manchester: Manchester
University Press, 1995), 93–101.

convinced the Soviets that they could remove as much industry as they desired from their own zone; moreover, that dismantling should be completed in the shortest possible time as, once the western and Soviet zones' economies were integrated into 'a single unit', mass removals would be unfeasible. This is one of the reasons why dismantling activity was so feverish during the 'crazy summer' of 1945, as the Soviets expected to reach an agreement on economic integration at Potsdam.

Provisions for the formation of the ARC were laid at Yalta, and it was charged with drawing up a viable reparations plan that promised to form the basis of agreements at Potsdam. The plan eventually drawn did not differentiate greatly between the dismantling of German military and heavy industry. This distinction became important later in Soviet–Allied disputes, but in early 1945 US Ambassador to the Soviet Union Averell Harriman accepted Stalin's argument that it was impossible to demilitarise Germany without removing both.[9] In any case, the Americans were keen to allow the Soviets to take what they needed from Germany to assist in their planned military operations against Japan.[10] And not only industrial plants, but labour as well. Harriman was excited by the idea of using German forced labour in the Soviet Union after the war and suggested that a million or so civilian workers would offset the problem of post-war unemployment in Germany which would invariably result from the removal of so much of its industry.[11]

The broad lines of agreement were detailed during a June ARC meeting in Moscow. I. M. Maiskii, deputy to the Commissar for Foreign Affairs V. M. Molotov, was central to this and most meetings with Pauley and Lubin, the other major American delegate. All agreed that they all should exert control over the German economy for another twenty-five years or so, far beyond the time when troops would be withdrawn. Pauley was quite pleased with the Soviet suggestion that the Ruhr be treated as an international concern controlled by the four occupation powers in Germany. Similarly, Pauley reiterated that the Americans would satisfy some of their reparations claims by sequestering German investments abroad rather than removing industrial equipment from Germany proper. Given that geographical boundaries between the occupation zones were

[9] For the Soviet record of Maiskii's discussion with Harriman in January 1945 see G. N. Sevost'ianov, ed., *Sovetsko-Amerikanskie otnosheniia 1939–1945: Dokumenty* (Moscow: Materik, 2004), 617.

[10] The Soviets and the Allies secretly agreed at Yalta that, approximately three months after the defeat of Germany, the Soviet Union would join the war against Japan. The use of German reparations to fund the Soviet war effort was discussed in May 1945 between Pauley and Molotov, see ibid., 684–6.

[11] Ibid., 617.

being finalised in Germany during this time, the idea of allowing the Soviets equal access to the most industrialised areas of Germany, all of which fell outside what would become Soviet territory, was certainly good news for the leadership. Although he noted the non-binding nature of their preliminary agreements, Maiskii went to some lengths to convince Molotov of the sincerity of American cordiality:

My general conclusion from the discussion with Pauley and Lubin is that their intentions are quite good (especially Lubin's who seems to be a Sovietophile [sic]) ... at the moment the Americans are alone as the British have no influence on them, yet it is still difficult to determine how the British will conduct themselves. It seems to me that we will encounter more opposition to our suggestions from the British side, than the American.[12]

Molotov immediately attempted to secure something binding in another meeting with Pauley a few days later. He again raised the issue of the dire economic situation facing the Soviets and their right to take advance reparations to satisfy their wartime or reconstruction needs. To this Pauley replied, 'I already told Maiskii that until the development of a final agreement with regard to reparations, it is possible to begin the removal of equipment from Germany towards reparations.'[13] Thus, despite future problems that emerged over the extent of Soviet 'advance removals', at this stage there was no obstruction to the fever-pitched dismantling during the 'crazy summer'. And although the final reparations agreement was long-coming, the final ARC proposal in late June accepted basic Soviet demands for half of the total reparations sum from Germany – almost 10 billion dollars.[14]

If the ARC plan was accepted by both parties as the basis for reparations agreements at Potsdam, why were some of its central tenets rejected only weeks later at the conference? The ARC was, after all, only a consultative body that on the Soviet side was staffed largely by People's Commissariat of International Affairs (NKID) bureaucrats. Their discussions with the Allied delegates did not reflect the breadth of the policy concerns which confronted the Soviet leadership and may not have exerted a significant influence on Stalin's post-war foreign policy making. Tension over Poland and the growing espionage war may have been more important in

---

[12] For Maiskii's report to Molotov on 12 June 1945 regarding his meeting with Pauley and Lubin see ibid., 697–8.

[13] A short record of their conversation is also found in Sevost'ianov, ed., *Sovetsko-Amerikanskie otnosheniia*, 699.

[14] Maiskii sent the copy of the American plan and his endorsement to Molotov on 10 June 1945. Ibid. 720–2.

this respect than agreements over Germany.[15] These arguments may help to explain why many historians have, for the most part, ignored the ARC. However, with regard to the broad role of the NKID in post-war decision-making, Geoffrey Roberts argues:

In short, it is reasonable to assume that the speculations of Gromyko, Litvinov, and Maiskii [NKID men] on the shape of the post-war world were not idiosyncratic but reflected the language and terms of the internal discourse on foreign policy and international relations that was taking place at the highest levels of decision-making.[16]

In Molotov's case, his views were reflective of the highest-level decision-making of which he was an integral part as Foreign Commissar and Stalin's chief lieutenant. The ARC experience clearly strengthened Soviet resolve to continue dismantling until the final reparations agreement was reached. The Soviets did not wait on Allied approval to implement their policies, but the leadership demonstrated a keen sensitivity to Allied concerns in Germany. In fact, they sought Allied approval incessantly for their behaviour. This conclusion squares poorly with the general western understanding of the central faultlines in Soviet–Allied post-war relations, which views reparations as one of the most divisive issues between the parties. It certainly became one of them, but there is little evidence to suggest now, as Nettl did in his 1951 study of the Soviet occupation, that the Soviets intentionally pursued this policy fully cognisant of its 'divisiveness'.[17]

This divisiveness began to become apparent at Potsdam. The Soviets had always received ambivalent indications as to the strength of their relationship with the Allies from various sections of their governments. That American/British intelligence and press services were disseminating anti-Soviet propaganda in western Germany during Potsdam was clear enough, but now it also seemed that the US State Department and broader diplomatic corps, the bastion of support for the Grand Alliance,

---

[15] Stalin did not seem to be too alarmed by the growth in espionage activity between Soviet and Allied forces in Germany by mid 1945. There is much evidence to suggest that he did not consider this growth 'out of the ordinary' or an accurate reflection of the complexity of Allied foreign policy attitudes towards the Soviet Union. In fact, Stalin suggested that those NKVD security reports which claimed the Allies were engaged in more subversive activity should be read carefully, given the possibility that anti-Soviet agents were inventing such information to cause a rift in the alliance. This was certainly the dominant (though inaccurate) understanding of the leadership with regard to NKVD reports that claimed the Allies were supporting Ukrainian nationalist rebels battling the Soviets throughout 1944 and much of 1945. J. Burds, 'The Early Cold War in West Ukraine', 20–3.

[16] Roberts, *Stalin's Wars*, 234.

[17] Nettl, *The Eastern Zone and Soviet Policy in Germany*, 303–4.

was wavering.[18] Truman's obstinate posturing over American atomic power and his refusal to accept previous agreements as to the Ruhr spoke of a resurgent British influence on an inexperienced president. The Soviets sensed an Allied betrayal. Tensions over Poland's new borders and the cessation of the wartime Lend–Lease agreement continued to exert serious pressure on the Alliance.[19]

However, the Soviets were not too unhappy with the final results of the conference. Fearing enormous Soviet claims for industrial equipment from their occupation zones, the Allies raised no objections to the Soviets continuing to dismantle their own. In addition, the Allies agreed to deliver 25 per cent of dismantled industrial plants deemed unnecessary for the German peacetime economy from their own zones to the Soviet in exchange for foodstuffs and other raw materials. What was 'unnecessary' and who deemed it so would become the crux of Soviet–Allied arguments. But at least these issues central to economic integration would be worked out by negotiating a Level of Industry Plan (LIP), expected to be signed no later than six months after the conference. Although the Soviets were unhappy that economic integration had been delayed for six months, American Secretary of State James Byrnes 'repeatedly assured Molotov that the two stage handling of the reparations question did nothing to alter the American determination that all four zones be treated as a single economic unit'.[20]

---

[18] The Soviet leadership was well aware of growing anti-Soviet propaganda in British and American newspapers, as well as the widespread dissemination of anti-Soviet propaganda in the western zones of Germany. The fact that the Soviets initially refused to conduct counter-propaganda in late 1945 for fear that it would endanger the alliance gives some indication as to the value they placed upon Soviet–Allied relations. Nevertheless, voices in the Department for Agitation and Propaganda in the Central Committee of the VKP (b) (Agitprop) gradually grew louder in protest to incessant anti-Soviet articles being published in leading western papers, especially with regard to the conduct of Soviet forces in the zone. By late 1945, a counter-propaganda campaign was being prepared. For Agitprop complaints and many examples of British and American anti-Soviet propaganda see RGASPI – f. 17, op. 125, d. 316. Pechatnov also traces the shift in Soviet attitudes towards Britain. V. O. Pechatnov, 'The Rise and Fall of Britansky Soyuznik: A Case Study in Soviet Response to British Propaganda of the mid-1940s', *The Historical Journal* 41, no. 1 (1998). It should be noted, however, that the *opis'* containing many of the Agitprop documents used by Pechatnov has since been reclassified in RGASPI and made unavailable to most researchers (f. 17, op. 128).

[19] Tensions over Poland reached a climax in May 1945 as Soviet security organs arrested sixteen Polish military and political figures, all of whom were considered 'democratic persons' by the Allies and with whom they planned to consult in the formation of a new Polish government. This elicited an 'international outrage' and Molotov was forced to field personal complaints about the arrests by Eden and Stettinius in San Francisco during May 1945. For the Soviet record of the May discussion see Sevost'ianov, ed., *Sovetsko-Amerikanskie otnosheniia*, 682–3.

[20] Loth, *Stalin's Unwanted Child*, 20.

Molotov was sceptical of Byrnes' assurances. He knew that if each power were to take reparations predominantly from their own zone it would be most difficult to regulate a common import/export balance for the entire country and thus treat the German economy as a whole. Some historians have argued that Byrnes' remark was most disingenuous, which betrayed his desire to inhibit any form of integration between the zones.[21] But for the time being, Molotov and Stalin expected to receive the reparations promised to them and the development of some form of economic integration to facilitate it.[22] The resumption of fever-pitched dismantling activity in the wake of the conference indicates that the Soviets understood now that they needed to finish it before the signing of the LIP, as any zone-wide plan, no matter how advantageous to them, would require a massive reduction of dismantling in their zone to support the country's economic sustainability better. The 'crazy summer' looked like turning into a 'crazy autumn'. Zhukov insisted on as much in his meeting with leading SVAG officers in mid August 1945:

We are not eternal guests here ... The situation cannot remain the same ... serious corrections to state and economic construction may also be introduced [i.e. LIP] ... Therefore, our primary task is to remove everything that is possible and necessary as quickly as we can.[23]

Zhukov's advice was symptomatic of broader strains of Soviet thinking of the leadership in Moscow throughout 1945. Even until mid 1946, the language of the reports sent back to the leadership by bureaucrats in Germany understood Soviet economic plans for the country within the framework of Allied cooperation. Within this framework, the Soviets

---

[21] M. Trachtenberg, *A Constructed Peace: The Making of the European Settlement, 1945–1963* (Princeton, NJ: Princeton University Press, 1999), 26.

[22] For Stalin's positive response to the reparations agreements at the conference see the memoirs of K. I. Koval'. K. I. Koval', *Poslednii svidetel': 'Germanskaia karta' v kholodnoi voine* (Moscow: Rosspen, 1997), 115–16.

[23] Zakharov, ed., *Deiatel'nost' sovetskikh voennykh komendatur*, 91. Just how many industrial plants were removed from Germany is difficult to calculate. Different Soviet sources provide conflicting information, reflecting the disorganised record-keeping practices of the immediate post-war period. A January 1946 report claimed that as the situation stood at 1 January, a total of 5,850,000 tonnes of equipment filling 450,000 locomotive wagons had been dismantled. Of this total much had already been sent to the Soviet Union or was in transit. Again, a similar report detailing activities for March 1946 claimed that a further 40,449 wagons had been filled with dismantled equipment, over 6,000 more than the planned target. GARF – f. r-7317, op. 4, d. 83, ll. 103–6. These figures square well with general estimates made by some historians who, although not citing the above source, estimate that by the end of 1946 some 6.2 million tonnes of equipment would have been removed from Germany, with over 50 per cent of it dismantled during the 'crazy summer' of 1945. B. Tsisla, 'Osobyi Komitet po Germanii', in *Sovetskaia voennaia administratsiia v Germanii*, ed. Doronin, Foitzik, and Tsarevskaia-Diakina, 113.

could pursue a range of measures in order to gain as much reparations as possible from the Allies without giving too much in return. That these measures included intransigent negotiating should not detract from the basic point that they were pursued within a broader context of cooperation that was required by the Soviets if they were to gain what was promised to them at Potsdam.

LIP negotiations were conducted through the Allied Control Council (ACC), the four-power body established to regulate occupation affairs. Until the plan was concluded, the Allies were obliged to dismantle and deliver a range of industrial plants to the Soviets as 'advance payments'. Still, only those plants considered unnecessary for the peacetime economy would be delivered. 'Military' plants naturally received primary focus. It was during these negotiations over 'advance payments' that the Soviets began to learn that the Allies, especially the British, did not intend to meet their reparations obligations under the Potsdam agreement – or at least the Soviet understanding of them. The crux of the problem was defining 'military' industries. Over the winter the Soviet delegation in the ACC requested a number of 'military' and 'military-related' plants from the Allies, most of which were rejected on the basis that they constituted neither.[24] With only preliminary information about these plants and whatever little details the Allies gave them, the Soviets could hardly protest – or at least protest successfully.[25] In response, Sokolovskii advised the Soviet delegation to do more research on the status of the western zones' economies in order to request in future plants that were undoubtedly military.[26] For the Soviets, then, it was a question of improving their own work in the ACC to achieve more profitable outcomes.

In April the Soviets began to receive secret economic data on the status of industry in the western zones which dashed this optimism. The data revealed that the Allies were applying an exceedingly strict definition of 'military' industry to all Soviet plant requests to reduce their reparations burden.[27] Part of the problem was that the Soviets regarded those plants that had been used to produce supplies for the war effort as 'military'

---

[24] For the structure of the Soviet delegation in the ACC see J. Foitzik, *Sowjetische Militäradministration in Deutschland (SMAD) 1945–1949: Struktur und Funktion* (Berlin: Akademie Verlag, 1999), 435–8.

[25] For the problems caused by the Soviets' lack of detailed knowledge of economic conditions in the western zones see GARF – f. r-7317, op. 5, d. 2, ll. 11–16.

[26] GARF – f. r-7317, op. 4, d. 83, ll. 151–3.

[27] The Soviets possessed basic information regarding Germany's economy. Much of this information was gathered from September 1944, as Soviet commissariats began to prepare reports on German industrial plants that could be appropriated in order to compensate for industrial or agricultural war losses incurred by the Soviet Union. The commissariats prepared detailed lists of German industries that they were interested in

industry, while the Allies rejected this definition if the plants could be converted for peacetime production. Conversion became more prominent as the Allies focused more on rebuilding aspects of western Germany's economy to ease the costs of providing for the occupied population. For instance, the Soviet delegation requested the delivery of furnace sites in the British zone which had produced chemical weapons. To support their case, they cited a 1944 Soviet–Allied reparations agreement that called for the destruction of all chemical wartime industries. With the support of the Americans, the British delegation denied that the sites had been used for this purpose and, in any case, poisonous chemicals had peacetime uses as well.[28]

The head of the Soviet Economic Department in the ACC and first deputy to the SVAG commander-in-chief on economic matters, K. I. Koval', had initially been most optimistic about negotiating reparation sums in the ACC.[29] By May 1946, however, he was at the end of his tether.[30] Whereas he and others in the delegation had been reluctant to express their concerns about Allied intransigence earlier in the year, by this time he was clearly indicating to Marshal Sokolovskii, Zhukov's successor, that current structures of Soviet–Allied cooperation in the ACC were inhibiting, rather than promoting, Soviet economic aims. Other members of the delegation followed suit as tensions with the Allies became even more heated when negotiating reparations from 'heavy industry'. The general secretary of the Soviet reparations delegation in the ACC, G. P. Arkad'ev, wrote to Moscow that according to the secret data there were at least 136 plants for the production of heavy machinery located in the British zone fit for reparations.[31] The British, however, had only put forward four of these plants on the 'advance lists' in the ACC.[32] Competing interpretations aside, now it was a matter of the Allies admitting a much smaller industrial capacity in their zones than that to which Soviet data attested.

appropriating from Germany for this purpose, noting their location, number of workers, production output, capital investment, etc. The Soviets drew on these reports when making requests for industrial plants and equipment from the western zones. It seems, however, that these reports were not detailed enough, forcing the Soviets to rely heavily on information from the Allies in the ACC. This information was not easily forthcoming and Soviet observers enjoyed only limited 'official' access to industrial sites in the western zones, as did western observers in the Soviet zones.

[28] GARF – f. r-7317, op. 4, d. 83, ll. 99–101.   [29] Koval', *Poslednii svidetel'*, 128.

[30] GARF – f. r-7317, op. 5. d. 2, l. 9.

[31] GARF – f. r-7317, op. 5, d. 2, ll. 23–4. Addressed to A. Ia. Vyshinskii and then forwarded to Minister of Foreign Trade A. I. Mikoyan.

[32] The Allies would submit advance lists to the ACC with those industrial plants that they thought were suitable for dismantling in accordance with the reparations agreement, while the Soviets would do the same. Each delegation would debate the suitability of the listed plants to be regarded as 'reparations', and then all delegations would try to form one joint reparations list.

This wave of reports demonstrated to the leadership that it would receive only a negligible amount of advance payments. More alarmingly, the reports also warned that the principal 25 per cent amount of reparations might not be delivered from the western zones. The structures of Soviet–Allied economic cooperation that had been formalised in March 1946 with the signing of the LIP seemed unworkable. The LIP struck a balance between reparations and domestic economic needs. It did this by setting the amount of industrial and agricultural production necessary to meet the requirements of the German peacetime economy, which made it possible to determine an industrial production surplus and thus quantify the amount of industrial equipment that could be delivered to the Soviets as reparations. Similarly, the amount of foodstuffs and raw materials that the Soviets were obliged to deliver to the western zones to meet the requirements of the peacetime economy was also quantified. Naturally, the Soviets pushed for lower industrial production levels in the western zones to allow for a greater surplus, and thus more reparations, as well as lower agricultural levels to limit the amount of food they were required to deliver. The Allies pushed for the opposite.

Despite this tension, in some cases the Soviets and the Allies were able to strike an impressive balance between industrial production and surplus, which promised the Soviets considerable quantities of reparations.[33] However, the production levels set tended to reflect political rather than chiefly economic considerations.[34] Moreover, important sections of the LIP could be given contradictory interpretations and be used by all sides in an attempt to avoid meeting their obligations to one another. The Allies proved to be masters of this practice. With the implementation of the LIP during May, the debates in the ACC shifted from those concerning advance to principal payments of reparations to the Soviets. But the Allies now refused to make principal payments on the basis that most of the remaining industrial capacity of the western zones was needed first to meet the production requirements of the peacetime economy. As significant surpluses in production could not be expected any time soon, reparations could not be delivered. The British even complained to Arkad'ev that reparations could not be delivered within the two-year period agreed

[33] See the debate over steel production in A. Cairncross, *A Country to Play With: Level of Industry Negotiations in Berlin 1945–46* (Gerrards Cross: Colin Smythe, 1987), 51–65.
[34] The reasons for its failures have been the subject of much attention ever since its inception. In fact, much of the criticism of the plan has come from its architects, ibid., C. Landauer, 'The German Reparations Problem', *The Journal of Political Economy* 56, no. 4 (1948) and B. U. Ratchford, *Berlin Reparations Assignment: Round One of the German Peace Settlement* (Chapel Hill, NC: University of North Carolina Press, 1947).

to at Potsdam, but only after four years.[35] The Allies were now applying a 'first-charge principle' to all forms of Soviet reparations, which meant that the Soviets would get nothing from the Allies until they deemed the German economy strong enough to afford it. According to this principle no occupying power should take reparations from the current production of German industry, as these products would be sold on the international market to pay for the import of goods necessary to sustain the German peacetime economy (at a level agreed to in the LIP). Similarly, the industries required to produce these goods could not be dismantled. Only once a surplus could be created in economic production would reparations be taken from this surplus, in the form of either production or industrial plants. This had been the British position all along, but now with the Americans following suit it was clear to the Soviets that they had miscalculated. They had misread both the 'spirit' of 1945, which seemed to clearly indicate that German reparations would fund Soviet post-war reconstruction, and the letter of the law in the Potsdam agreement that exempted the 25 per cent reparations amount from 'first charge'.[36] The Soviets cited these exemptions and claimed that the LIP only quantified reparations and did not subject them to new restrictions until they were blue in the face, but the Allies refused to budge.

The Allies' position was understandable. Broader relations with the Soviets were souring and the growing knowledge of economic damage done to the Soviet zone by mass dismantling made economic integration a less attractive prospect. If the Allies had lost faith in economic cooperation,

---

[35] GARF – f. r-7317, op. 5, d. 2, l. 18.

[36] The Soviets went away from Potsdam with the impression that reparations from the western zones were still exempt from the 'first-charge principle'. The British and the Americans were so insistent on implementing this principle because it would ensure that they would not have to supplement the German economy for it to be used for Soviet reparations demands. Soviet consternation over this plan was understandable, given that if 'first charge' were applied, the reparations necessary for their domestic economic reconstruction would be subject to whimsical post-war international market forces of which the British and Americans played a leading role. Nevertheless, the Soviets were able to alleviate the possible damaging effects that 'first charge' would have had by restricting it solely to goods from current production during ARC meetings. Principle seven of the 'Statement of Principles Agreed to by the Moscow [Allied] Commission' stated that 'first charge' did not apply to 'reparations in kind' loosely defined as industrial plants and plant machinery. This suited the Soviets well, as the first few months of the occupation had already demonstrated that they were more concerned with dismantling and removing actual industrial plants and their machinery than with putting them back into production. Therefore, current dismantling practice was 'approved', despite some protests over the scale of removals. However, by December 1945 the Allies were giving the Soviets mixed signals about the future application of the principle. In fact, Harriman's correspondence with Vyshinskii is indicative of the ambiguous position taken by the Americans over the matter. GARF – f. r-7317, op. 4, d. 83, ll. 31–8.

then their next move in the negotiations was just the thing to end it. Until these imaginary sufficient surpluses could be produced, they demanded that the Soviets deliver the agreed amount of foodstuffs and raw materials. The demands grew louder from March 1946, as the world food crisis significantly affected food supplies in the British zone, forcing a massive reduction in ration levels. The Soviets were incandescent, sensing that the Allies wanted something for nothing, and refused to make these deliveries until they first received the reparations that had been promised to them. In response, the American Military Governor in Germany, Lucius Clay, temporarily suspended all future reparations deliveries to the Soviets on 4 May 1946.[37]

Cold war historians have investigated this gridlock since the 1970s.[38] Now with the aid of declassified sources, we can identify what made this gridlock unresolvable. Essentially, whichever interpretation of Potsdam/ LIP was more valid was not relevant to the negotiations during May 1946. The ability of both sides to enforce their differing interpretations to support their claims was of primary importance, rather than the 'accuracy' of the interpretations themselves. And by May 1946 the Allies were in a much better position to enforce their understanding of the agreements than the Soviets, best demonstrated by Clay's heated correspondence with Sokolovskii. Clay wrote to him in late April 1946, complaining that his dismantling teams had removed a maize processing plant near Leipzig. For Clay, the removal of such plants was prohibited under both the Potsdam and LIP agreements. To make matter worse, he claimed the plant was American, rather than German-owned. Laced with the tone of latent threat not uncommon to Clay's correspondence by mid 1946, he warned Sokolovskii that 'if this is to be the practice, I feel that reparations deliveries must be stopped as a whole until our program can be reviewed'.[39] Clay was effectively testing the Soviets' commitment to allowing a sufficient industrial capacity to remain in their own zone in order to meet the agreed upon production requirements set out by the LIP.

Sokolovskii failed the test in his reply to Clay a month later, after the 4 May suspension. He refuted each of Clay's claims, but most importantly he indicated the sense of betrayal felt by the Soviets. Clay's refusal to deliver

---

[37] The temporary suspension became permanent on 26 May 1945. Clay claimed that industrial plants and equipment already allocated for shipment to the Soviet zone under the LIP would still be delivered. According to Kuklick, however, even by October 1946 'the Allies had removed only five of the 1850 plants scheduled for dismantling in the west under the LIP'. Kuklick, *American Policy and the Division of Germany*, 233.

[38] Ibid.

[39] GARF – f. r-7317, op. 4, d. 83, l. 122. For Clay's recollections see L. D. Clay, *Decision in Germany* (Garden City, NY: Doubleday, 1950).

reparations to the Soviets and his demand that they limit dismantling made it impossible for the Soviets to use the German economy to help reconstruct their own. The 'spirit' of the reparations programme was being undermined. Not without a trace of incredulity, then, the final part of Sokolovskii's reply to Clay reads:

> I would consider it unfair to relate the issue of dismantling to this particular factory in any such way with the fulfilment of our agreed reparations programme . . . You know that our food industry was destroyed by the German occupation, including nearly all the factories in southern Russia that produce maize.[40]

Unfair or not, the Soviets had little recourse against Allied threats and their broader intransigent position that hardened throughout May in the wake of the Soviet 'failure'.[41] The gridlock continued until the Soviets finally took decisive action in June. The growing prospect of economic isolation from the western zones cast new light on the devastation wrought on their own zone by dismantling and highlighted the need for change. The leadership now started to listen to SVAG's arguments calling for alternative economic policies.

Some historians have noted that the breakdown of economic cooperation in Germany gave the essential impetus to those in Moscow and Berlin pushing for an end to dismantling policy.[42] The push became stronger in June 1946 when the Americans announced plans to unify their zone with the British, and an investigation launched by the Central Committee criticised the failures of dismantling policy.[43] The chief criticism was

---

[40] GARF – f. r-7317, op. 4, d. 85, l. 80.

[41] The reason for the shift in American thinking towards cooperation with the Soviets has long been a contentious issue in the literature. Clay's greater independence from Washington has often led to a closer focus on his behaviour towards the Soviets, which, at least initially, was quite positive in comparison towards the French. For a discussion of the shift in behaviour that takes a broader view of the situation, particularly how US foreign policy thinking discouraged cooperation with the Soviets and led to the division of Germany see C. Eisenberg, *Drawing the Line: The American Decision to Divide Germany, 1944–1949* (New York: Cambridge University Press, 1996). For another work that analyses a range of policy influences on the Truman administration see M. Wala, *The Council on Foreign Relations and American Foreign Policy in the Early Cold War* (Providence, RI: Berghahn Books, 1994). For a more traditional 'western' understanding of the shift that allocates primary blame to the Soviets see J. Gimbel, *The Origins of the Marshall Plan* (Stanford, Calif.: Stanford University Press, 1976). Kuklick's 'revisionist' critique of Gimbel's work is also most useful. B. Kuklick, 'The Origins of the Marshall Plan?', *Reviews in American History* 5, no. 2 (1977).

[42] Loth, *Stalin's Unwanted Child*, 44–5.

[43] This investigation was launched by A. A. Zhdanov and N. A. Voznesenskii, chief rivals of the head of the dismantling programme, G. M. Malenkov. R. Medvedev, *All Stalin's Men*, trans. H. Shukman (Oxford: Blackwell, 1983), 147–8. Other 'investigations' were launched against Malenkov during this time as well. For instance, Malenkov was implicated in the 'Shakurin affair', where the former People's Commissar of the Aviation

that poor and incomplete dismantling practices often damaged German factories and machines so badly that they could not be reconstructed in the Soviet Union, hampering the post-war recovery. The environment was thus most conducive to policy change. Yet historians have failed to note that it was SVAG's most intelligent dealings with Moscow within this new environment that really sealed the fate of dismantling. SVAG reports promised to use Germany's economy to assist in the homeland's post-war reconstruction, but their fine print struck a balance between rebuilding both.

Sokolovskii was somewhat more sensitive than Zhukov to the economic and social consequences caused by dismantling. After he replaced Zhukov as commander-in-chief of SVAG in March 1946, he warned Moscow that it was impossible to regulate the Soviet zone's economy with the dismantling organs running rampant.[44] The leadership began listening to his warnings in the summer of 1945, but it was only when Sokolovskii began discussing the negative impact of dismantling in Germany on the Soviet economy that it really took notice. When he and his new allies in Moscow demonstrated how he could deliver greater reparations from Germany by ending the dismantling programme, he gained the leadership's full attention.

In June the Council of Ministers (Sovmin) ordered that 300,000 tonnes of scrap metal were to be removed from Germany and sent to the Soviet Union to fulfil the five-year plan. SVAG economic chiefs co-authored a letter with Minister of Foreign Trade A. I. Mikoyan to Sovmin which argued that this was impossible. The independent dismantling organs, particularly the Special Committee, could not achieve set reparations goals because their members dismantled plants only on behalf of the commissariats/ministries[45] to which they belonged, rather than in accordance with common reparations goals. Poor dismantling practice also made most of the industrial booty unusable when it arrived back home. The only way that this quota could be met was if these organs were disbanded and SVAG were given complete control over this project and the entire dismantling programme, that is, if SVAG were given complete control over the zone. And it was only to be expected that the letter should promise that a unified and technically efficient reparations approach under SVAG control would deliver not 300,000 tonnes of scrap metal,

Industry A. I. Shakurin was charged with allowing the production of defective airplanes during the war. G. Ra'anan, *International Policy Formation in the USSR: Factional 'Debates' during the Zhdanovschina* (Hamden, Conn.: Archon Books), 22–3.

[44] GARF – f. r-7317, op. 4, d. 85, ll. 1–2.

[45] The Council of People's Commissars (Sovnarkom) changed its name to the Council of Ministers (Sovmin) in March 1946, when all commissars and commissariats became ministers and ministries respectively.

but 600,000. Mikoyan was well aware that the promise of huge industrial booty was the best lubricant possible to help quicken the usually sluggish gears of change in the Soviet bureaucratic machine.[46]

The letter also promised that a SVAG-controlled dismantling programme would achieve its set goals in the shortest possible time. SVAG would then be able to scale down and eventually terminate the dismantling policy. It would not be abandoned, but completed.[47] This didn't mean that the Soviets would cease to take reparations, but that they would try to take them in a way that didn't hamper the long-term sustainability of the zone's economy. In short, the letter provided a blueprint of policy change from 'economic destruction' to 'economic sustainability'. The blueprint was accepted by Sovmin immediately and without amendment.[48] Perhaps this was to be expected. Mikoyan was a deputy president of Sovmin and the Special Committee was technically under Sovmin's jurisdiction. The chief of the dismantling process, Malenkov, was hardly able to protest, as he was skating on thin ice in the Far East and his opponents were gathering strength in highlighting his failures in Germany and at home.

The blueprint for 'economic sustainability' was timetabled. Special Committee representatives were ordered to leave the zone by 1 August 1946, except for engineers and other technically capable staff that were to be transferred to SVAG.[49] Sokolovskii expected to complete the entire dismantling project by the end of the year. To replace reparations lost from dismantling, provisions were made to establish Soviet–German-owned joint-stock companies (SGAOs) under the control of the Foreign Ministry of Trade. Now the Soviets would invest in local production and take reparations in the form of finished industrial product. It seems that this prospect was certainly another factor in gathering Mikoyan's support for policy change.[50] Yet even though the Soviets continued to bleed SGAO production lines and German ownership of them was only

---

[46] GARF – f. r-7317, op. 4, d. 85, l. 123. Attaining the scrap metal target did not require the removal of many new factories. Dismantlers tended to remove mostly valuable machinery from factories, either destroying their metal infrastructure in the process or leaving it on site. Now SVAG would focus on recuperating these structures and other scraps. By 1 November 1946, 325,000 tonnes of scrap metal had already been removed. Of this amount, 144,000 tonnes had already been sent to the Soviet Union. GARF – f. r-7317, op. 7, d. 37, l. 166.

[47] GARF – f. r-7317, op. 4, d. 85, l. 125.   [48] GARF – f. r-7317, op. 4, d. 85, ll. 135–6.

[49] GARF – f. r-7317, op. 4, d. 85, l. 137.

[50] Import/export groups under the jurisdiction of the Ministry of Foreign Trade were already working closely with the SVAG Reparations and Supply Administration, removing finished industrial product from German production lines for reparations purposes. SVAG's new control over the reparations programme promised Mikoyan greater access to German products that could be used for Soviet exports.

nominal, SGAOs were eventually important in rejuvenating the economy and laying the foundation for the future economic sustainability of the GDR. In fact, most SGAOs were handed over to the GDR after 1949. Such transfers of wealth and power were inconceivable without such an entity as the SED to facilitate them.[51]

The schedule for achieving economic sustainability was not uninterrupted. The ministries in Moscow had lost the main mechanism for satisfying their appetite for industrial booty with the dissolution of the Special Committee, but they found others. The June Sovmin order failed to dissolve all dismantling groups, meaning that they continued to rampage across the zone until Sokolovskii could pick them off one by one. He was successful by the end of the year, at least in administrative terms. Another Sovmin order called for all remaining groups to be dissolved and, by New Year's Day 1947, their staff and equipment transferred to SVAG.[52] The policy change was complete and remaining dismantling works were to be wound up within four months.

This was a massive achievement for Sokolovskii. As long as armies of dismantlers pillaged the zone of factories and materials, SVAG had found it most difficult to plan local economies and avoid massive shortfalls in materials and even essential services. This difficulty was compounded by having to satisfy dismantling orders for power stations etc. from commissariats in Moscow who cared nothing about the impact of such removals on the local area. Now it was possible for SVAG to begin working closely with the SED and related organs such as the German Economic Commission (DWK) to plan for economic growth without interference from the dismantlers and even the troops.[53] The massive reduction of

---

[51] A. L. Phillips, *Soviet Policy toward East Germany Reconsidered: The Postwar Decade* (Westport, Conn.: Greenwood Press, 1986), 33.

[52] GARF – f. r-7317, op. 1, d. 87, ll. 116–17. In a letter to Voznesenskii on 29 November 1946, Sokolovskii complained that some ten battalions attached to GSOVG and under the jurisdiction of the Ministry of Defence were continuing to fulfil dismantling orders from various Soviet ministries for a range of non-military industrial equipment months after the Sovmin order had come into effect. He suggested that instead of simply dissolving the battalions and sending the men home, it would be more profitable to bring them all under SVAG control. The fact is that by December 1946, Sokolovskii realised that he was short of skilled manpower and argued that with thousands more experienced dismantlers at his disposal, and only at his disposal, SVAG would be able to complete the final and most difficult stage of the dismantling and disarmament programme within the promised four months. Sokolovskii requested 4,100 dismantling supervisors (one for every ten German workers), 1,800 guards to protect dismantling sites, and another 750 for transport duties. GARF – f. r-7317, op. 1, d. 87, ll. 113–15.

[53] For the gradual development of central economic planning in the zone see B. Niedbalski, 'Deutsche Zentralverwaltungen und Deutsche Wirtschaftskommission (DWK): Ansätze zur zentralen Wirtschaftsplanung in der SBZ 1945–1948', *Vierteljahrshefte für Zeitgeschichte* 33, no. 3 (1985).

occupation forces by the middle of 1947 made it easier to keep them sequestered in the barracks, which severely limited the violence and the arbitrary requisitioning of food from German farmers. Significant problems still remained, but the reduction of violence, more secure levels of food and industrial supply, and the greater delegation of power to the SED finally brought an end to the chaos of the first years of the occupation.

The extent to which Soviet policy changed in response to a range of factors, including a breakdown of Allied cooperation and leadership stoushes in Moscow, suggests that Soviet thinking about Germany after the war was inherently flexible and even 'opportunistic', to use Naimark's term.[54] Yet by 1947 the flexible Soviet approach had less room to bend in the more rigid relationship with the Allies. The growing rift with the Allies empowered those sections of the leadership who saw Germany as the first line of defence against western intervention into Eastern Europe rather than a space in which Soviet–Allied cooperation could develop. This understanding of Soviet policy change is irreconcilable with the view proposed by Petrov and others that Stalin always intended to 'sovietise' the zone.

But this doesn't mean that SVAG did not go about rebuilding war-torn Germany in the only way it knew – 'Soviet style' – or that Stalin did not desire a broader 'security belt' of other Eastern European nations to defend the Soviet Union from future invasions. The creation of a monolithic mass party, the nationalisation of banks, land reform, etc. in the zone were all structures of economic and political control that resembled those built during the development of the young Soviet revolutionary state. But these structures were not fixed or exclusively 'Soviet' in nature. Statebuilders on the ground learnt how to establish control over an occupied territory in completely unfamiliar conditions of electoral politics requiring more refined tactics than back home. It was on these structures, initially built to reconstruct a war-torn country and establish Soviet control, that the Soviet satellite, or the GDR, was eventually built. Petrov may be accurate in arguing that many of these structures inhibited economic/ political integration with the western zones. Yet the problem lies in assuming that Stalin and the Soviet leadership understood that this was the case during 1945 and 1946 and proceeded with building them anyway. The evidence presented here suggests otherwise. There was no straight line from establishing control in 1945 and the birth of the GDR in 1949. The Soviets initially desired cooperation with the Allies, yet failed to achieve it on terms advantageous to them. That their failure may have

---

[54] Naimark, *The Russians in Germany*, 9.

resulted, at least in part, from their mis/understanding of how to reconstruct a war-torn country was indeed, to use Petrov's term, more a fault of
habit than intention.[55]

Tragically, the Soviets only realised they had failed once it was too late.
In their December 1948 meeting in Moscow, Stalin advised SED leaders
that their attempts at building socialism in the zone would be compromised as long as Germany remained divided. He suggested that they not
only propagandise in favour of zonal unification, but that they pursue
'opportunist polices' aimed at increasing their popularity in the western
zones, rather than the 'Soviet style' socialisation measures that they were
proposing, such as smashing the 'kulaks'.[56] Thus even at the height of the
Berlin blockade and, perhaps, partly because of it, it seems that Stalin still
believed that Soviet–Allied relations could be mended, the zones united,
and that the SED could play a dominant political role in a new and unified
Germany. He wanted to turn the clock back to 1945, when this thinking
was dominant and much more feasible.

By the end of 1948 it was neither. The Allies were deaf to Stalin's offers
of unification envisaging a united Germany based on 'democratic principles', and only a few of his lieutenants remained open to the idea. Upon
Stalin's death in 1953, Malenkov and Beria sparred bitterly with the
ideologues in the leadership over this question. Both supported zonal
unification on a 'bourgeois–democratic basis' in their own way and were
willing to relinquish considerable influence to an all-German elected
government to realise this aim. They reasoned that Soviet–Allied cooperation over Germany promised to be far more advantageous to the long-
term security of the Soviet Union than simply continuing the current
divisive policy of supporting an isolated and economically feeble satellite
state.[57] Despite the soundness of their reasoning, Beria's fall in the immediate aftermath of Stalin's death gave ultimate victory to the ideologues,
destroying any possibility of unification that remained.

[55] This conclusion has some parallels with those made by Zubok and Pleshakov in their work
on the Cold War, particularly those regarding Stalin's desire to continue the Grand
Alliance in the post-war period. C. Pleshakov and V. Zubok, *Inside the Kremlin's Cold
War: From Stalin to Khrushchev* (Cambridge, Mass.: Harvard University Press, 1996),
275–7.
[56] A. D. Chernev, "Nuzhno idti k sotsializmu ne priamo, a zigzagami": Zapis' besedy I. V.
Stalina s rukovoditeliami SEPG. Dekabr' 1948 g.', *Istoricheskii Arkhiv* 5 (2002): 11.
[57] A. M. Filitov, 'Germany will Be a Bourgeois–Democratic Republic: The New Evidence
from the Personal File of Georgiy Malenkov', *Cold War History* 6, no. 4 (2006).

Conclusion

Zhukov never saw the 'end of chaos' for which he had fought so long. Stalin removed him from his major posts in March 1946 and eventually appointed him to a lower-level district military command in the Soviet hinterland. This was perhaps to be expected given Stalin's growing concerns about the power of the military brass operating far beyond Soviet borders. In any case, Stalin's new title of Generalissimus and Soviet propaganda's lauding of him as the most outstanding war leader in history sat uneasily with Zhukov's growing popularity as the most outstanding general of the war at home and especially in the West. There could be only one sun in the socialist universe.[1]

Yet Zhukov's sun did not set in March 1946, as his influence on the occupation endured long after his removal. His successes in establishing law and order, greater ones in reconstructing essential services, agriculture, and the political landscape under the most unpropitious circumstances, helped to stabilise the zone and made more feasible the adoption of a long-term occupation strategy towards Germany by 1947. He inspired some of his men to contemplate seriously their duty as occupiers before history and the gravity of this historical moment. At his meeting with SVAG and army chiefs in August 1945, he offered them a 'choice' – either allow the violence to continue and sow the seeds of hatred in Germany for generations to come, or do everything they can to end the violence and lay the foundation for mutual respect between the two nations.[2] His chiefs listened intently and spread his message to their subordinates. Some understood it better than others, especially in SVAG, and fought with a fanaticism to secure law and order in their *komendaturas* far beyond the limited mandate which they were given to do so. As with Zhukov, the horrors of German occupation had inspired

---

[1] For the political intrigue surrounding Zhukov's removal see Petrov, *Pervyi predsedatel' KGB Ivan Serov*, 68–9.

[2] Zakharov, ed., *Deiatel'nost' sovetskikh voennykh komendatur*, 95.

them less to seek vengeance, and more the peace which they craved after years at war.

These idealists found little peace in the zone. The war may have been over, but it had not ended for those soldiers committing the violence and their officers who allowed it to continue. Having lost more in victory than their enemies in defeat, both were deaf to Zhukov's magnanimous tones – the millions of liberated slaves even more so. Many soldiers would not return to families ready to embrace them as the heroes in those moving scenes which filled Soviet film screens after the war, but to destroyed villages and towns that left no trace of their loved ones – at least above ground. This sense of foreboding was ever present among occupation forces in Germany awaiting return and even among SVAG officers and men who needed to wait longer. Zhukov and his fellows refused to accept that their pain should interfere with their duty as occupiers. Anticipating a positive response to his ultimatum at the August meeting, Zhukov continued to the point of delusion:

In my capacity as Supreme Commander, I demand that this situation [the violence] quickly cease and will not take into account any complications of this matter. If we are required ... to shoot several tens of thousands of people, then we shall do it.[3]

Ever the ruthless humanitarian, he could have shot them and more, but it would not have tackled the roots of the problem. It was simply beyond his or anyone else's control. Stalin understood that his troops needed to keep fighting after the war ended against civilians and even each other, Zhukov did not. The structure of occupation governance which emerged in Germany ensured that they did continue fighting and that Zhukov and his dutiful men could do little to stop them.

A chorus of historians has long indicted Stalin for devising a paradoxical occupation strategy in Germany, which engendered this structure unable to function efficiently under the weight of its own ineptitude. He allowed and even encouraged occupation organs to pursue conflicting aims, and in their bureaucratic wrangling over resources and jurisdictional power they struggled to function, let alone achieve these aims. We may add that with jurisdictional lines blurred to a much greater extent than in the Soviet Union and without a dominant organ in Germany to keep the others in check, a new type of conflict emerged in Germany unseen back home. Stalin's sporadic interventions in occupation affairs exacerbated it. By stifling Zhukov's draconian measures to put an end to troop violence in September 1945, Stalin allowed it to become the central dispute between

---

[3] GARF – f. r-7317, op. 7, d. 14, l. 12.

the wrangling organs. SVAG's attempts to tackle the problem independently by arresting more and more army officers and men only aggravated the jurisdictional tension that hindered the cooperation which may have reduced the violence. As the same chorus of historians argues, violence and broader repressive policies engendered an everlasting hatred of the Soviet occupiers and their German allies across the country, rendering their creation, the GDR, illegitimate in German eyes. Occupiers are thus cast by the chorus as boorish fools incapable of anticipating the consequences of their actions.

But Stalin was no fool. Bad blood between SVAG, the army, and especially the NKVD was preferable to unity in his system, especially when operating far beyond Soviet borders. The more they gnawed at one another's throats, the less they could gnaw at his. And as long as the dismantled factories kept on coming from Germany, which was part of the broader aim of eliminating the country's war-making potential, nothing else really mattered too much. Why then was SVAG assigned the conflicting aims of assisting with dismantling and reconstructing local economies? For Moscow at least, these aims were not necessarily contradictory, as it only afforded SVAG enough jurisdictional power to achieve the first. This was very much the point, that local concerns in Germany were second-tier and, as it turned out, were to be pursued in the dust storm of economic devastation and mass resentment created by dismantling and the continuation of troop violence. This was SVAG's lot, which makes their successes in rebuilding Germany until mid 1946 all the more impressive.

Until then much of the leadership in Moscow still envisaged a short-term occupation giving way to a weak quasi-government to administer a unified country. The consequences of their economic policies were unimportant because they would not be there to suffer them. In fact, until mid 1946 these were not 'consequences' at all. They became such when strains between the Allies emerged, making unification unlikely and forcing Stalin to reckon on a long-term occupation. The devastated economy of the zone was now less a guarantor of German neutrality and more a burden on the Soviets who needed to rebuild what they had destroyed. Ending the dismantling programme, SGAOs, and pushing for an end to the violence were all part of this shift in outlook. Until then, Stalin had little reason to be too concerned about how his policies reflected poorly on the KPD/SED. Now they and the electorate assumed greater importance. Some in his close circle had always afforded them such, and the natural inclination of 'political officers' on the ground better reflected their positions, particularly in building the SED. There was, therefore, a basis upon which the leadership in Moscow and Berlin could make this shift and rebuild the country in its distorted image. This shift gained greater momentum as the violence eventually subsided in 1947. By the middle of the year mass demobilisation had reduced the occupation force to 350,000 troops, who were much easier to lock in the barracks and keep away from the population – the only way really to deal with the problem. But in many ways the damage had already been done. Much of the population despised the Soviet-sponsored party which Stalin needed now more than ever to control the zone, which had become a violent industrial wasteland.

However, it did not become one of the dead zones (*Tote Zonen*) that the Germans had left strewn across the western parts of the Soviet Union. For all of the violence, terror, and arbitrary rule which characterised daily life in the zone during the first years of the occupation, there were no mass killings, forced starvations, and the millions of corpses these left. We should not lose sight of what was at stake in 1945, that the most pressing question during the advance was whether the Soviets would now let the Germans live – life which the Germans had denied them. They did. SVAG's Herculean efforts to feed the German population so soon after German occupation forces starved millions of Soviet citizens to death remains an enduring testimony to the intelligence and humanity of its officers. It did not improve relations between occupiers and occupied for long, however, as Zhukov was correct to fear that the violence would undo much of the Soviets' good work and help sow the seeds of German hatred for decades to come. But at least they were left alive to spit it. Twenty million of Zhukov's civilian countrymen and ten million of his comrades were stripped of their chance to hate or forgive, as were their children who were never born.[4]

---

[4] Krivosheev's work is at the forefront of the fraught casualties' debate. G. F. Krivosheev, ed. *Rossiia i SSSR v voinakh* xx *veka: Poteri vooruzhennykh sil. Istoriko-statisticheskoe issledovanie* (Moscow: Olma-Press, 2001).

Map

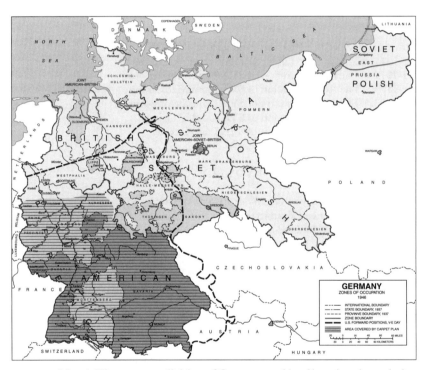

Map 1 The post-war division of Germany and land/province boundaries in the Soviet occupation zone. After E. F. Ziemke, *The U.S. Army in the Occupation of Germany 1944–1946*. Army Historical Series (Washington, DC: Center of Military History, United States Army, 1990), back cover.

Bibliography

PRIMARY SOURCES

ARCHIVES

State Archive of the Russian Federation – GARF
f. r-7317   The Soviet Military Administration in Germany (SVAG)
f. r-7077   The Administration of SVA Land Brandenburg
f. r-7103   The Administration of SVA Land Mecklenburg
f. r-7133   The Administration of SVA Land Saxony-Anhalt
f. r-7184   The Administration of SVA Land Thuringia
f. r-7212   The Administration of SVA Land Saxony
f. r-5446   Sovnarkom/Sovmin
f. r-7021   ChGK
f. r-9401   Secretariat of the NKVD/MVD

Russian State Archive of Socio-Political History – RGASPI
f. 644   State Defence Committee (GKO)
f. 17   Central Committee of the Communist Party – TsK VKP (b)

Russian State Economic Archive (RGAE)
f. 1562   Central Statistical Administration of the USSR

SOURCE COLLECTIONS/PUBLISHED DOCUMENTS

Adibekov, G. M., K. M. Anderson, and L. A. Rogovaia. *Politbiuro Tsk RKP(b) – VKP(b). Povestki dnia zasedanii. 1919–1952: Katalog v 3-kh tomakh.* Moscow: Rosspen, 2000–1.

Bonvech [Bonwetsch], B., G. A. Bordiugov, L. P. Kosheleva, and L. A. Rogovaia. 'Nasha liniia takaia: Dokumenty o vstreche I. V. Stalina s rukovoditeliami SEPG. Ianvar'–fevral' 1947 g'. *Istoricheskii Arkhiv* 4 (1994): 22–44.

Bonvech [Bonwetsch], B., G. Bordiugov, and N. Neimark [Naimark], eds. *Sovetskaia voennaia administratsiia v Germanii: Upravlenie propagandy (infor-matsii) i S. I. Tiul'panov. 1945–1949 gg. Sbornik dokumentov.* Moscow and St Petersburg: AIRO–Pervaia Publikatsiia, 2006.

Chernev, A. D. '"Nuzhno idti k sotsializmu ne priamo, a zigzagami": Zapis' besedy I. V. Stalina s rukovoditeliami SEPG. Dekabr' 1948 g'. *Istoricheskii Arkhiv* 5 (2002): 3–26.

Doronin, A. V., J. Foitzik, and T. V. Tsarevskaia-Diakina, eds. *Sovetskaia voennaia administratsiia v Germanii, 1945–1949: Spravochnik.* Moscow: Rosspen, 2009.

Erlikhman, V. *Poteri narodonaseleniia v XX veke: Spravochnik.* Moscow: Russkaia Panorama, 2004.

Filitov, A. M. 'SSSR i Germanskii vopros. 1941–1949; Dokumenty iz arkhiva vneshnei politiki MID Rossii'. *Novaia i Noveishaia Istoriia* 4 (2000): 128–39.

Foitzik, J., and N. P. Timofeeva, eds. *Politika SVAG v oblasti kul'tury, nauki i obrazovaniia: Tseli, metody, rezul'taty 1945–1949. Sbornik dokumentov.* Moscow: Rosspen, 2006.

Great Britain Foreign Office. 'Weekly Political Intelligence Summaries'. October 1947.

Khlevniuk, O., ed. *Politbiuro Tsk VKP(b) i Sovet Ministrov SSSR 1945–1953.* Moscow: Rosspen, 2002.

Kosheleva, G. A., A. I. Miniuk, L. A. Rogovaia, and E. I. Zubkova, eds. *Sovetskaia zhizn, 1945–1953: Dokumenty sovetskoi istorii.* Moscow: Rosspen, 2003.

Kynin, G. P. *SSSR i germanskii vopros 1941–1949: Dokumenty iz arkhiva vneshnei politiki MID Rossiiskoi Federatsii.* Moscow: Mezhdunarodnye Otnosheniia, 1996.

Mironenko, S. V., ed. *Spetsial'nye lageria NKVD/MVD SSSR v Germanii 1945–1950: Sbornik dokumentov i statei.* Vol. II. Moscow: Rosspen, 2001.

Office of Military Government for Germany, US. 'Report of the Military Governor: Statistical Annex', no. 34, April 1948.

Petrov, N. V., ed. *SVAG i nemetskie organy samoupravleniia 1945–1949: Sbornik dokumentov.* Moscow: Rosspen, 2006.

Russkii arkhiv: Velikaia Otechestvennaia voina. Bitva za Berlin. Vol. XV. Moscow: Terra, 1995.

Sevost'ianov, G. N., ed. *Sovetsko-Amerikanskie otnosheniia 1939–1945: Dokumenty.* Moscow: Materik, 2004.

    ed. *Sovetsko-amerikanskie otnosheniia 1945–1948: Dokumenty.* Moscow: Materik, 2004.

UN. 'Monthly Bulletin of Statistics'. New York, July 1948.

Velikaia Otechestvennaia voina. Prikazy narodnogo kommisara oborony SSSR, 22 iiunia 1941g.–1942 g. Vol. XIII. Moscow: Terra 1997.

Zakharov, V. V., ed. *Deiatel'nost' sovetskikh voennykh komendatur po likvidatsii posledstvii voiny i organizatsii mirnoi zhizni v sovetskoi zone okkupatsii Germanii 1945–1949: Sbornik dokumentov.* Moscow: Rosspen, 2005.

    ed. *Deiatel'nost' Sovetskoi voennoi administratsii v Germanii (SVAG) po demilitarizatsii Sovetskoi zony okkupatsii Germanii, 1945–1949: Sbornik dokumentov.* Moscow: Rosspen, 2004.

PERIODICALS

Izvestiia, 1941–7.
Krasnaia Zvezda, 1941–5.
Pravda, 1941–7.

MEMOIRS

Anonymous. *A Woman in Berlin: Eight Weeks in the Conquered City, A Diary.* Translated by P. Boehm. New York: Metropolitan Books/Henry Holt, 2005.

Bokov, F. E. *Vesna pobedy.* Moscow: Mysl', 1985.

Cairncross, A. *A Country to Play With: Level of Industry Negotiations in Berlin 1945–46.* Gerrards Cross: Colin Smythe, 1987.

Clay, L. D. *Decision in Germany.* Garden City, NY: Doubleday, 1950.

Djilas, M. *Conversations with Stalin.* Translated by M. B. Petrovich. New York: Harcourt, Brace & World, 1962.

Kahn, A. D. *Experiment in Occupation: Witness to the Turnabout. Anti-Nazi War to Cold War, 1944–6.* University Park, Pa.: State University Press, 2004.

Klimov, G. *The Terror Machine: The Inside Story of the Soviet Administration in Germany.* Translated by H. C. Stevens. New York: Praeger, 1953.

Kolesnichenko, I. S. *Bitva posle voiny: O poslevoennoi zhizni v Germanii.* Moscow: Voenizdat, 1987.

Koval', K. I. 'Na postu zamestitelia glavnonachal'stvuiushchego SVAG 1945–1949 gg.'. *Novaia i Noveishaia Istoriia* (1987), no. 3: 130–48.

Poslednii svidetel': 'germanskaia karta' v kholodnoi voine. Moscow: Rosspen, 1997.

'Rabota v Germanii po zadaniiu GKO'. *Novaia i Noveishaia Istoriia* (1995), no. 2: 101–14.

'Zapiski upolnomochennogo GKO na territorii Germanii'. *Novaia i Noveishaia Istoriia* (1994), no. 3: 124–47.

Leonhard, W. *Child of the Revolution.* Translated by C. M. Woodhouse. Chicago: H. Regnery Co., 1956.

Mikoyan, A. *Tak bylo.* Edited by S. I. Mikoyan. Moscow: Vagrius, 1999.

Ratchford, B.U. *Berlin Reparations Assignment: Round One of the German Peace Settlement.* Chapel Hill, NC: University of North Carolina Press, 1947.

Resis, A., ed. *Molotov Remembers: Inside Kremlin Politics. Conversations with Felix Chuev.* Chicago: I. R. Dee, 1993.

Schaffer, G. *Russian Zone.* London: published for the Co-operative Press by G. Allen & Unwin, 1947.

Semiriaga, M. I. *Kak my upravliali Germaniei: Politika i zhizn'.* Moscow: Rosspen, 1995.

Solzhenitsyn, A. *Prussian Nights: A Narrative Poem.* Translated by R. Conquest. London: Collins and Harvil Press, 1977.

Zhukov, G. K. *Vospominaniia i razmyshleniia.* Moscow: OLMA-Press, 2002.

Zhukova, M. G. *Marshal Zhukov – moi otets.* Moscow: Izdatel'stvo Sretenskogo monastyria, 2005.

SECONDARY SOURCES

BOOKS AND ARTICLES

Abrams, L., and E. Harvey, eds. *Gender Relations in German History: Power, Agency, and Experience from the Sixteenth to the Twentieth Century.* Durham: Duke University Press, 1997.

Adomeit, H. *Imperial Overstretch: Germany in Soviet Policy from Stalin to Gorbachev. An Analysis Based on Archival Evidence, Memoirs, and Interviews.* Baden-Baden: Nomos Verlagsgesellschaft, 1998.

Allen, D. J. *The Oder–Neisse Line: The United States, Poland, and Germany in the Cold War.* Westport, Conn.: Praeger 2003.

Barnes, S. A. 'All for the Front, All for Victory! The Mobilization of Forced Labor in the Soviet Union During World War Two'. *International Labor and Working-Class History* 58 (2000): 239–60.

Beisel, D. R. 'The German Suicide, 1945'. *Journal of Psychohistory* 34, no. 4 (Spring 2007): 302–13.

Bellinger, E. G., and N. M. Dronin. *Climate Dependence and Food Problems in Russia 1900–1990: The Interaction of Climate and Agricultural Policy and their Effect on Food Problems.* New York: Central European University Press, 2005.

Bergson, A., J. H. Blackman, and A. Erlich. 'Postwar Economic Reconstruction and Development in the U.S.S.R.'. *Annals of the American Academy of Political and Social Science* 263 (1949): 52–72.

Bessel, R. *Germany 1945: From War to Peace.* New York: HarperCollins, 2009.

'Hatred after War: Emotion and the Postwar History of East Germany'. *History and Memory* 17, nos. 1–2 (2005): 195–216.

Bessel, R., and D. Schumann, eds. *Life after Death: Approaches to a Cultural and Social History During the 1940s and 1950s.* New York: Cambridge University Press, 2003.

Biddiscombe, P. 'Dangerous Liaisons: The Anti-Fraternization Movement in the U.S. Occupation Zones of Germany and Austria, 1945–1948'. *Journal of Social History* 34, no. 3 (2001): 611–47.

Werwolf! The History of the National Socialist Guerrilla Movement, 1944–1946. Toronto: University of Toronto Press, 1998.

Biess, F. 'Pioneers of a New Germany: Returning POWs from the Soviet Union and the Making of East German Citizens, 1945–1950'. *Central European History* 32, no. 2 (1999): 143–80.

Biess, F., and R. G. Moeller, eds. *Histories of the Aftermath: The Legacies of the Second World War in Europe.* New York: Berghahn Books, 2010.

Bletzer, K. V. 'A Voice for Every Woman and the Travesties of War'. *Violence against Women* 12, no. 7 (2006): 700–5.

Bodenman, P. S. *Education in the Soviet Zone of Germany.* Washington: U.S. Dept. of Health, Education and Welfare, 1959.

Bramsted, E. K. *Goebbels and National Socialist Propaganda, 1925–1945.* Michigan: Cresset Press, 1965.

Brand, E. 'Nazi Criminals on Trial in the Soviet Union (1961–1965)'. *Yad Vashem Bulletin* 19 (1966): 36–44.

Bruce, G. *Resistance with the People: Repression and Resistance in Eastern Germany 1945–55.* Lanham: Rowman & Littlefield, 2003.

Budde, G. F. 'Der Körper der "Sozialistischen Frauenpersönlichkeit": Weiblichkeits-Vorstellungen in der SBZ und frühen DDR'. *Geschichte und Gesellschaft* 26, no. 4 (2000): 602–28.

Buhite, R. D., ed. *Major Crises in Contemporary American Foreign Policy: A Documentary History.* Westport, Conn.: Greenwood Press, 1997.

Burds, J. *The Early Cold War in Soviet West Ukraine 1944–1948*. Russian and East European Studies no. 1505, 2001.

    'Sexual Violence in Europe in World War II 1939–1945'. *Politics and Society* 37, no. 1 (2009): 35–73.

Collingham, E. M. *The Taste of War: World War Two and the Battle for Food*. London: Allen Lane, 2011.

Conquest, R. *The Great Terror: A Reassessment*. New York: Oxford University Press, 1990.

Creuzberger, S. 'The Soviet Military Administration and East German Elections'. *Australian Journal of Political History* 45, no. 1 (1999): 89–98.

Croan, M. 'Soviet Uses of the Doctrine of the "Parliamentary Road" to Socialism: East Germany 1945–1946'. *American Slavic and East European Review* 17, no. 3 (1958): 302–15.

Crowfoot, J., and H. M. Harrison. 'The USSR Council of Ministers under Late Stalinism, 1945–1954: Its Production Branch Composition and the Requirements of National Economy and Policy'. *Soviet Studies* 42, no. 1 (1990): 39–58.

Dallin, A. *German Rule in Russia, 1941–1945: A Study in Occupation Policies*. London: Macmillan, 1981.

Davies, R. W., M. Harrison, and S. G. Wheatcroft, eds. *The Economic Transformation of the Soviet Union, 1913–1945*. Cambridge and New York: Cambridge University Press, 1994.

Davies, S., and J. Harris, eds. *Stalin: A New History*. New York: Cambridge University Press, 2005.

De Zayas, A. M. *A Terrible Revenge: The Ethnic Cleansing of the East European Germans, 1944–50*. New York: St. Martin's Press, 1994.

Dennis, M. *The Rise and Fall of the German Democratic Republic, 1945–1990*. Harlow: Longman, 2000.

Diehl, J. M. 'Germany in Defeat, 1918 and 1945: Some Comparisons and Contrasts'. *The History Teacher* 22, no. 4 (1989): 397–409.

Duffy, C. R. *Red Storm on the Reich: The Russians March on Germany, 1945*. New York: Routledge, 1991.

Dunmore, T. *The Stalinist Command Economy: The Soviet State Apparatus and Economic Policy 1945–53*. London: Macmillan, 1980.

Dunn, W. S. *Hitler's Nemesis: The Red Army, 1930–1945*. Westport, Conn.: Praeger, 1994.

Duskin, E. J. *Stalinist Reconstruction and the Confirmation of a New Elite*. Wiltshire: Palgrave, 2001.

Edele, M. 'A "Generation of Victors?" Soviet Second World War Veterans from Demobilisation to Organisation 1941–1956', unpublished PhD thesis, University of Chicago, 2004.

    'Paper Soldiers: The World of the Soldier Hero according to Soviet Wartime Posters'. *Jahrbücher für Geschichte Osteuropas* 47, no. 1 (1999): 89–108.

Eisenberg, C. *Drawing the Line: The American Decision to Divide Germany, 1944–1949*. New York: Cambridge University Press, 1996.

Elliott, M. 'The United States and Forced Repatriation of Soviet Citizens, 1944–47'. *Political Science Quarterly* 88, no. 2 (1973): 253–5.

Emel'ianov, I. V. *Stalin: na vershine vlasti.* Moscow: Veche, 2003.

Evans, J. V. 'Bahnof Boys: Policing Male Prostitution in Post-Nazi Berlin'. *Journal of the History of Sexuality* 12, no. 4 (2003): 605–36.

Evdokimov, R. B., ed. *Liudskie poteri SSSR v period vtoroi mirovoi voiny: Sbornik statei.* St Petersburg: Russko-Baltiiskii Informatsionnyi Tsentr BLITS, 1995.

Farquharson, J. E. 'Anglo-American Policy on German Reparations from Yalta to Potsdam'. *The English Historical Review* 112, no. 448 (1997): 904–26.

The Western Allies and the Politics of Food: Agrarian Management in Postwar Germany. Leamington Spa: Berg, 1985.

Figes, O. 'The Red Army and Mass Mobilization during the Russian Civil War 1918–1920'. *Past & Present* 129 (1990): 168–211.

Filitov, A. M. *Germanskii vopros: Ot raskola k ob''edineniiu. Novoe prochtenie.* Moscow: Mezhdunarodnye Otnosheniia, 1993.

'Germany will Be a Bourgeois–Democratic Republic: The New Evidence from the Personal File of Georgiy Malenkov'. *Cold War History* 6, no. 4 (2006): 549–57.

Fischer, K. P. *Nazi Germany: A New History.* New York: Continuum, 1995.

Fitzpatrick, S. *Everyday Stalinism: Ordinary Life in Extraordinary Times. Soviet Russia in the 1930s.* New York: Oxford University Press, 1999.

'How the Mice Buried the Cat: Scenes from the Great Purges of 1937 in the Russian Provinces'. *Russian Review* 52, no. 3 (1993): 299–320.

Stalin's Peasants: Resistance and Survival in the Russian Village after Collectivization. New York: Oxford University Press, 1994.

Foitzik, J. *Sowjetische Militäradministration in Deutschland (SMAD) 1945–1949: Struktur und Funktion.* Berlin: Akademie Verlag, 1999.

Gailus, M., and H. Volkmann, eds. *Der Kampf um das tägliche Brot: Nahrungsmangel, Versorgungspolitik und Protest 1770–1990.* Opladen: Westdeutscher Verlag, 1994.

Gertjejanssen, W. 'Victims, Heroes, Survivors: Sexual Violence on the Eastern Front During World War II', unpublished PhD thesis, University of Minnesota, 2004.

Getty, J. A., and R. T. Manning, eds. *Stalinist Terror: New Perspectives.* Cambridge and New York: Cambridge University Press, 1993.

Geyer, M., and S. Fitzpatrick, eds. *Beyond Totalitarianism: Stalinism and Nazism Compared.* New York: Cambridge University Press, 1999.

Gimbel, J. *The Origins of the Marshall Plan.* Stanford, Calif.: Stanford University Press, 1976.

Glantz, D. M. *The Role of Intelligence in Soviet Military Strategy in World War II.* Novato: Presidio, 1990.

Goeschel, C. 'Suicide at the End of the Third Reich'. *Journal of Contemporary History* 41, no. 1 (Jan. 2006): 153–73.

Gorlizki, Y. 'Ordinary Stalinism: The Council of Ministers and the Soviet Neopatrimonial State, 1946–1953'. *The Journal of Modern History* 74 (2002): 699–736.

'Stalin's Cabinet: The Politburo and Decision Making in the Post-War Years'. *Europe–Asia Studies* 53, no. 2 (2001): 291–312.

Gorlizki, Y., and O. Khlevniuk, eds. *Cold Peace: Stalin and the Soviet Ruling Circle, 1945–1953.* Oxford and New York: Oxford University Press, 2004.

Gottlieb, M. *The German Peace Settlement and the Peace Crisis.* New York, 1960.

Graziosi, A. 'The New Soviet Archival Sources: Hypotheses for a Critical Assessment'. *Cahiers du Monde Russe* 40, nos. 1–2 (1999): 13–64.

Grossman, A. 'A Question of Silence: The Rape of German Women by Occupation Soldiers'. *October* 72 (1995): 42–63.

'Grams, Calories, and Food: Languages of Victimization, Entitlement, and Human Rights in Occupied Germany, 1945–1949'. *Central European History* 44 (2011): 118–48.

Hahn, W. G. *Postwar Soviet Politics: The Fall of Zhdanov and the Defeat of Moderation, 1946–53.* Ithaca, NY: Cornell University Press, 1982.

Hamburger Institut für Sozialforschung. *Verbrechen der Wehrmacht: Dimensionen des Vernichtungskrieges 1941–1944. Ausstellungskatalog.* Hamburg: Hamburger Edition, 2002.

Harrison, H. M. *Accounting for War: Soviet Production, Employment, and the Defence Burden, 1940–1945.* New York: Cambridge University Press, 1996.

Harsch, D. 'Approach/Avoidance: Communists and Women in East Germany, 1945–9'. *Social History* 25, no. 2 (2000): 156–82.

Revenge of the Domestic: Women, the Family, and Communism in the German Democratic Republic. Princeton, NY: Princeton University Press, 2007.

Haupts, L. 'Die Blockparteien in der DDR und der 17. Juni 1953'. *Vierteljahrshefte für Zeitgeschichte* 40, no. 3 (1992): 383–412.

Hollander, P. *The Survival of the Adversary Culture: Social Criticism and Political Escapism in American Society.* New Brunswick, NJ: Transaction Books, 1988.

Holz, M. *Evakuierte, Flüchtlinge und Vertriebene auf der Insel Rügen 1943–1961.* Cologne: Böhlau Verlag, 2004.

Homze, E. L. *Foreign Labor in Nazi Germany.* Princeton, NJ: Princeton University Press, 1967.

Judt, T. *Postwar: A History of Europe since 1945.* London: Pimlico, 2007.

Kamenetsky, I. *Secret Nazi Plans for Eastern Europe: A Study of Lebensraum Policies.* New York: Bookman Associates, 1961.

Kay, A. J. 'Germany's Staatssekretäre, Mass Starvation and the Meeting of 2 May 1941'. *Journal of Contemporary History* 41, no. 4 (Oct. 2006): 685–700.

Keeble, C., ed. *The Soviet State: The Domestic Roots of Soviet Foreign Policy.* Boulder, Colo.: Westview Press, 1985.

Keep, J., and A. Litvin. *Stalinism: Russian and Western Views at the Turn of the Millennium.* New York: Routledge, 2005.

Keiderling, G. 'Scheinpluralismus und Blockparteien: Die KPD und die Gründung der Parteien in Berlin 1945'. *Vierteljahrshefte für Zeitgeschichte* 45, no. 2 (1997): 257–96.

Kennedy-Pipe, C. *Stalin's Cold War: Soviet Strategies in Europe, 1943 to 1956.* Manchester: Manchester University Press, 1995.

Kessler, R., and H. R. Peter. 'Antifaschisten in der SBZ: Zwischen elitärem Selbstverständnis und politischer Instrumentalisierung'. *Vierteljahrshefte für Zeitgeschichte* 43, no. 4 (1995): 611–33.

Konasov, V. B. 'Preemniki Stalina i problema nemetskikh voennoplennykh'. *Otechestvennaia Istoriia* 5 (1998): 167–74.

Kondoyanidi, A. 'The Liberating Experience: War Correspondents, Red Army Soldiers, and the Nazi Extermination Camps'. *The Russian Review* 69 (2010): 438–62.

Krisch, H. *German Politics under Soviet Occupation*. Princeton, NJ: Princeton University Press, 1974.

Krivosheev, G. F., ed. *Rossiia i SSSR v voinakh XX veka: Poteri vooruzhennykh sil. Istoriko-statisticheskoe issledovanie*. Moscow: Olma-Press, 2001.

Kuklick, B. *American Policy and the Division of Germany: The Clash with Russia over Reparations*. Ithaca, NY: Cornell University Press, 1972.

   'The Origins of the Marshall Plan?', *Reviews in American History* 5, no. 2 (1977): 292–8.

Kulz, H. R. 'The Soviet Zone of Germany: A Study of Development and Policies'. *International Affairs* 27, no. 2 (1951): 156–66.

Kynin, G. P. 'Germanskii vopros vo vzaimootnosheniiakh SSSR, SSHA i Velikobritanii 1944–1945'. *Novaia i Noveishaia Istoriia* (1995), no. 4: 105–32.

Landauer, C. 'The German Reparations Problem'. *The Journal of Political Economy* 56, no. 4 (1948): 344–7.

Landsman, M. *Dictatorship and Demand: The Politics of Consumerism in East Germany*. Cambridge, Mass.: Harvard University Press, 2005.

Lauckhuff, P. 'German Reaction to Soviet Policy, 1945–1953'. *Journal of International Affairs* 8, no. 1 (1954): 62–72.

Lavrenov, S. I., and I. M. Popov. *Krakh Tret'ego reikha*. Moscow: AST, 2000.

Le Tissier, T. *Zhukov at the Oder: The Decisive Battle for Berlin*. Westport, Conn.: Praeger, 1996.

Leffler, M. P. 'The Cold War: What Do "We Now Know"?' *The American Historical Review* 104, no. 2 (1999): 501–24.

Lewin, M. *Russian Peasants and Soviet Power: A Study of Collectivisation*. London: Allen & Unwin, 1968.

   ed. *Taking Grain: Soviet Policies of Agricultural Procurement before the War: The Making of the Soviet System. Essays in the Social History of Interwar Russia*. New York: Pantheon, 1985.

Liebman, S., and A. Michelson. 'After the Fall: Women in the House of the Hangmen'. *October* 72 (1995): 4–14.

Littlewood, R. 'Military Rape'. *Anthropology Today* 13, no. 2 (Apr. 1997): 7–16.

Loth, W. *Stalin's Unwanted Child: The Soviet Union, the German Question and the Founding of the GDR*. Translated by R. F. Fogg. London: Macmillan, 1998.

Lozhkin, A. G. *Pravo pobeditelei: Pravovaia deiatel'nost' Sovetskoi voennoi administratsii v Germanii 1945–1949 gg*. Moscow: AIRO-XXI, 2006.

Lumey, L. H., and A. Vaiserman, eds. *Early Life Nutrition, Adult Health, and Development: Lessons from Changing Diets, Famines, and Experimental Studies*. New York: Nova Science Publishers Inc., 2013.

MacDonogh, G. *After the Reich: The Brutal History of the Allied Occupation*. New York: Basic Books, 2007.

Mark, J. 'Remembering Rape: Divided Social Memory and the Red Army in Hungary 1944–1945'. *Past and Present* 188 (2005): 133–61.

Marshall, B. 'German Attitudes to British Military Government 1945–47'. *Journal of Contemporary History* 15, no. 4 (1980): 655–84.

Mastny, V. *The Cold War and Soviet Insecurity: The Stalin Years.* New York: Oxford University Press, 1996.

Mathers, J. C., and E. M. Widdowson, eds. *The Contribution of Nutrition to Human and Animal Health.* Cambridge and New York: Cambridge University Press, 1992.

McCagg, W. O. *Stalin Embattled 1943–1948.* Detroit, Mich.: Wayne State University Press, 1978.

Medvedev, R. *All Stalin's Men.* Translated by H. Shukman. Oxford: Blackwell, 1983.

Meimberg, R. *The Economic Development in West Berlin, and in the Soviet zone.* Berlin: Duncker und Humblot, 1952.

Merridale, C. *Ivan's War: Life and Death in the Red Army, 1939–1945.* New York: Metropolitan Books, 2006.

Merritt, R. L. *Democracy Imposed: U.S. Occupation Policy and the German Public, 1945–1949.* New Haven, Conn. and London: Yale University Press, 1995.

Messerschmidt, J. W. 'The Forgotten Victims of World War II: Masculinities and Rape in Berlin, 1945'. *Violence against Women* 12, no. 7 (2006): 706–12.

Moeller, R. G. 'War Stories: The Search for a Usable Past in the Federal Republic of Germany'. *The American Historical Review* 101, no. 4 (Oct. 1996): 1008–48.

Morina, C. 'Instructed Silence, Constructed Memory: The SED and the Return of German Prisoners of War as "War Criminals" from the Soviet Union to East Germany, 1950–1956'. *Contemporary European History* 13, no. 3 (2004): 323–43.

Morsch, G., ed. *Mord und Massermord im Konzentrationlager Sachsenhausen 1936–1945.* Berlin: Metropol-Verlag, 2005.

Moskoff, W. *The Bread of Affliction: The Food Supply in the USSR during World War II.* Cambridge and New York: Cambridge University Press, 1990.

Mulligan, T. P. *The Politics of Illusion and Empire: German Occupation Policy in the Soviet Union 1942–1943.* New York: Praeger, 1988.

Naimark, N. *Fires of Hatred: Ethnic Cleansing in Twentieth-Century Europe.* Cambridge, Mass.: Harvard University Press, 2001.
  'Stalin and Europe in the Postwar Period, 1945–53: Issues and Problems'. *Journal of Modern European History* 2, no. 1 (2004): 28–57.
  The Russians in Germany: A History of the Soviet Zone of Occupation. Cambridge, Mass.: Harvard University Press, 1995.
  'The Soviets and the Christian Democrats: The Challenge of a "Bourgeois" Party in Eastern Germany, 1945–1949'. *East European Politics and Societies* 9, no. 3 (1995): 369–92.

Nettl, J. P. *The Eastern Zone and Soviet Policy in Germany.* London: Oxford University Press, 1951.

Niedbalski, B. 'Deutsche Zentralverwaltungen und Deutsche Wirtschaftskommission (DWK): Ansätze zur zentralen Wirtschaftsplanung in der SBZ 1945–1948'. *Vierteljahrshefte für Zeitgeschichte* 33, no. 3 (1985): 456–77.

Pechatnov, V. O. 'The Rise and Fall of Britansky Soyuznik: A Case Study in Soviet Response to British Propaganda of the mid-1940s'. *The Historical Journal* 41, no. 1 (1998): 293–301.

Peterson, E. N. *Russian Commands and German Resistance: The Soviet Occupation 1945–1949*. New York: Peter Lang Publishing, 1999.

The Many Faces of Defeat: The German People's Experience in 1945. New York: Peter Lang, 1990.

Petrov, I. A. 'Istoriia poslevoennykh Sovetsko- i Rossiisko-Germanskikh otnoshenii: Konferentsiia v Maintse (FRG)'. *Otechestvennaia Istoriia* 1 (1996): 208–15.

Petrov, N. V. *Pervyi predsedatel' KGB Ivan Serov*. Moscow: Materik, 2005.

Peukert, D. J. K. *Inside Nazi Germany: Conformity, Opposition and Racism in Everyday Life*. Translated by R. Deveson. London: Batsford, 1987.

Phillips, A. L. *Soviet Policy toward East Germany Reconsidered: The Postwar Decade*. Westport, Conn.: Greenwood Press, 1986.

Pike, D. 'Cultural Politics in Soviet-Occupied Germany 1945–46'. *Journal of Contemporary History* 24, no. 1 (1989): 91–123.

Pinfold, D. '"Das Mündel will Vormund sein": The GDR State as Child'. *German Life and Letters* 64, no. 2 (2011): 283–304.

Pinnow, K. M. *Lost to the Collective: Suicide and the Promise of Soviet Socialism, 1921–1929*. Ithaca, NY: Cornell University Press, 2010.

Pleshakov, C., and V. Zubok. *Inside the Kremlin's Cold War: From Stalin to Khrushchev*. Cambridge, Mass.: Harvard University Press, 1996.

Polian, P. *Zhertvy dvukh diktatur: Ostarbaitery i voennoplennye v Tret'em reikhe i ikh repatriatsiia*. Moscow: Vash Vybor TSIRZ, 1996.

Pritchard, G. 'Schwarzenberg 1945: Antifascists and the "Third Way" in German Politics'. *European History Quarterly* 35 (2005): 499–522.

The Making of the GDR, 1945–53: From Antifascism to Stalinism. Manchester: Manchester University Press, 2000.

'The Occupation of Germany in 1945 and the Politics of German History'. *History Compass* 7/2 (2009): 447–73.

Proudfoot, M. J. *European Refugees, 1939–52: A Study in Forced Population Movement*. London: Faber, 1957.

Prusin, A. V. 'Fascist Criminals to the Gallows! The Holocaust and Soviet War Crimes Trials, December 1945–February 1946'. *Holocaust and Genocide Studies* 17 (2003): 1–30.

Ra'anan, G. D. *International Policy Formation in the USSR: Factional 'Debates' during the Zhdanovschina*. Hamden, Conn.: Archon Books, 1983.

Raack, R. C. 'Stalin Plans his Post-War Germany'. *Journal of Contemporary History* 28, no. 1 (1993): 53–73.

Stalin's Drive to the West, 1938–1945: The Origins of the Cold War. Stanford, Calif.: Stanford University Press, 1995.

Raup, P. M. 'The Agricultural Significance of German Boundary Problems'. *Land Economics* 26, no. 2 (1950): 101–14.

Rees, E. A., ed. *The Nature of Stalin's Dictatorship: The Politburo, 1924–1953*. New York: Palgrave Macmillan, 2003.

Reese, R. R. *The Soviet Military Experience: A History of the Soviet Army, 1917–1991*. London: Routledge, 2000.

Stalin's Reluctant Soldiers: A Social History of the Red Army, 1925–1941. Lawrence, Kans.: University Press of Kansas, 1996.

Reitlinger, G. *The House Built on Sand: The Conflicts of German Policy in Russia, 1939–1945.* New York: Viking Press, 1960.

Roberts, G. 'Ideology, Calculation, and Improvisation: Spheres of Influence and Soviet Foreign Policy'. *Review of International Studies* 25 (1999): 655–73.

Stalin's Wars: From World War to Cold War, 1939–1953. New Haven and London: Yale University Press, 2006.

Rodovich, I. V. *Germanskaia problema v 1945–1955 gg. i pozitsiia SSSR: Kontseptsiia i istoricheskaia praktika.* Tula: Grif i K, 1997.

Rzheshevskii, O. A. 'Sekretnye voennye plany U. Cherchullia protiv SSSR v mae 1945 g.'. *Novaia i Noveishaia Istoriia* (1999), no. 3: 98–123.

Schneider, D. M. 'Renaissance und Zerstörung der kommunalen Selbstverwaltung in der sowjetischen Besatzungszone'. *Vierteljahrshefte für Zeitgeschichte* 37, no. 3 (1989): 457–97.

Schulte, T. J. *The German Army and Nazi Policies in Occupied Russia.* New York: St. Martin's Press, 1989.

Semystiaha, V. 'The Role and Place of Secret Collaborators in the Informal Informational Activity'. *Cahiers du Monde Russe* 42/2, nos. 3–4 (2001): 231–44.

Seniavskaia, E. S. *Frontovoe pokolenie, 1941–1945: Istoriko-psikhologicheskoe issledovanie.* Moscow: In-t Rossiiskoi Istorii RAN, 1995.

Sevost'ianov, G. N., and V. A. Zolotarev, eds. *Velikaia Otechestvennaia voina 1941–1945.* Vol. IV. Moscow: Nauka, 1999.

Shapoval, I. I. 'The Mechanisms of the Informational Activity of the GPU-NKVD: The Surveillance File of Mykhailo Hrushevsky'. *Cahiers du Monde Russe* 42/2, nos. 3–4 (2001): 207–30.

Sharp, T. *The Wartime Alliance and the Zonal Division of Germany.* Oxford: Clarendon Press, 1975.

Shepherd, B. 'Hawks, Doves and Tote Zonen: A Wehrmacht Security Division in Central Russia, 1943'. *Journal of Contemporary History* 37, no. 3 (2002): 349–69.

Shishkin, V. I., ed. *Sovetskaia istoriia: Problemy i uroki.* Novosibirsk: Nauka, 1992.

Shtemenko, S. M. *The Soviet General Staff at War, 1941–1945.* Translated by R. Daglish. Moscow: Progress Publishers, 1985.

Siljak, A., and P. Ther, eds. *Redrawing Nations: Ethnic Cleansing in East–Central Europe, 1944–1948*, Harvard Cold War Studies Book Series. Lanham, Md.: Rowman & Littlefield, 2001.

Slaveski, F. 'Competing Occupiers: Bloody Conflicts between Soviet and Polish Authorities in the Borderlands of Post-War Germany and Poland, 1945–46'. *New Zealand Slavonic Journal* 42 (2008): 137–55.

'Violence and Xenophobia as Means of Social Control in Times of Collapse: The Soviet Occupation of Post-War Germany, 1945–1947'. *Australian Journal of Politics and History* 54, no. 3 (2008): 389–402.

Slusser, R., ed. *Soviet Economic Policy in Postwar Germany.* New York: Research Program on the USSR., 1953.

Smyser, W. R. *From Yalta to Berlin: The Cold War Struggle over Germany*. *New York:* St Martin's Press, 1999.

Spilker, D. *The East German Leadership and the Division of Germany: Patriotism and Propaganda 1945–1953*. Oxford and New York: Oxford University Press, 2006.

Statiev, A. 'Penal Units in the Red Army'. *Europe-Asia Studies* 62, no. 5 (2010): 721–47.

Steege, P. *Black Market, Cold War: Everyday Life in Berlin, 1946–1949*. New York: Cambridge University Press, 2007.

Steinberg, J. 'The Third Reich Reflected: German Civil Administration in the Occupied Soviet Union'. *The English Historical Review* 110, no. 437 (1995): 620–51.

Stelzl-Marx, B. 'Die unsichtbare Generation: Kinder sowjetischer Besatzungssoldaten in Österreich und Deutschland'. *Historical Social Research* 34, no. 3 (2009): 352–72.

Stites, R., ed. *Culture and Entertainment in Wartime Russia*. Bloomington, Ind.: Indiana University Press, 1995.

Swain, G. 'Stalin's Wartime Vision of the Postwar World'. *Diplomacy & Statecraft* 7, no. 1 (1996): 73–96.

Ther, P. 'The Integration of Expellees in Germany and Poland after World War II: A Historical Reassessment'. *Slavic Review* 55, no. 4 (1996): 779–805.

Timm, A. F. 'The Legacy of *"Bevölkerungspolitik"*: Venereal Disease Control and Marriage Counselling in Post-WWII Berlin'. *Canadian Journal of History* 33, no. 2 (1998): 173–214.

Trachtenberg, M. *A Constructed Peace: The Making of the European Settlement, 1945–1963*. Princeton, NJ: Princeton University Press, 1999.

Unger, A. L. 'The Public Opinion Reports of the Nazi Party'. *The Public Opinion Quarterly* 29, no. 4 (1965–6): 565–82.

Viola, L. *Peasant Rebels under Stalin: Collectivization and the Culture of Peasant Resistance*. New York: Oxford University Press, 1996.

Vogt, T. R. *Denazification in Soviet-Occupied Germany: Brandenburg, 1945–8*. Cambridge, Mass.: Harvard University Press, 2000.

von Hagen, M. *Soldiers in the Proletarian Dictatorship: The Red Army and the Soviet Socialist State, 1917–1930*. Ithaca, NY: Cornell University Press, 1990.

Wachsmann, N. 'Annihilation through Labour: The Killing of State Prisoners in the Reich'. *The Journal of Modern History* 71, no. 3 (1999): 624–59.

Wala, M. *The Council on Foreign Relations and American Foreign Policy in the Early Cold War*. Providence, RI: Berghahn Books, 1994.

Wehner, J. *Kulturpolitik und Volksfront: Ein Beitrag zur Geschichte der sowjetischen Besatzungszonedeutschlands 1945–1949*. New York: Peter Lang, 1992.

Wheatcroft, S. G., ed. *Challenging Traditional Views of Russian History*. New York: Palgrave Macmillan, 2002.

'The Soviet Famine of 1946–1947, the Weather and Human Agency in Historical Perspective'. *Europe–Asia Studies* 64, no. 6 (2012): 987–1005.

'Towards a Thorough Analysis of Soviet Forced Labor Statistics'. *Soviet Studies* 35, no. 2 (1983): 223–37.

Widdell, M., and F. Wemheuer, eds. *Hunger, Ernährung und Rationierungssysteme unter dem Staatssozialismus (1917–2006)*. Frankfurt am Main: Peter Lang, 2011.

Wille, M. 'Compelling the Assimilation of Expellees in the Soviet zone of Occupation and the GDR'. *Redrawing Nations* (2001): 263–83.

Wood, J. E. 'Variation in Sexual Violence during War'. *Politics and Society* 34, no. 3 (2006): 307–41.

Wunderlich, F. 'Agriculture and Farm Labor in the Soviet Zone of Germany'. *Social Research* 19, no. 2 (1952): 198–220.

Wyman, M. *DP: Europe's Displaced Persons, 1945–1951.* London: Associated University Presses, 1989.

Zaleski, E. *Stalinist Planning for Economic Growth, 1933–1952.* Translated by M. C. MacAndrew and J. H. Moore. Chapel Hill, NC: University of North Carolina Press, 1980.

Zhukov, I. N. *Inoi Stalin.* Moscow: Vagrius, 2005.

Ziemke, E. F. *The U.S. Army in the Occupation of Germany 1944–1946.* Army Historical Series. Washington, DC: Center of Military History, United States Army, 1990.

Zubkova, E. I. 'Obshchestvo, vyshedshee iz voiny: Russkie i nemtsy v 1945 godu'. *Otechestvennaia Istoriia* 3 (1995): 95–100.

Pribaltika i Kreml', 1940–1953. Moscow: Rosspen, 2008.

Russia after the War: Hopes, Illusions, and Disappointments, 1945–1957. Translated by H. Ragsdale. New York: Armonk, 1998.

Index